ASSASSIN'S CREED®

HOMECOMING

TITAN
COMICS

Assassin's Creed: Homecoming

9781782763109
Published by Titan Comics
A division of Titan Publishing Group Ltd.
144 Southwark St.
London
SE1 0UP

A CIP catalogue record for this title is available from the British Library

First edition: April 2017

10 9 8 7 6 5 4 3 2 1

Printed in China.
Titan Comics. 0733

TITAN COMICS

EDITOR: TOM WILLIAMS
SENIOR DESIGNER: ANDREW LEUNG

Senior Comics Editor: Andrew James
Titan Comics Editorial: Jessica Burton, Amoona Saohin, Lauren McPhee
Production Supervisions: Jackie Flook, Maria Pearson
Production Assistant: Peter James
Production Manager: Obi Onuora
Art Director: Oz Browne
Senior Sales Manager: Steve Tothill
Press Officer: Will O'Mullane
Senior Marketing & Press Executive: Owen Johnson
Direct Sales & Marketing Manager: Ricky Claydon
Head of Rights: Jenny Boyce
Publishing Manager: Darryl Tothill
Publishing Director: Chris Teather
Operations Director: Leigh Baulch
Executive Director: Vivian Cheung
Publisher: Nick Landau

WWW.TITAN-COMICS.COM

Follow us on Twitter @ComicsTitan

Visit us at facebook.com/comicstitan

ACKNOWLEDGEMENTS:
Many thanks to Aymar Azaïzia, Anouk Bachman, Richard Farrese,
Raphaël Lacoste, Caroline Lamache and Clémence Deleuze.

ASSASSIN'S CREED

HOMECOMING

WRITERS
ANTHONY DEL COL &
CONOR MCCREERY

ARTIST
NEIL EDWARDS

COLORIST
IVAN NUNES

LETTERER
RICHARD STARKINGS AND COMICRAFT'S
JIMMY BETANCOURT

TITAN
COMICS

ASSASSIN'S CREED:
TRIAL BY FIRE

ASSASSIN'S CREED:
SETTING SUN

◆ **ASSASSIN'S CREED:
HOMECOMING**

\ STORY SO FAR...

For centuries, the Assassin Brotherhood has fought a covert war against their sworn enemies, the Templar Order. Via the Pieces of Eden – advanced relics left behind by a precursor race – the Templars seek to create a 'perfect' world governed by discipline and unity, directly contrasting the ideals of the Brotherhood, who strive to safeguard humanity's free-will.

Charlotte de la Cruz is the latest initiate to enter this shadowy world. Through the memories of her ancestors' Charlotte's journey led her from the violence and hysteria of the Salem Witch Trials, to the heart of the Inca Empire, and beyond, in a bid to dig deeper into the inner workings of the Brotherhood.

Now, with little to go on and no backup on the way, Charlotte has convinced her fellow Assassins to follow her into the unknown - a meeting with the elusive hacktivist collective, Erudito - where the hidden truths about an immnient Templar plot are about to come to light...

CHAPTER
ELEVEN

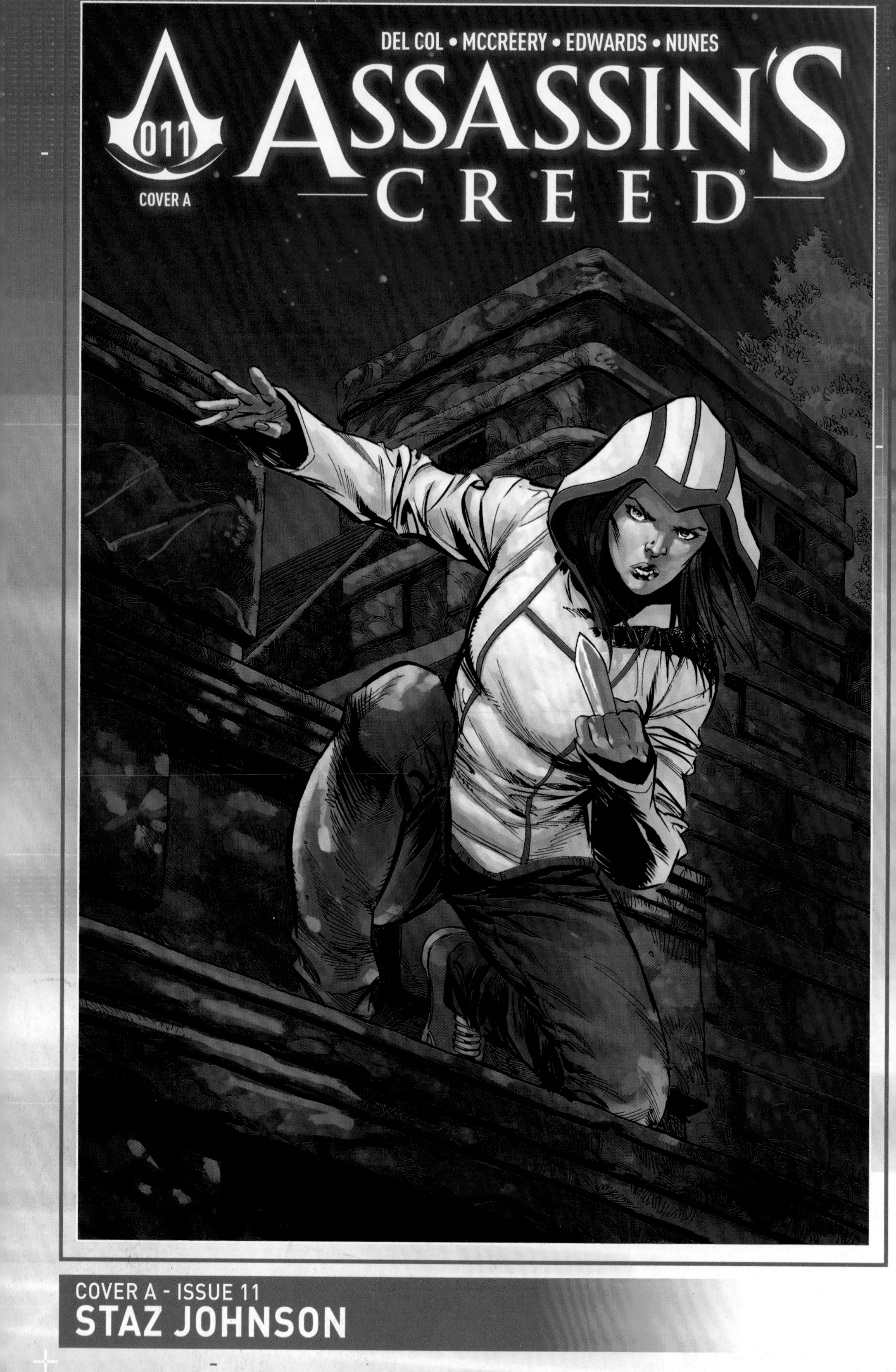
DEL COL • MCCREERY • EDWARDS • NUNES
ASSASSIN'S CREED
011
COVER A

COVER A - ISSUE 11
STAZ JOHNSON

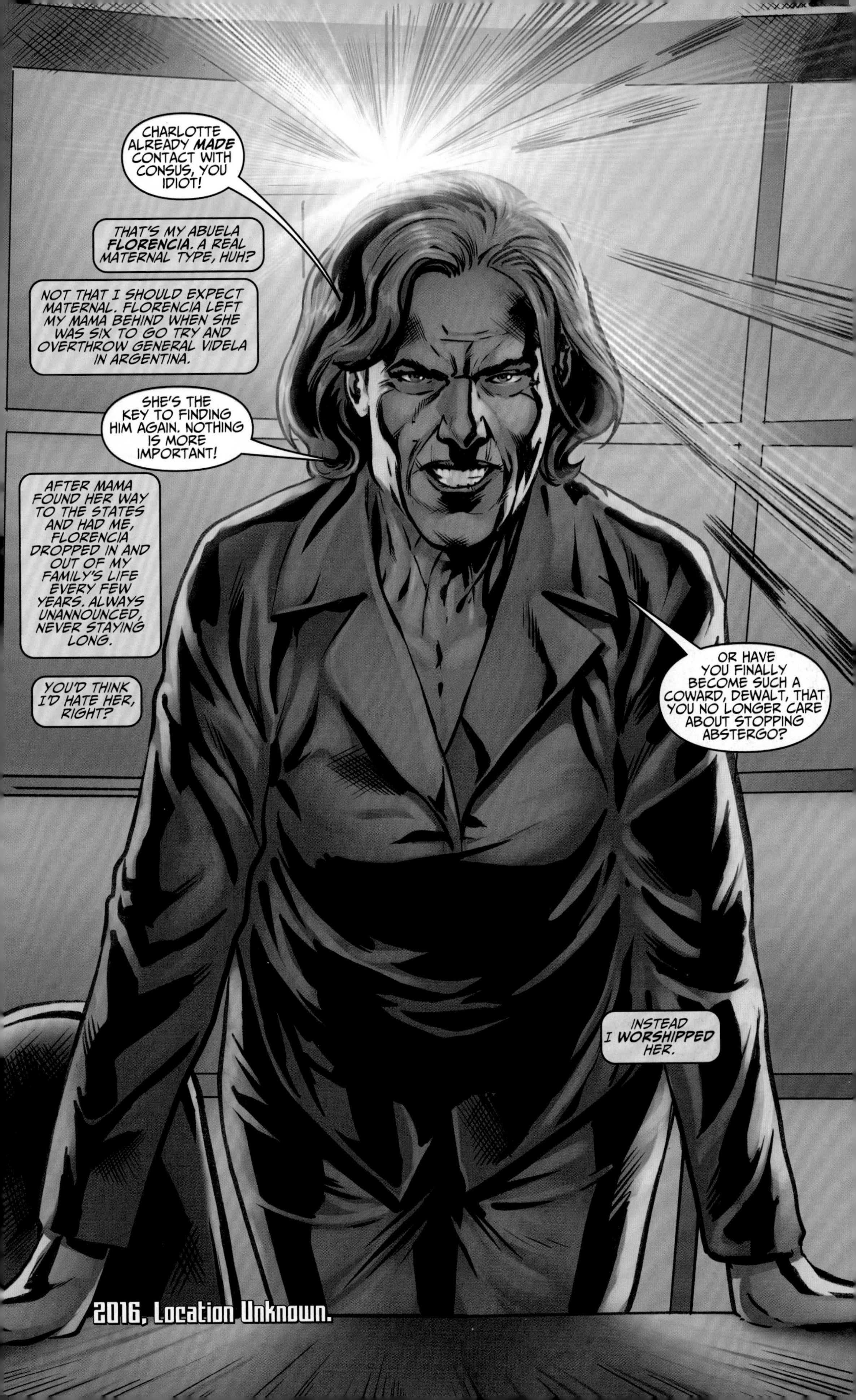

CHARLOTTE ALREADY MADE CONTACT WITH CONSUS, YOU IDIOT!
THAT'S MY ABUELA FLORENCIA. A REAL MATERNAL TYPE, HUH?
NOT THAT I SHOULD EXPECT MATERNAL. FLORENCIA LEFT MY MAMA BEHIND WHEN SHE WAS SIX TO GO TRY AND OVERTHROW GENERAL VIDELA IN ARGENTINA.
SHE'S THE KEY TO FINDING HIM AGAIN. NOTHING IS MORE IMPORTANT!
AFTER MAMA FOUND HER WAY TO THE STATES AND HAD ME, FLORENCIA DROPPED IN AND OUT OF MY FAMILY'S LIFE EVERY FEW YEARS. ALWAYS UNANNOUNCED, NEVER STAYING LONG.
YOU'D THINK I'D HATE HER, RIGHT?
OR HAVE YOU FINALLY BECOME SUCH A COWARD, DEWALT, THAT YOU NO LONGER CARE ABOUT STOPPING ABSTERGO?
INSTEAD I WORSHIPPED HER.
2016, Location Unknown.

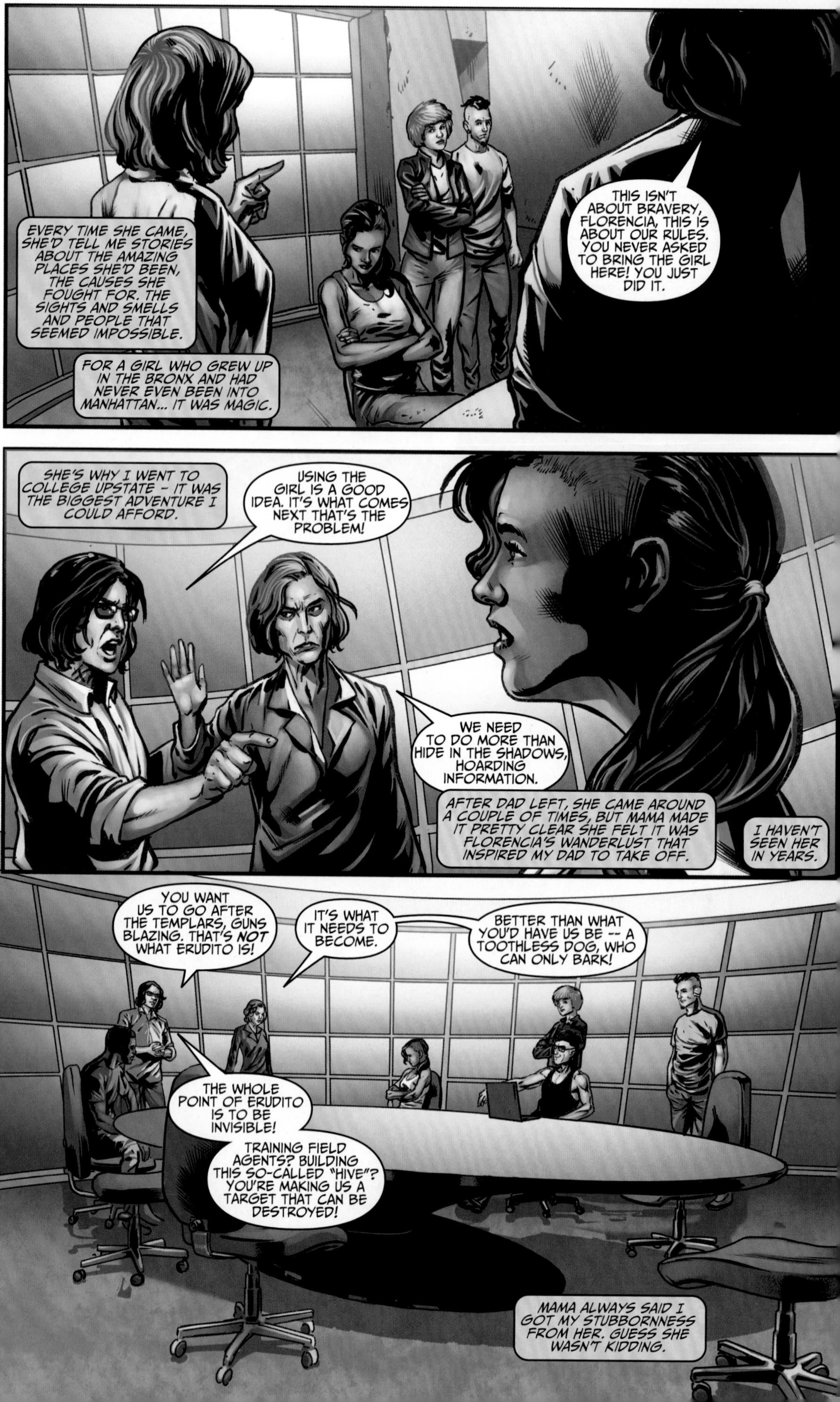
EVERY TIME SHE CAME, SHE'D TELL ME STORIES ABOUT THE AMAZING PLACES SHE'D BEEN, THE CAUSES SHE FOUGHT FOR. THE SIGHTS AND SMELLS AND PEOPLE THAT SEEMED IMPOSSIBLE.
FOR A GIRL WHO GREW UP IN THE BRONX AND HAD NEVER EVEN BEEN INTO MANHATTAN... IT WAS MAGIC.
THIS ISN'T ABOUT BRAVERY, FLORENCIA, THIS IS ABOUT OUR RULES. YOU NEVER ASKED TO BRING THE GIRL HERE! YOU JUST DID IT.
SHE'S WHY I WENT TO COLLEGE UPSTATE – IT WAS THE BIGGEST ADVENTURE I COULD AFFORD.
USING THE GIRL IS A GOOD IDEA. IT'S WHAT COMES NEXT THAT'S THE PROBLEM!
WE NEED TO DO MORE THAN HIDE IN THE SHADOWS, HOARDING INFORMATION.
AFTER DAD LEFT, SHE CAME AROUND A COUPLE OF TIMES, BUT MAMA MADE IT PRETTY CLEAR SHE FELT IT WAS FLORENCIA'S WANDERLUST THAT INSPIRED MY DAD TO TAKE OFF.
I HAVEN'T SEEN HER IN YEARS.
YOU WANT US TO GO AFTER THE TEMPLARS, GUNS BLAZING. THAT'S NOT WHAT ERUDITO IS!
IT'S WHAT IT NEEDS TO BECOME.
BETTER THAN WHAT YOU'D HAVE US BE -- A TOOTHLESS DOG, WHO CAN ONLY BARK!
THE WHOLE POINT OF ERUDITO IS TO BE INVISIBLE!
TRAINING FIELD AGENTS? BUILDING THIS SO-CALLED "HIVE"? YOU'RE MAKING US A TARGET THAT CAN BE DESTROYED!
MAMA ALWAYS SAID I GOT MY STUBBORNNESS FROM HER. GUESS SHE WASN'T KIDDING.

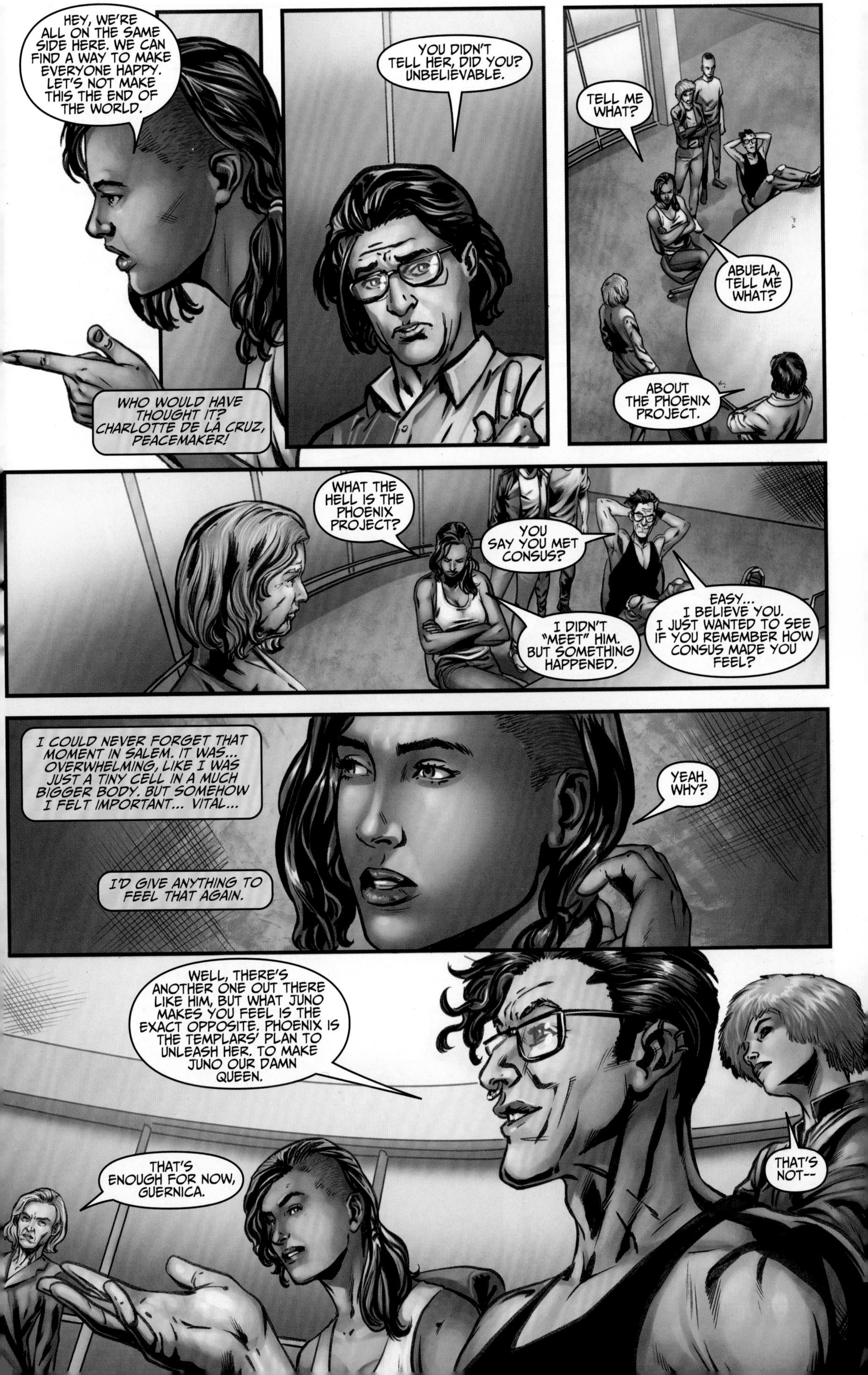
HEY, WE'RE ALL ON THE SAME SIDE HERE. WE CAN FIND A WAY TO MAKE EVERYONE HAPPY. LET'S NOT MAKE THIS THE END OF THE WORLD.
WHO WOULD HAVE THOUGHT IT? CHARLOTTE DE LA CRUZ, PEACEMAKER!
YOU DIDN'T TELL HER, DID YOU? UNBELIEVABLE.
TELL ME WHAT?
ABUELA, TELL ME WHAT?
ABOUT THE PHOENIX PROJECT.
WHAT THE HELL IS THE PHOENIX PROJECT?
YOU SAY YOU MET CONSUS?
I DIDN'T "MEET" HIM. BUT SOMETHING HAPPENED.
EASY... I BELIEVE YOU. I JUST WANTED TO SEE IF YOU REMEMBER HOW CONSUS MADE YOU FEEL?
I COULD NEVER FORGET THAT MOMENT IN SALEM. IT WAS... OVERWHELMING, LIKE I WAS JUST A TINY CELL IN A MUCH BIGGER BODY. BUT SOMEHOW I FELT IMPORTANT... VITAL...
YEAH. WHY?
I'D GIVE ANYTHING TO FEEL THAT AGAIN.
WELL, THERE'S ANOTHER ONE OUT THERE LIKE HIM, BUT WHAT JUNO MAKES YOU FEEL IS THE EXACT OPPOSITE. PHOENIX IS THE TEMPLARS' PLAN TO UNLEASH HER. TO MAKE JUNO OUR DAMN QUEEN.
THAT'S ENOUGH FOR NOW, GUERNICA.
THAT'S NOT--

THERE'S NO NEED TO OVERWHELM MY GRANDDAUGHTER ANYMORE THAN SHE ALREADY IS.

AH, THE FLORENCIA LAWS! IF YOU DON'T LIKE THE DISCUSSION, CUT IT OFF. THAT'S NOT THE WAY ERUDITO SHOULD WORK!.

IT IS WHILE I SIT AT THE HEAD OF THE TABLE. UNLESS YOU WANT TO GO BACK TO THE OLD DAYS OF A THOUSAND VOICES SCREAMING TO BE HEARD?

BETTER THAN ONE THAT'S EVERYTHING WE SHOULD BE FIGHTING AGAINST. RULES. HIERARCHY. CONTROL.

I CALL FOR A VOTE OF NON-CONFIDENCE.

FINE. LET'S VOTE. I HAVE MORE SUPPORT IN THIS ROOM THAN YOU DO, AND YOU KNOW IT.

IT'S MY RIGHT TO INSIST ON A FULL-MEMBERSHIP VOTE. MEMBERS WILL HAVE AN HOUR TO CONVENE.

YOU'RE STALLING.

HE'S RIGHT. WE HAVE AN OBLIGATION TO INFORM ALL MEMBERS OF THE COLLECTIVE.

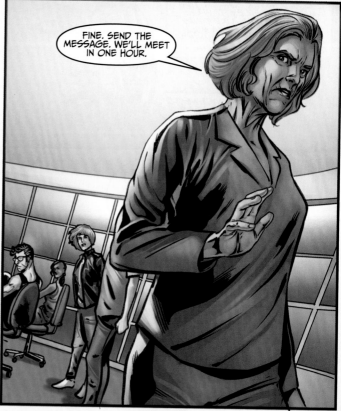

FINE. SEND THE MESSAGE. WE'LL MEET IN ONE HOUR.

I'M SORRY, I SHOULD HAVE ANTICIPATED THAT. HE'S JUST A SMALL MIND THAT HAS NO IDEA WHAT WE CAN REALLY ACCOMPLISH.

COULD THEY REALLY GET RID OF YOU? KILL THIS WHOLE PLAN?

BAH. DEWALT HAS THE CHARISMA OF A SEA URCHIN. AS SOON AS HE SPEAKS, THE REST OF ERUDITO WILL REMEMBER WHY THEY IGNORED HIM WHEN THEY FIRST GAVE ME THE POWER TO CHANGE THINGS.

WHAT *IS* THE PHOENIX PROJECT? WHY DIDN'T YOU TELL ME ABOUT IT?

I DIDN'T WANT TO PUT ANY MORE PRESSURE ON YOU.

WHAT IS THIS MISSION? EXACTLY, I MEAN? I'VE BEEN HERE FOR TWO DAYS AND ALL I KNOW IS I'M GOING TO BE LOOKING FOR CONSUS.

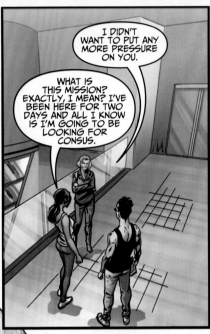

ABUELA... I CAN'T DO MY JOB IF I DON'T KNOW WHAT I'M GOING TO BE SEEING.

PLEASE, YOU CAN TRUST ME.

WE WERE INTRIGUED WHEN WE FOUND OUT CONSUS HAD CONTACTED YOU. WE THOUGHT HE'D ONLY SPOKEN TO A YOUNG ASSASSIN NAMED GIOVANNI BORGIA, AND THEN, ONLY ONCE WHEN HE WAS VERY YOUNG.

NOW WE THINK CONSUS COMMUNICATED WITH GIOVANNI MORE THAN ONCE. WE THINK HE'S HIDDEN A MESSAGE.

WOULDN'T THE TEMPLARS HAVE IT? THEY HAVE ACCESS TO ALL OF GIOVANNI'S MEMORIES, RIGHT?

AH... NOW I GET TO DO SOMETHING I HATE. BRAG.

OH YEAH, I CAN TELL IT REALLY KILLS YOU.

THIS IS A VISUAL REPRESENTATION OF WHAT MEMORIES LOOK LIKE WHEN THEY'RE CODED INTO THE ANIMUS. DO YOU SEE WHAT I'M POINTING AT HERE?

NO.

EXACTLY. AND NEITHER CAN ABSTERGO, BUT TRUST ME WHEN I TELL YOU WE SAW SOMETHING. AND THAT SOMETHING ISN'T QUITE RIGHT.

OUR BEST GUESS: IT'S SOME KIND OF FALSE MEMORY. THE TEMPLARS DON'T KNOW ABOUT A SECOND ENCOUNTER BECAUSE GIOVANNI DOESN'T REMEMBER IT.

BUT ONE OF MY ANCESTORS DID WITNESS IT...

BOOM.

YOUR ANCESTOR WAS WITH GIOVANNI TWICE. ONCE IN 1515, AND A SECOND TIME IN 1516.

WE THINK YOUR EAGLE VISION WILL LET YOU SEE THE TRUTH. OUR FAMILY HAS ALWAYS BEEN STRONG WITH THE SIGHT.

ABUELA, I WANT TO FIND OUT MORE ABOUT THAT. ABOUT EVERYTHING IN OUR FAMILY. I HAVE SO MANY QUESTIONS —

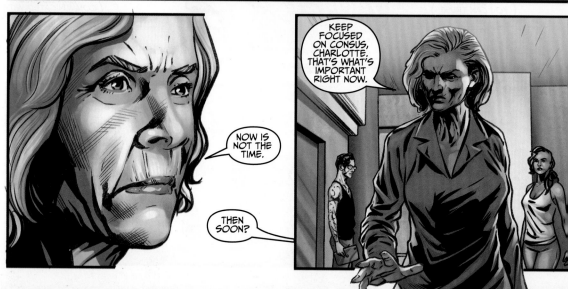

NOW IS NOT THE TIME.

KEEP FOCUSED ON CONSUS, CHARLOTTE. THAT'S WHAT'S IMPORTANT RIGHT NOW.

THEN SOON?

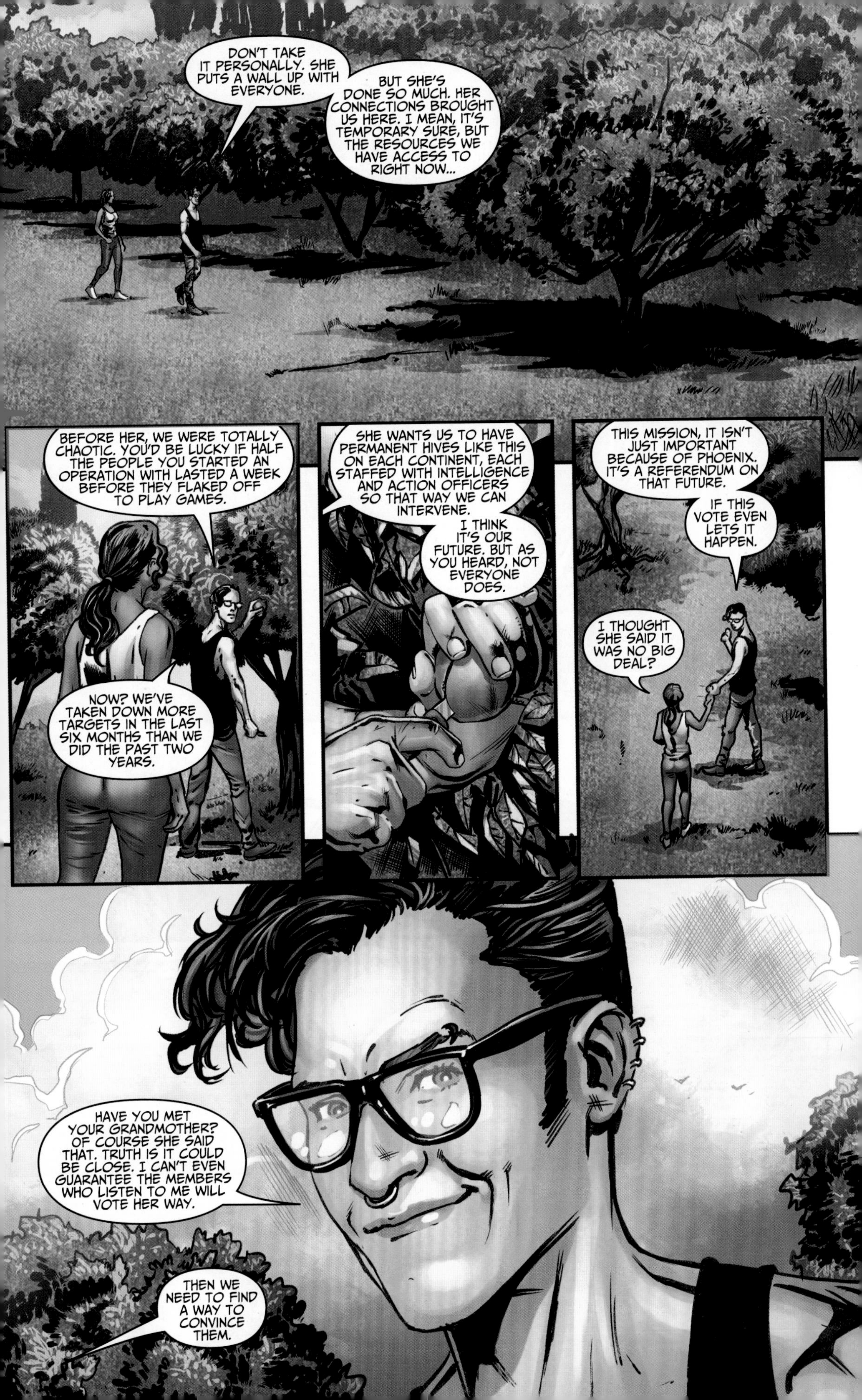
DON'T TAKE IT PERSONALLY. SHE PUTS A WALL UP WITH EVERYONE.
BUT SHE'S DONE SO MUCH. HER CONNECTIONS BROUGHT US HERE. I MEAN, IT'S TEMPORARY SURE, BUT THE RESOURCES WE HAVE ACCESS TO RIGHT NOW...
BEFORE HER, WE WERE TOTALLY CHAOTIC. YOU'D BE LUCKY IF HALF THE PEOPLE YOU STARTED AN OPERATION WITH LASTED A WEEK BEFORE THEY FLAKED OFF TO PLAY GAMES.
NOW? WE'VE TAKEN DOWN MORE TARGETS IN THE LAST SIX MONTHS THAN WE DID THE PAST TWO YEARS.
SHE WANTS US TO HAVE PERMANENT HIVES LIKE THIS ON EACH CONTINENT, EACH STAFFED WITH INTELLIGENCE AND ACTION OFFICERS SO THAT WAY WE CAN INTERVENE.
I THINK IT'S OUR FUTURE. BUT AS YOU HEARD, NOT EVERYONE DOES.
THIS MISSION, IT ISN'T JUST IMPORTANT BECAUSE OF PHOENIX. IT'S A REFERENDUM ON THAT FUTURE.
IF THIS VOTE EVEN LETS IT HAPPEN.
I THOUGHT SHE SAID IT WAS NO BIG DEAL?
HAVE YOU MET YOUR GRANDMOTHER? OF COURSE SHE SAID THAT. TRUTH IS IT COULD BE CLOSE. I CAN'T EVEN GUARANTEE THE MEMBERS WHO LISTEN TO ME WILL VOTE HER WAY.
THEN WE NEED TO FIND A WAY TO CONVINCE THEM.

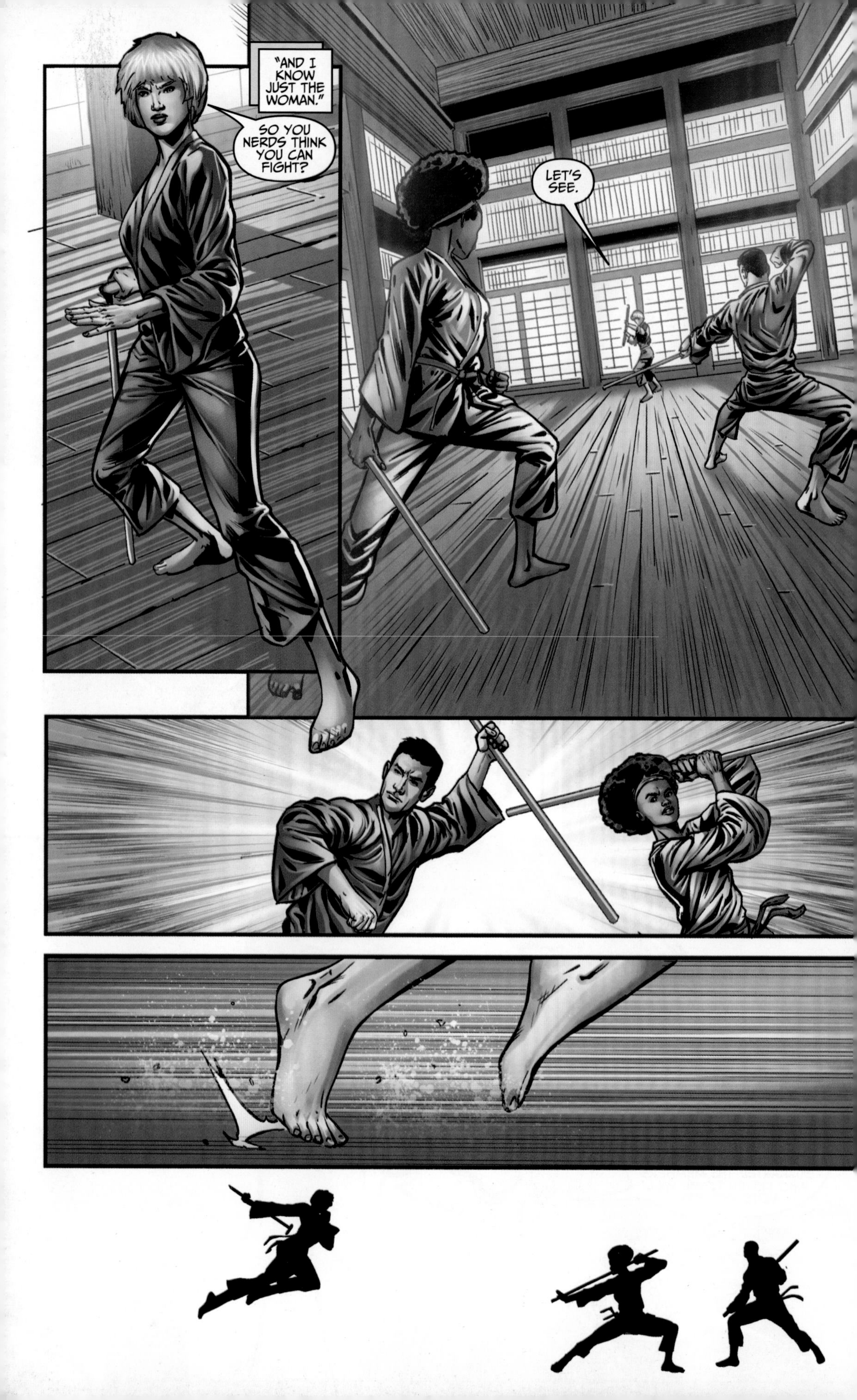
"AND I KNOW JUST THE WOMAN."
SO YOU NERDS THINK YOU CAN FIGHT?
LET'S SEE.

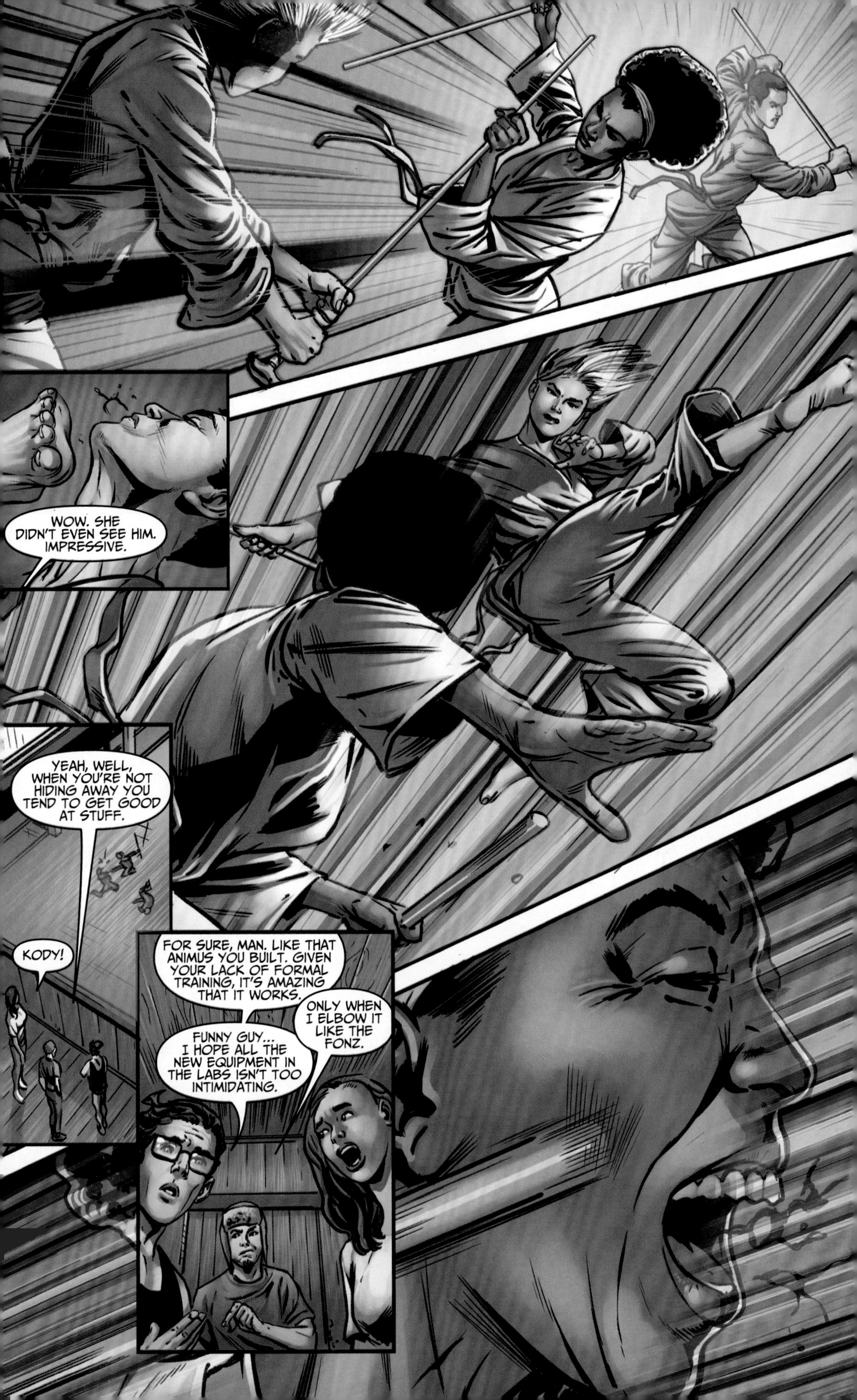
WOW. SHE DIDN'T EVEN SEE HIM. IMPRESSIVE.
YEAH, WELL, WHEN YOU'RE NOT HIDING AWAY YOU TEND TO GET GOOD AT STUFF.
KODY!
FOR SURE, MAN. LIKE THAT ANIMUS YOU BUILT. GIVEN YOUR LACK OF FORMAL TRAINING, IT'S AMAZING THAT IT WORKS.
ONLY WHEN I ELBOW IT LIKE THE FONZ.
FUNNY GUY... I HOPE ALL THE NEW EQUIPMENT IN THE LABS ISN'T TOO INTIMIDATING.

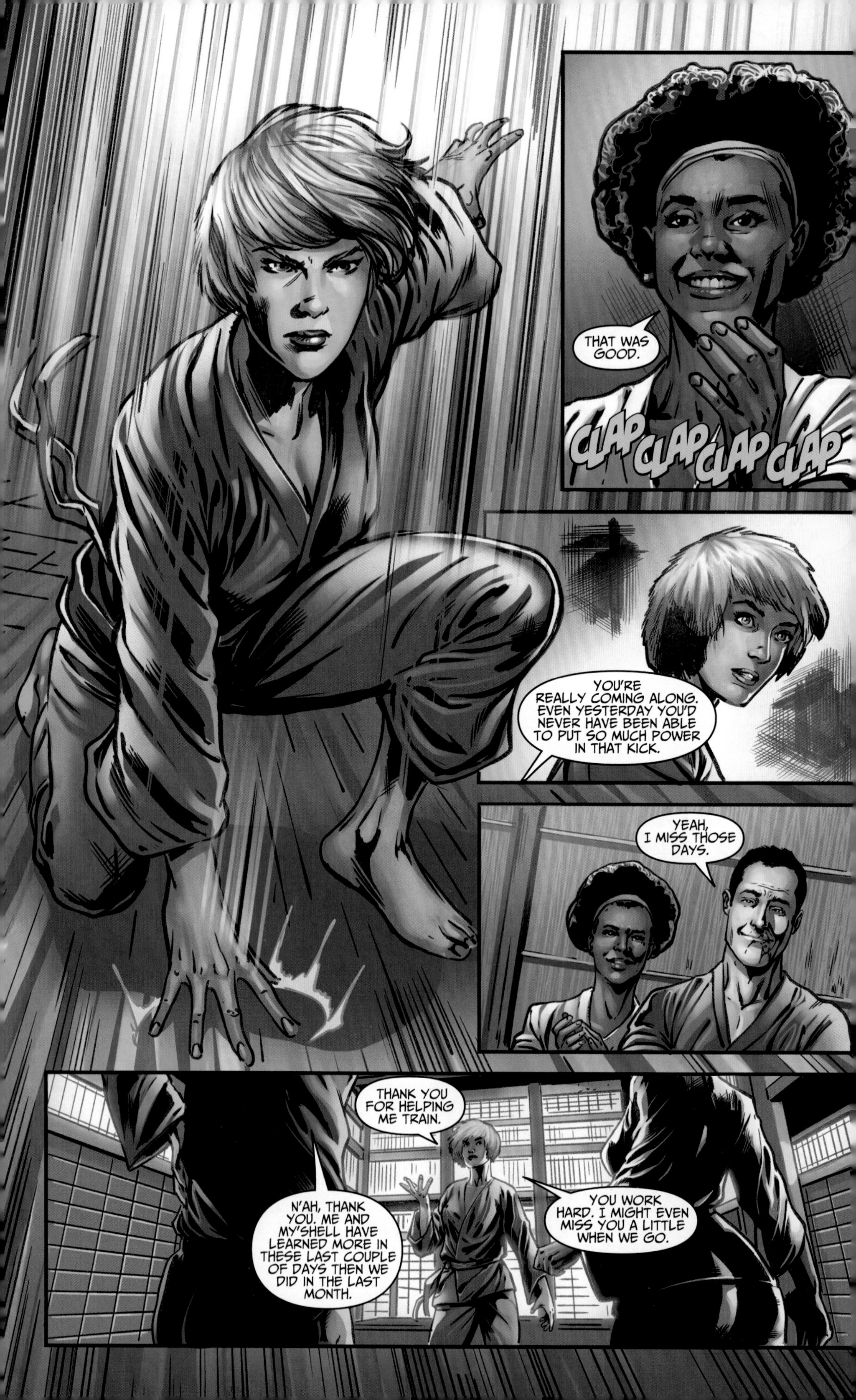
THAT WAS GOOD.
CLAP CLAP CLAP CLAP
YOU'RE REALLY COMING ALONG. EVEN YESTERDAY YOU'D NEVER HAVE BEEN ABLE TO PUT SO MUCH POWER IN THAT KICK.
YEAH, I MISS THOSE DAYS.
THANK YOU FOR HELPING ME TRAIN.
N'AH, THANK YOU. ME AND MY'SHELL HAVE LEARNED MORE IN THESE LAST COUPLE OF DAYS THEN WE DID IN THE LAST MONTH.
YOU WORK HARD. I MIGHT EVEN MISS YOU A LITTLE WHEN WE GO.

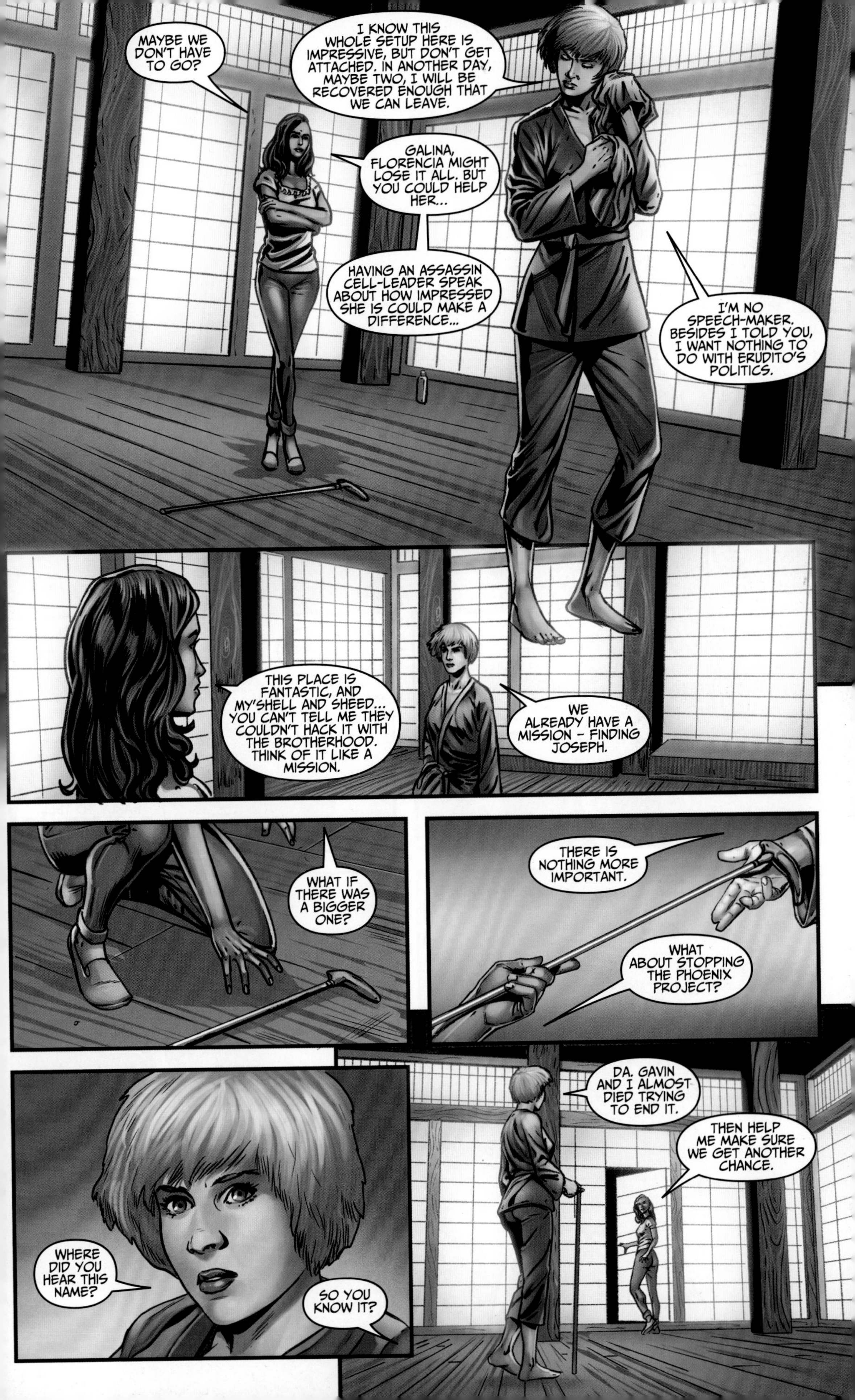
MAYBE WE DON'T HAVE TO GO?
I KNOW THIS WHOLE SETUP HERE IS IMPRESSIVE, BUT DON'T GET ATTACHED. IN ANOTHER DAY, MAYBE TWO, I WILL BE RECOVERED ENOUGH THAT WE CAN LEAVE.
GALINA, FLORENCIA MIGHT LOSE IT ALL. BUT YOU COULD HELP HER...
HAVING AN ASSASSIN CELL-LEADER SPEAK ABOUT HOW IMPRESSED SHE IS COULD MAKE A DIFFERENCE...
I'M NO SPEECH-MAKER. BESIDES I TOLD YOU, I WANT NOTHING TO DO WITH ERUDITO'S POLITICS.
THIS PLACE IS FANTASTIC, AND MY'SHELL AND SHEED... YOU CAN'T TELL ME THEY COULDN'T HACK IT WITH THE BROTHERHOOD. THINK OF IT LIKE A MISSION.
WE ALREADY HAVE A MISSION - FINDING JOSEPH.
WHAT IF THERE WAS A BIGGER ONE?
THERE IS NOTHING MORE IMPORTANT.
WHAT ABOUT STOPPING THE PHOENIX PROJECT?
WHERE DID YOU HEAR THIS NAME?
SO YOU KNOW IT?
DA. GAVIN AND I ALMOST DIED TRYING TO END IT.
THEN HELP ME MAKE SURE WE GET ANOTHER CHANCE.

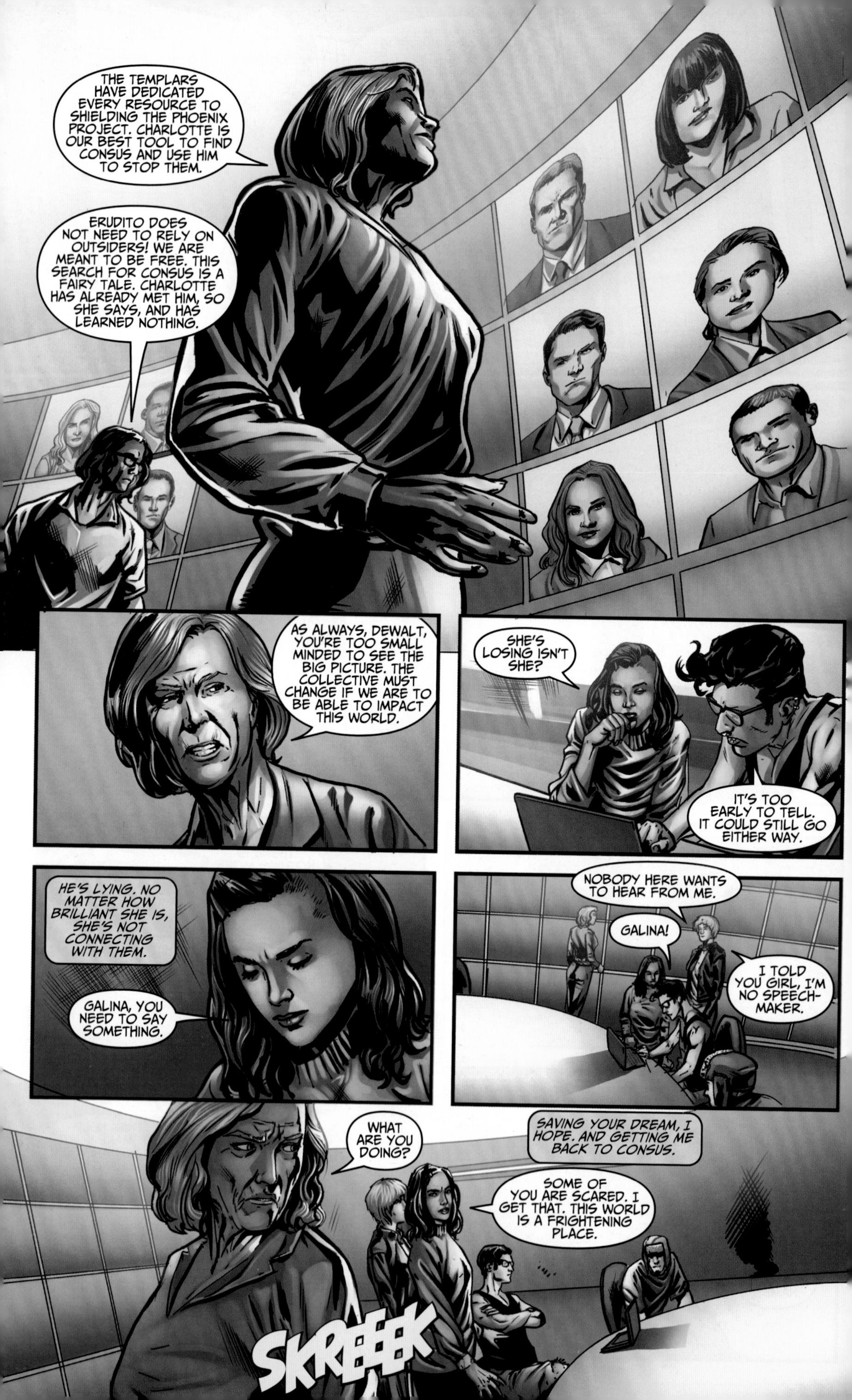
THE TEMPLARS HAVE DEDICATED EVERY RESOURCE TO SHIELDING THE PHOENIX PROJECT. CHARLOTTE IS OUR BEST TOOL TO FIND CONSUS AND USE HIM TO STOP THEM.
ERUDITO DOES NOT NEED TO RELY ON OUTSIDERS! WE ARE MEANT TO BE FREE. THIS SEARCH FOR CONSUS IS A FAIRY TALE. CHARLOTTE HAS ALREADY MET HIM, SO SHE SAYS, AND HAS LEARNED NOTHING.
AS ALWAYS, DEWALT, YOU'RE TOO SMALL MINDED TO SEE THE BIG PICTURE. THE COLLECTIVE MUST CHANGE IF WE ARE TO BE ABLE TO IMPACT THIS WORLD.
SHE'S LOSING ISN'T SHE?
IT'S TOO EARLY TO TELL. IT COULD STILL GO EITHER WAY.
HE'S LYING. NO MATTER HOW BRILLIANT SHE IS, SHE'S NOT CONNECTING WITH THEM.
GALINA, YOU NEED TO SAY SOMETHING.
NOBODY HERE WANTS TO HEAR FROM ME.
GALINA!
I TOLD YOU GIRL, I'M NO SPEECH-MAKER.
WHAT ARE YOU DOING?
SAVING YOUR DREAM, I HOPE. AND GETTING ME BACK TO CONSUS.
SOME OF YOU ARE SCARED. I GET THAT. THIS WORLD IS A FRIGHTENING PLACE.
SKREEEEK

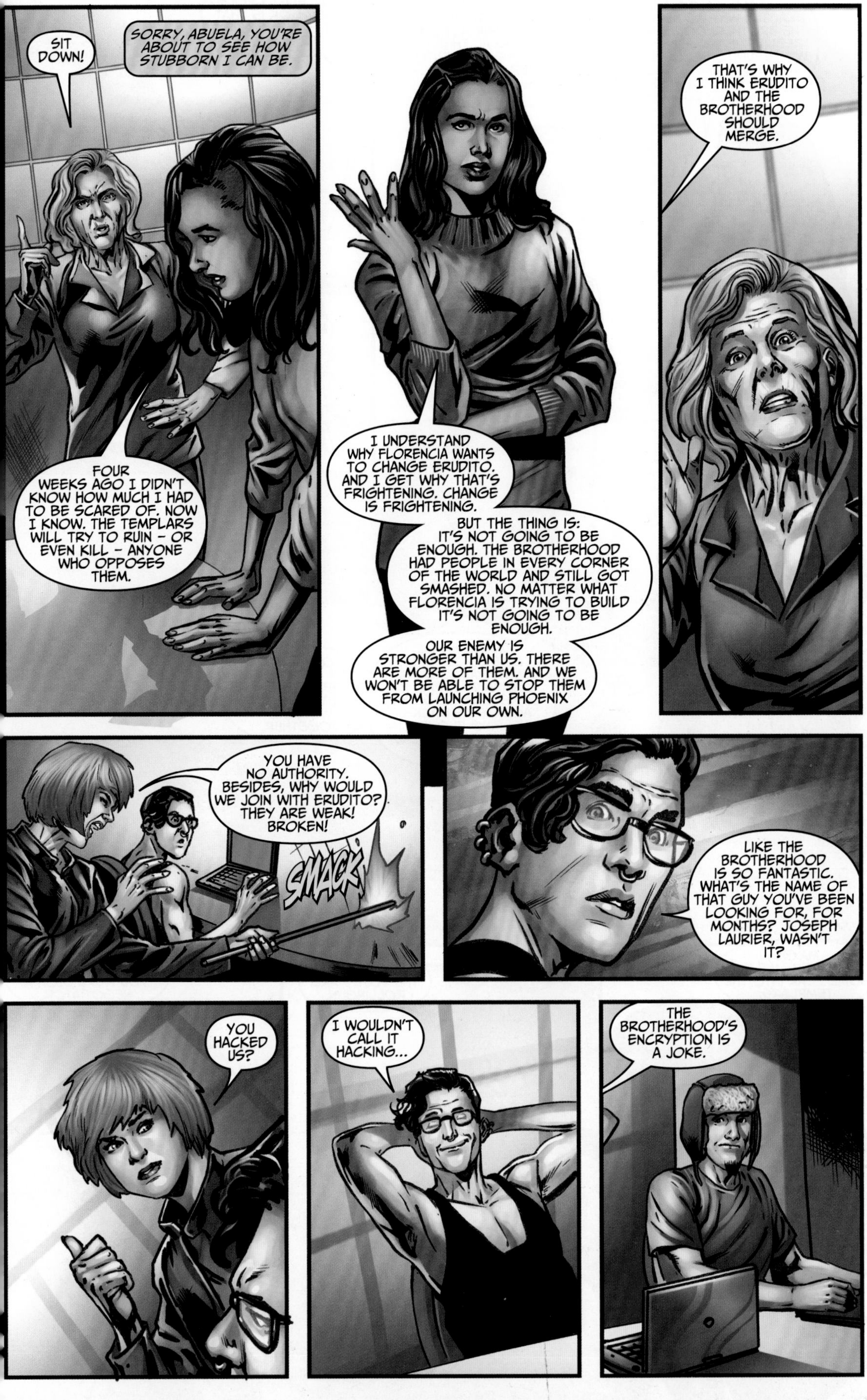

SIT DOWN!
SORRY, ABUELA, YOU'RE ABOUT TO SEE HOW STUBBORN I CAN BE.
FOUR WEEKS AGO I DIDN'T KNOW HOW MUCH I HAD TO BE SCARED OF. NOW I KNOW. THE TEMPLARS WILL TRY TO RUIN – OR EVEN KILL – ANYONE WHO OPPOSES THEM.
I UNDERSTAND WHY FLORENCIA WANTS TO CHANGE ERUDITO. AND I GET WHY THAT'S FRIGHTENING. CHANGE IS FRIGHTENING.
BUT THE THING IS: IT'S NOT GOING TO BE ENOUGH. THE BROTHERHOOD HAD PEOPLE IN EVERY CORNER OF THE WORLD AND STILL GOT SMASHED. NO MATTER WHAT FLORENCIA IS TRYING TO BUILD IT'S NOT GOING TO BE ENOUGH.
OUR ENEMY IS STRONGER THAN US. THERE ARE MORE OF THEM. AND WE WON'T BE ABLE TO STOP THEM FROM LAUNCHING PHOENIX ON OUR OWN.
THAT'S WHY I THINK ERUDITO AND THE BROTHERHOOD SHOULD MERGE.
YOU HAVE NO AUTHORITY. BESIDES, WHY WOULD WE JOIN WITH ERUDITO? THEY ARE WEAK! BROKEN!
SMACK
LIKE THE BROTHERHOOD IS SO FANTASTIC. WHAT'S THE NAME OF THAT GUY YOU'VE BEEN LOOKING FOR, FOR MONTHS? JOSEPH LAURIER, WASN'T IT?
YOU HACKED US?
I WOULDN'T CALL IT HACKING...
THE BROTHERHOOD'S ENCRYPTION IS A JOKE.

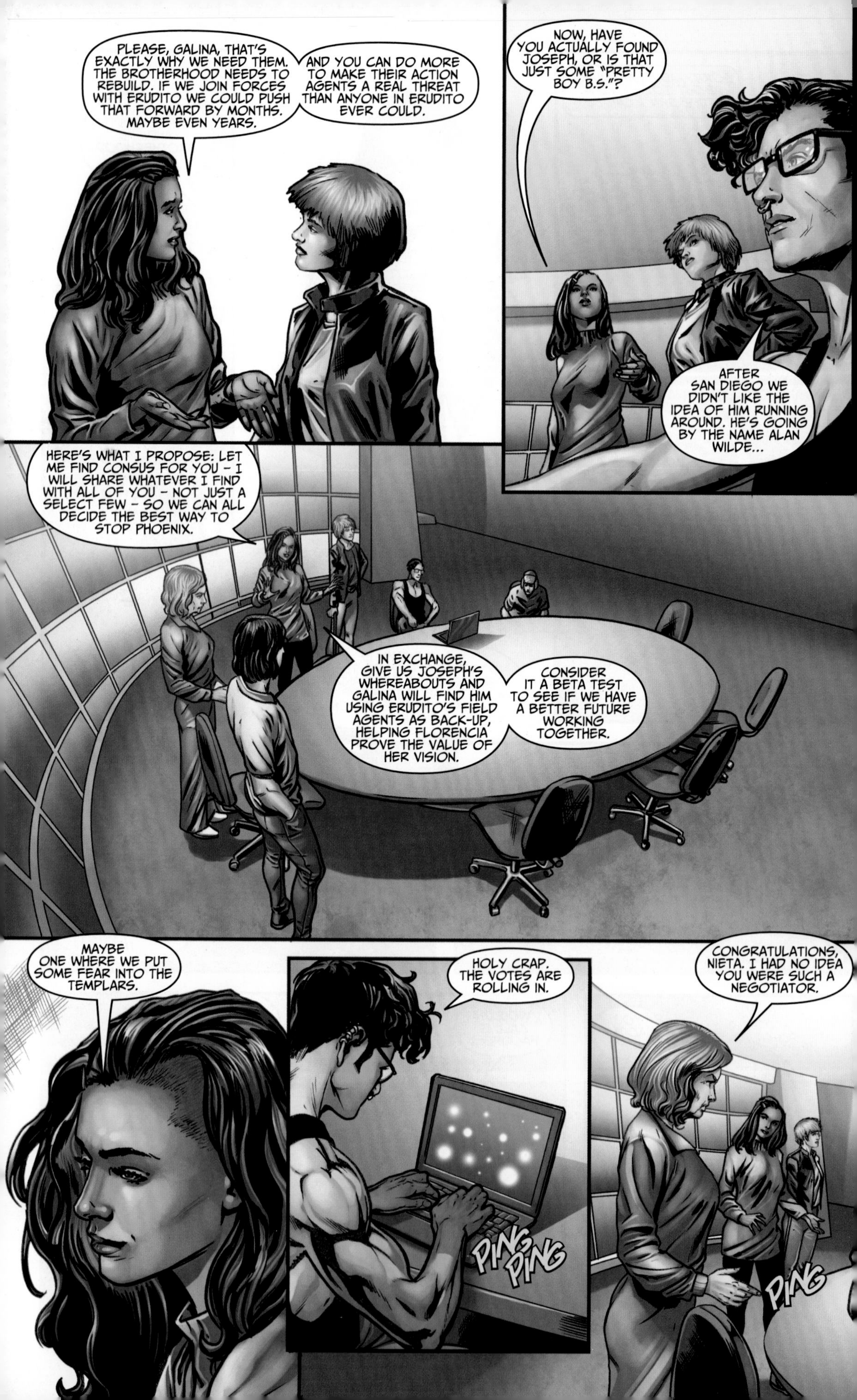
PLEASE, GALINA, THAT'S EXACTLY WHY WE NEED THEM. THE BROTHERHOOD NEEDS TO REBUILD. IF WE JOIN FORCES WITH ERUDITO WE COULD PUSH THAT FORWARD BY MONTHS. MAYBE EVEN YEARS.
AND YOU CAN DO MORE TO MAKE THEIR ACTION AGENTS A REAL THREAT THAN ANYONE IN ERUDITO EVER COULD.
NOW, HAVE YOU ACTUALLY FOUND JOSEPH, OR IS THAT JUST SOME "PRETTY BOY B.S."?
AFTER SAN DIEGO WE DIDN'T LIKE THE IDEA OF HIM RUNNING AROUND. HE'S GOING BY THE NAME ALAN WILDE...
HERE'S WHAT I PROPOSE: LET ME FIND CONSUS FOR YOU – I WILL SHARE WHATEVER I FIND WITH ALL OF YOU – NOT JUST A SELECT FEW – SO WE CAN ALL DECIDE THE BEST WAY TO STOP PHOENIX.
IN EXCHANGE, GIVE US JOSEPH'S WHEREABOUTS AND GALINA WILL FIND HIM USING ERUDITO'S FIELD AGENTS AS BACK-UP, HELPING FLORENCIA PROVE THE VALUE OF HER VISION.
CONSIDER IT A BETA TEST TO SEE IF WE HAVE A BETTER FUTURE WORKING TOGETHER.
MAYBE ONE WHERE WE PUT SOME FEAR INTO THE TEMPLARS.
HOLY CRAP. THE VOTES ARE ROLLING IN.
PING PING
CONGRATULATIONS, NIETA. I HAD NO IDEA YOU WERE SUCH A NEGOTIATOR.
PING

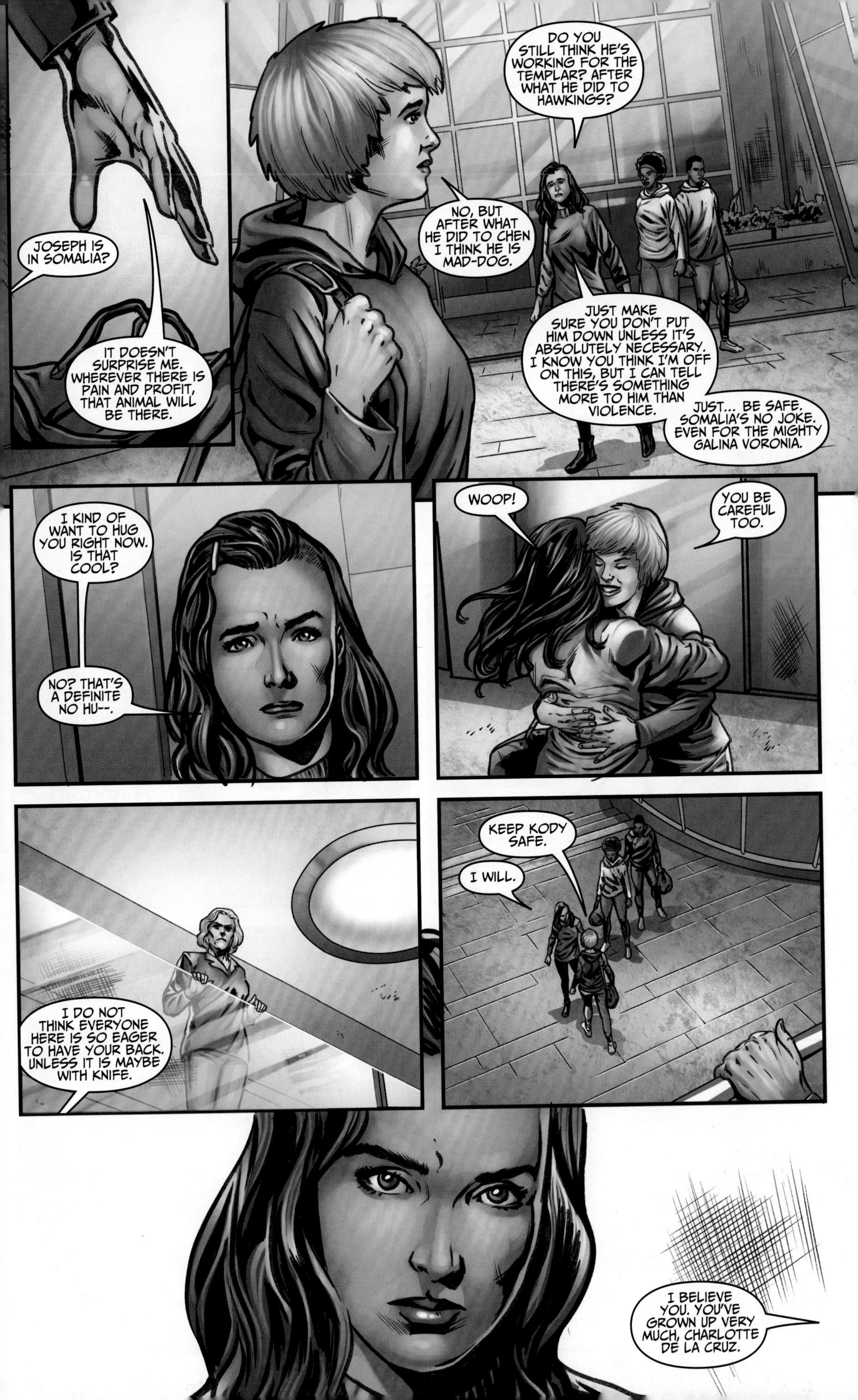
JOSEPH IS IN SOMALIA?
IT DOESN'T SURPRISE ME. WHEREVER THERE IS PAIN AND PROFIT, THAT ANIMAL WILL BE THERE.
DO YOU STILL THINK HE'S WORKING FOR THE TEMPLAR? AFTER WHAT HE DID TO HAWKINGS?
NO, BUT AFTER WHAT HE DID TO CHEN I THINK HE IS MAD-DOG.
JUST MAKE SURE YOU DON'T PUT HIM DOWN UNLESS IT'S ABSOLUTELY NECESSARY. I KNOW YOU THINK I'M OFF ON THIS, BUT I CAN TELL THERE'S SOMETHING MORE TO HIM THAN VIOLENCE.
JUST... BE SAFE. SOMALIA'S NO JOKE. EVEN FOR THE MIGHTY GALINA VORONIA.
I KIND OF WANT TO HUG YOU RIGHT NOW. IS THAT COOL?
NO? THAT'S A DEFINITE NO HU--.
WOOP!
YOU BE CAREFUL TOO.
I DO NOT THINK EVERYONE HERE IS SO EAGER TO HAVE YOUR BACK. UNLESS IT IS MAYBE WITH KNIFE.
KEEP KODY SAFE.
I WILL.
I BELIEVE YOU. YOU'VE GROWN UP VERY MUCH, CHARLOTTE DE LA CRUZ.

SO, ASIDE FROM THE FACT THAT I'M GOING TO MEET THIS GIOVANNI BORGIA, CAN YOU MAYBE TELL ME WHICH ANCESTOR I'M GOING TO JUMP INTO?

I'M GONNA KEEP THAT A SURPRISE. BUT TRUST ME, I THINK YOU'LL LIKE IT.

OH, SO NOW YOU THINK I KNOW WHAT I LIKE?

I THINK I HAVE AN IDEA.

EXCUSE ME. THE AMAZING, UNTRAINED IDIOT NEEDS TO GET AT THE MACHINE HE BUILT.

GO AHEAD, CHARLOTTE AND I CAN WAIT.

IF YOU THREE ARE FINISHED WITH YOUR SOAP OPERA, I'D LIKE TO KNOW THE RESULTS OF THE STRESS TEST.

EXCEPT FOR A LITTLE PUNCTURE MARK, SHE'S GREAT.

PUNCTURE? WHAT PUNCTURE?

I HADN'T ASKED... I MEAN EVERYTHING CAME UP CLEAN....

YOU DIDN'T ASK?

YEAH... I GOT JABBED BY THIS TEMPLAR NAMED SANCHEZ. HE WAS JUST TRYING TO INTIMIDATE ME. AFTER A DAY WHEN NOTHING HAPPENED, I JUST DIDN'T THINK IT WAS A BIG DEAL.

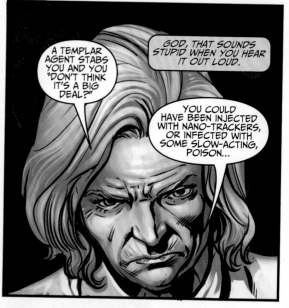

A TEMPLAR AGENT STABS YOU AND YOU "DON'T THINK IT'S A BIG DEAL?"

GOD, THAT SOUNDS STUPID WHEN YOU HEAR IT OUT LOUD.

YOU COULD HAVE BEEN INJECTED WITH NANO-TRACKERS, OR INFECTED WITH SOME SLOW-ACTING, POISON...

WHAT LEVEL SCAN DID YOU DO?

STANDARD EPSILON. I DIDN'T WANT TO KEEP HER IN THERE TOO LONG.

TAP TAP

I'M SORRY, ABUELA. I HAD NO IDEA.

RRRrr

THERE ARE A LOT OF THINGS YOU HAVE NO IDEA ABOUT. DO YOU THINK DEWALT REALLY WANTS A MERGER WITH THE BROTHERHOOD?

HE'LL USE YOU TO GET RID OF ME.

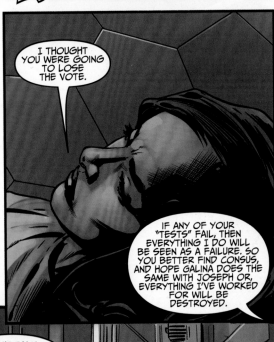

I THOUGHT YOU WERE GOING TO LOSE THE VOTE.

IF ANY OF YOUR "TESTS" FAIL, THEN EVERYTHING I DO WILL BE SEEN AS A FAILURE. SO YOU BETTER FIND CONSUS, AND HOPE GALINA DOES THE SAME WITH JOSEPH OR, EVERYTHING I'VE WORKED FOR WILL BE DESTROYED.

ABUELA...

DON'T TALK. THE SCAN WILL TAKE TWO HOURS. TRY TO KEEP YOUR MOUTH SHUT THIS TIME OR ELSE WE'LL HAVE TO RESTART.

GIVE ME THE RESULTS AS SOON AS YOU GET THEM.

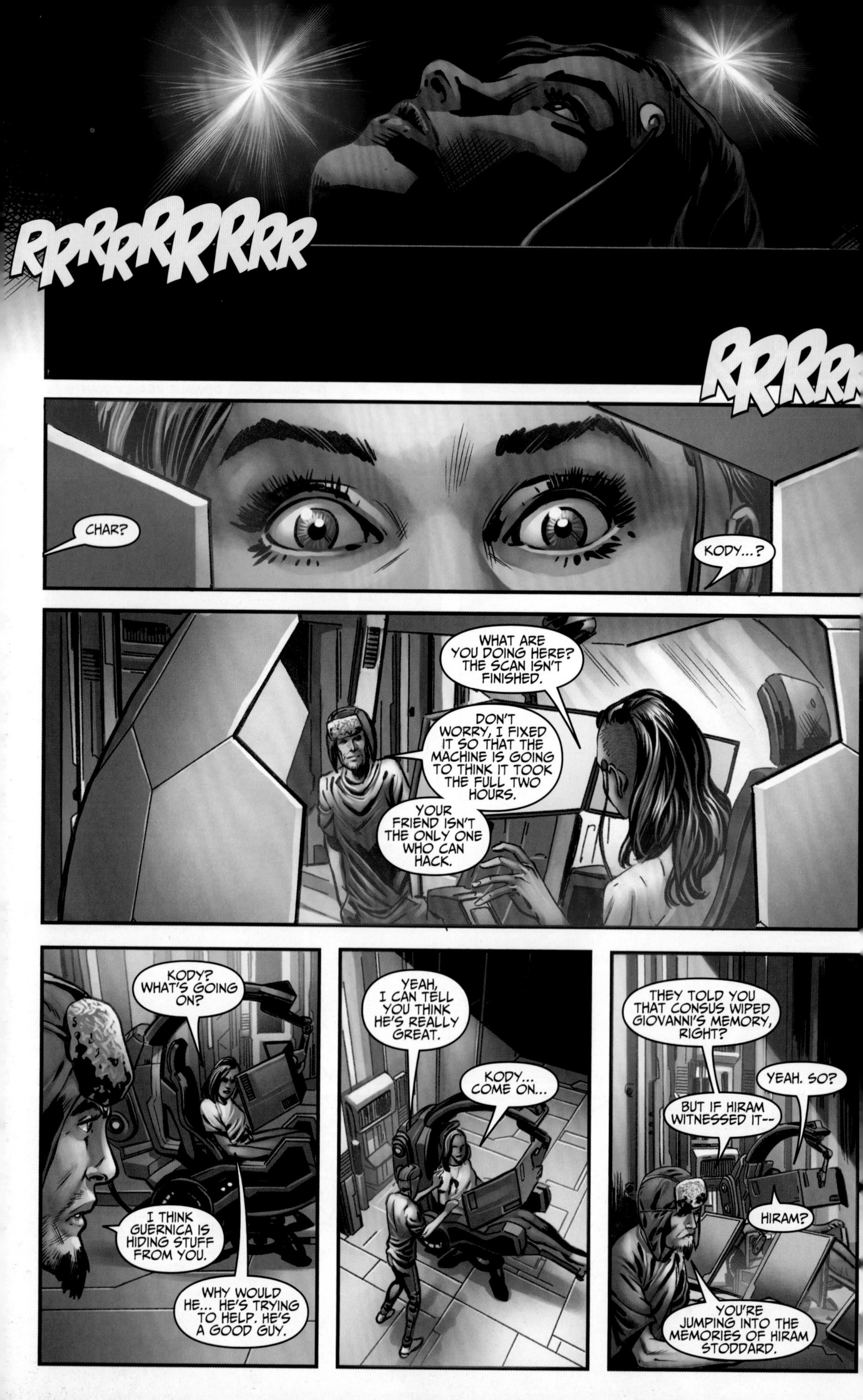
RRRRRRRRR
RRRRR
CHAR?
KODY...?
WHAT ARE YOU DOING HERE? THE SCAN ISN'T FINISHED.
DON'T WORRY, I FIXED IT SO THAT THE MACHINE IS GOING TO THINK IT TOOK THE FULL TWO HOURS.
YOUR FRIEND ISN'T THE ONLY ONE WHO CAN HACK.
KODY? WHAT'S GOING ON?
I THINK GUERNICA IS HIDING STUFF FROM YOU.
WHY WOULD HE... HE'S TRYING TO HELP. HE'S A GOOD GUY.
YEAH, I CAN TELL YOU THINK HE'S REALLY GREAT.
KODY... COME ON...
THEY TOLD YOU THAT CONSUS WIPED GIOVANNI'S MEMORY, RIGHT?
YEAH. SO?
BUT IF HIRAM WITNESSED IT--
HIRAM?
YOU'RE JUMPING INTO THE MEMORIES OF HIRAM STODDARD.

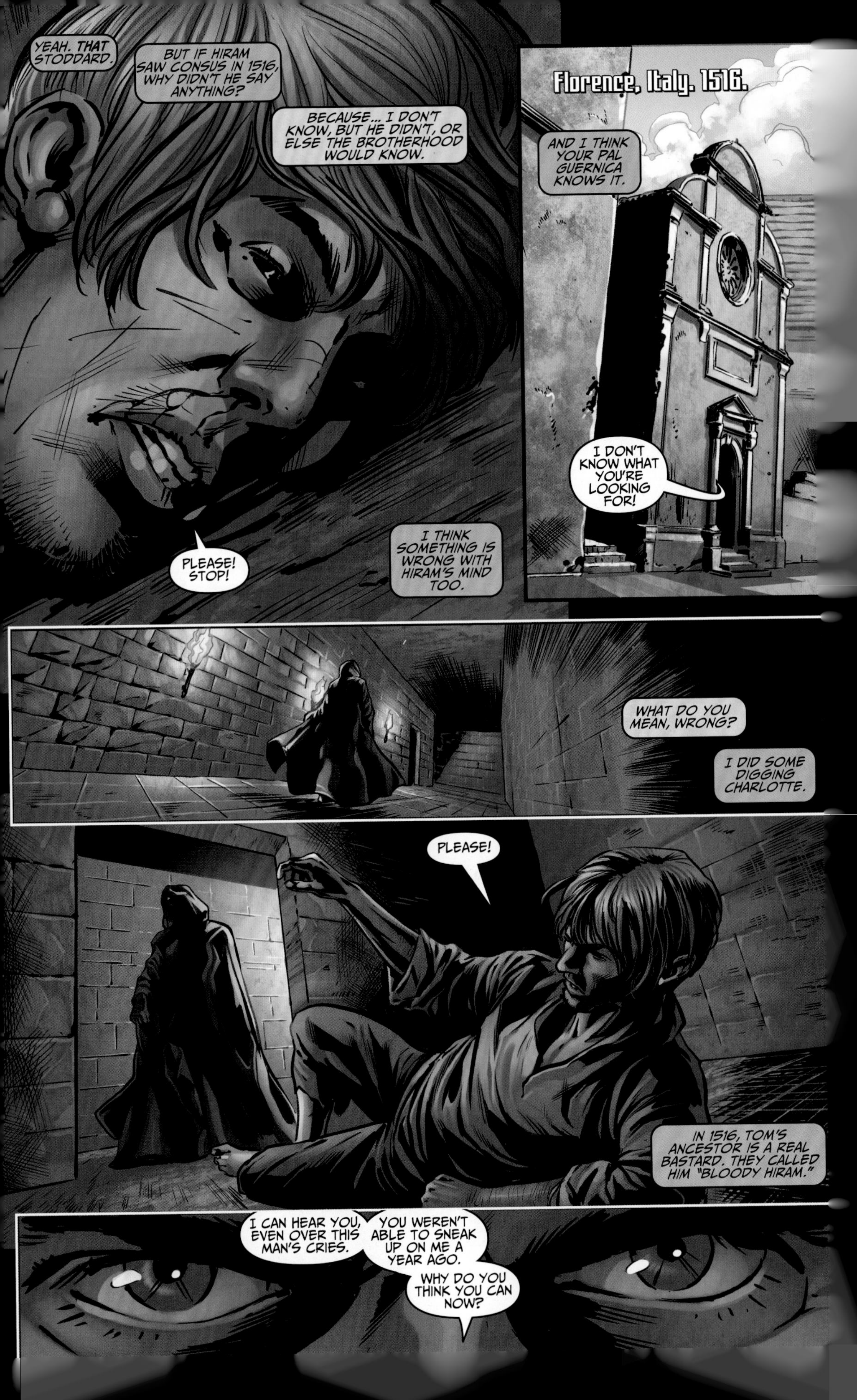
YEAH. THAT STODDARD.
BUT IF HIRAM SAW CONSUS IN 1516, WHY DIDN'T HE SAY ANYTHING?
BECAUSE... I DON'T KNOW, BUT HE DIDN'T, OR ELSE THE BROTHERHOOD WOULD KNOW.
PLEASE! STOP!
I THINK SOMETHING IS WRONG WITH HIRAM'S MIND TOO.
Florence, Italy. 1516.
AND I THINK YOUR PAL GUERNICA KNOWS IT.
I DON'T KNOW WHAT YOU'RE LOOKING FOR!
WHAT DO YOU MEAN, WRONG?
I DID SOME DIGGING CHARLOTTE.
PLEASE!
IN 1516, TOM'S ANCESTOR IS A REAL BASTARD. THEY CALLED HIM "BLOODY HIRAM."
I CAN HEAR YOU, EVEN OVER THIS MAN'S CRIES.
YOU WEREN'T ABLE TO SNEAK UP ON ME A YEAR AGO.
WHY DO YOU THINK YOU CAN NOW?

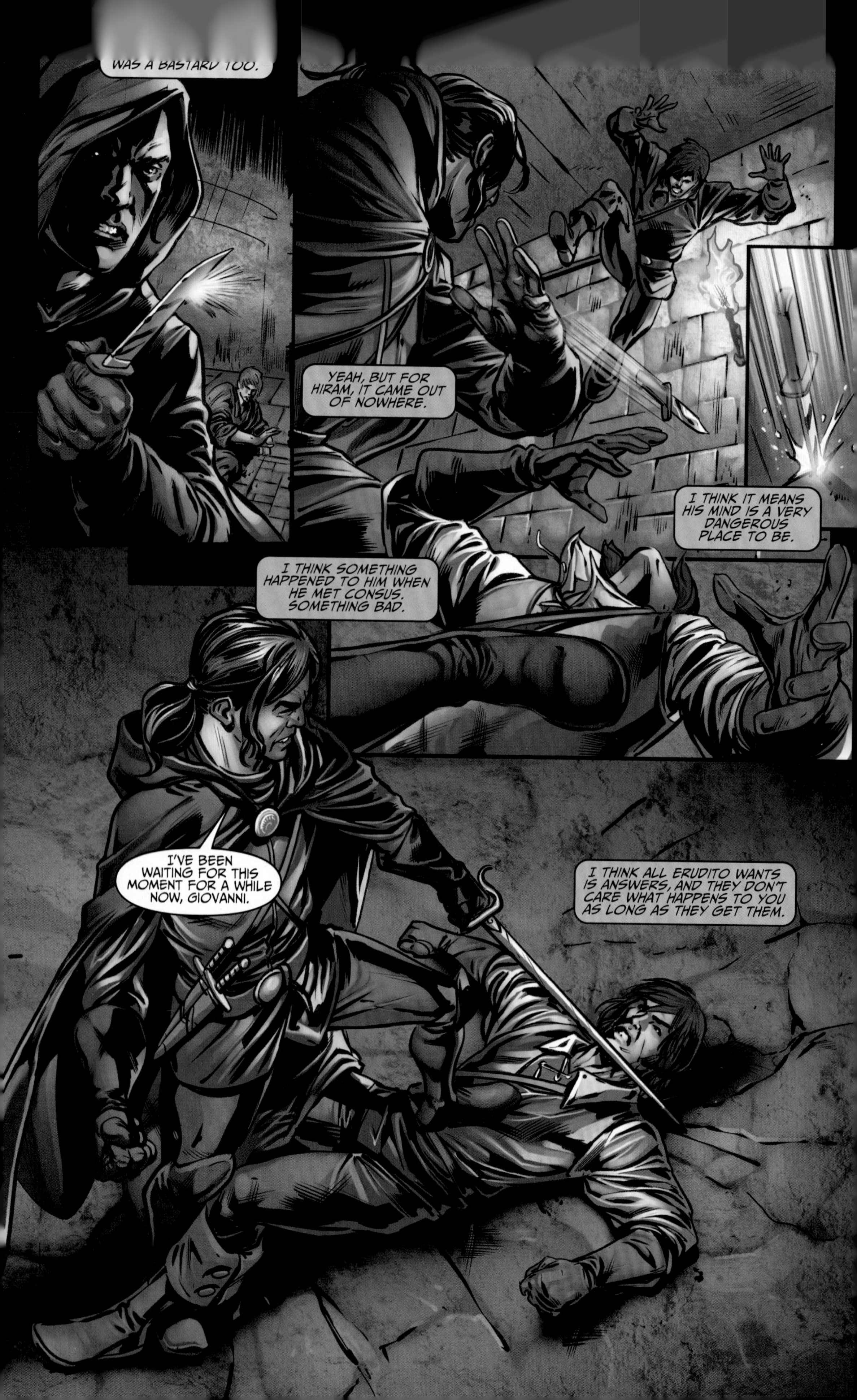
WAS A BASTARD TOO.
YEAH, BUT FOR HIRAM, IT CAME OUT OF NOWHERE.
I THINK IT MEANS HIS MIND IS A VERY DANGEROUS PLACE TO BE.
I THINK SOMETHING HAPPENED TO HIM WHEN HE MET CONSUS. SOMETHING BAD.
I'VE BEEN WAITING FOR THIS MOMENT FOR A WHILE NOW, GIOVANNI.
I THINK ALL ERUDITO WANTS IS ANSWERS, AND THEY DON'T CARE WHAT HAPPENS TO YOU AS LONG AS THEY GET THEM.

CHAPTER
TWELVE

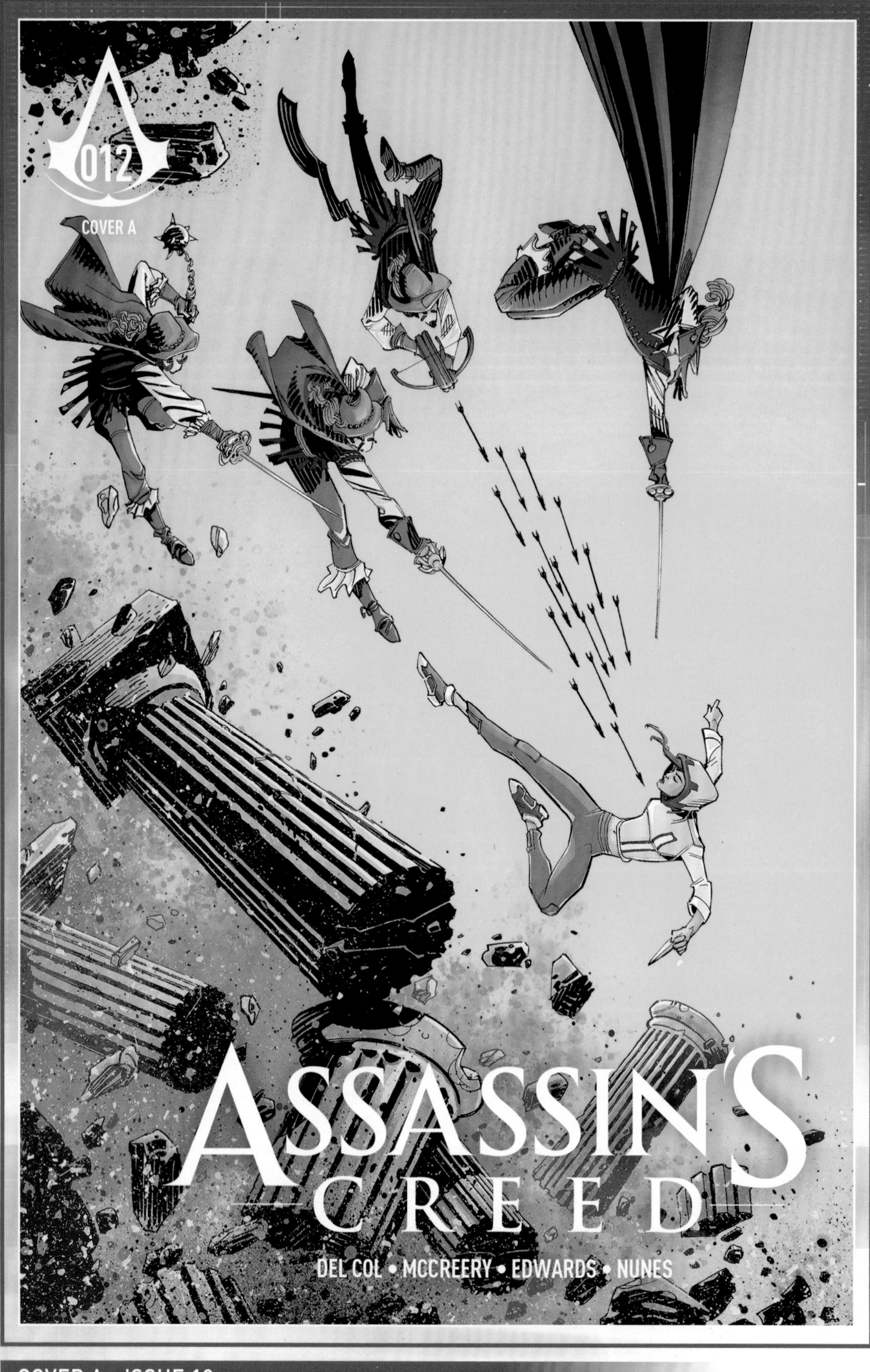
012
COVER A
ASSASSIN'S
CREED
DEL COL • MCCREERY • EDWARDS • NUNES

COVER A - ISSUE 12
JOHN MCCREA

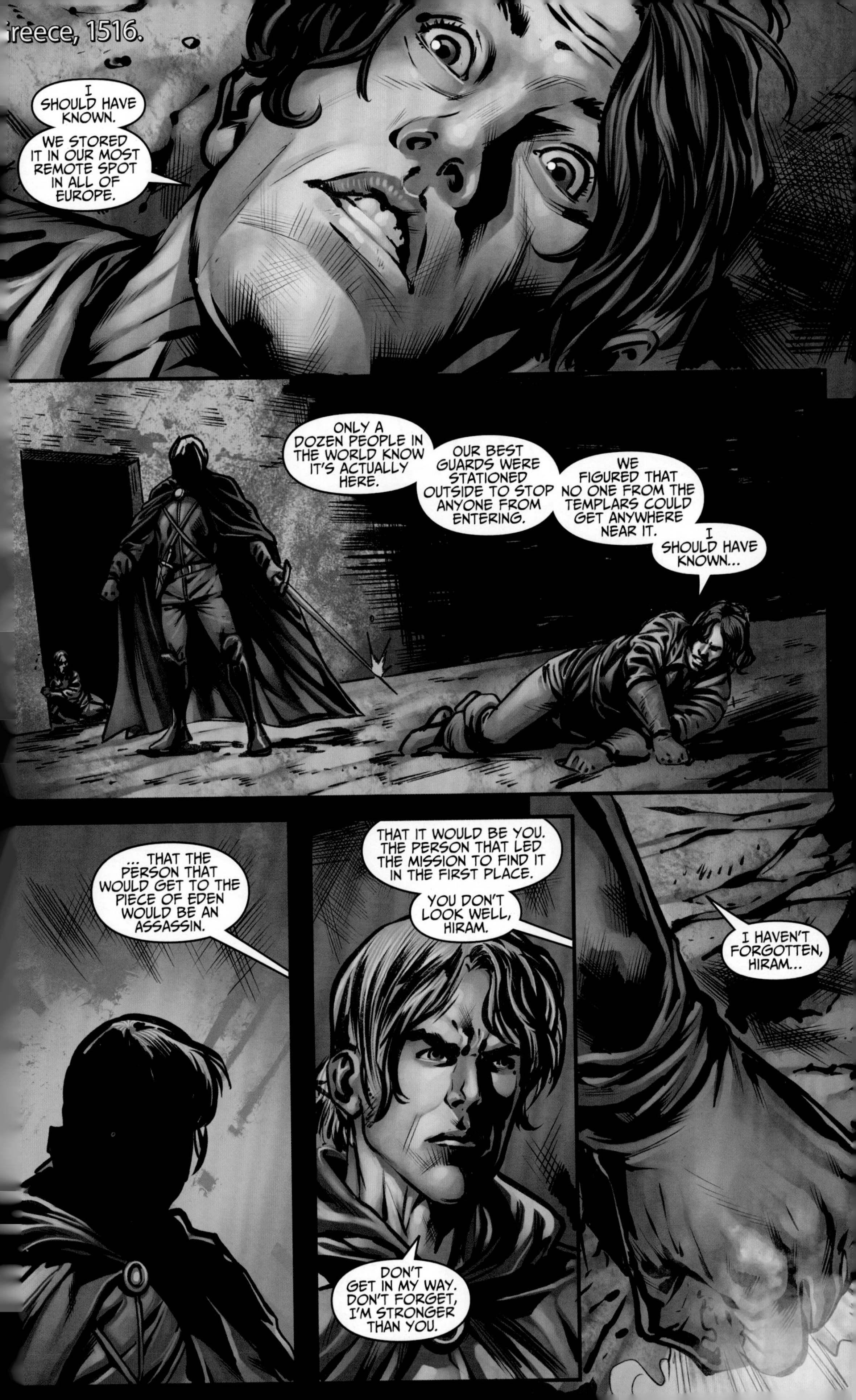
reece, 1516.
I SHOULD HAVE KNOWN.
WE STORED IT IN OUR MOST REMOTE SPOT IN ALL OF EUROPE.
ONLY A DOZEN PEOPLE IN THE WORLD KNOW IT'S ACTUALLY HERE.
OUR BEST GUARDS WERE STATIONED OUTSIDE TO STOP ANYONE FROM ENTERING.
WE FIGURED THAT NO ONE FROM THE TEMPLARS COULD GET ANYWHERE NEAR IT.
I SHOULD HAVE KNOWN...
... THAT THE PERSON THAT WOULD GET TO THE PIECE OF EDEN WOULD BE AN ASSASSIN.
THAT IT WOULD BE YOU. THE PERSON THAT LED THE MISSION TO FIND IT IN THE FIRST PLACE.
YOU DON'T LOOK WELL, HIRAM.
I HAVEN'T FORGOTTEN, HIRAM...
DON'T GET IN MY WAY. DON'T FORGET, I'M STRONGER THAN YOU.

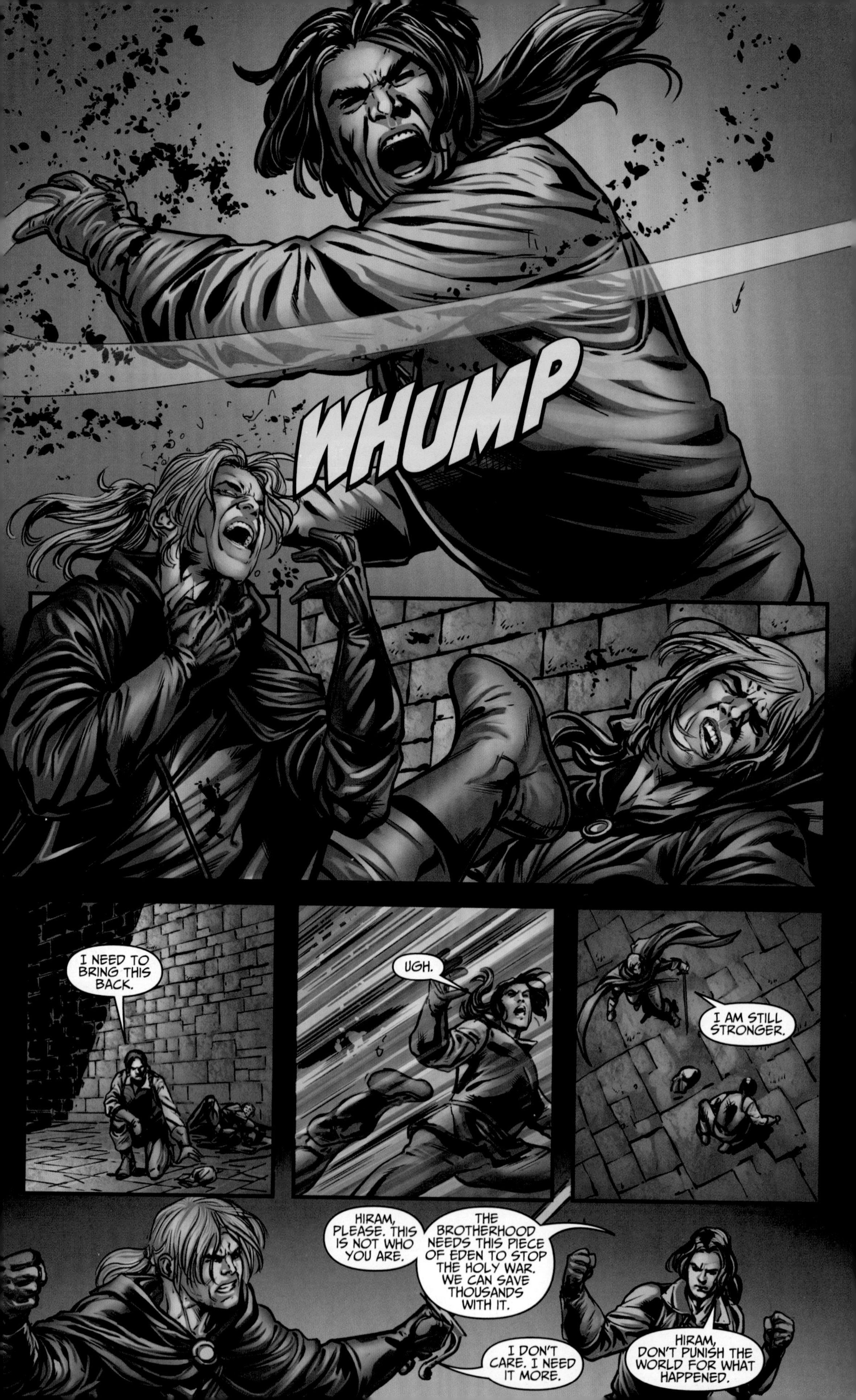
WHUMP
I NEED TO BRING THIS BACK.
UGH.
I AM STILL STRONGER.
HIRAM, PLEASE. THIS IS NOT WHO YOU ARE.
THE BROTHERHOOD NEEDS THIS PIECE OF EDEN TO STOP THE HOLY WAR. WE CAN SAVE THOUSANDS WITH IT.
I DON'T CARE. I NEED IT MORE.
HIRAM, DON'T PUNISH THE WORLD FOR WHAT HAPPENED.

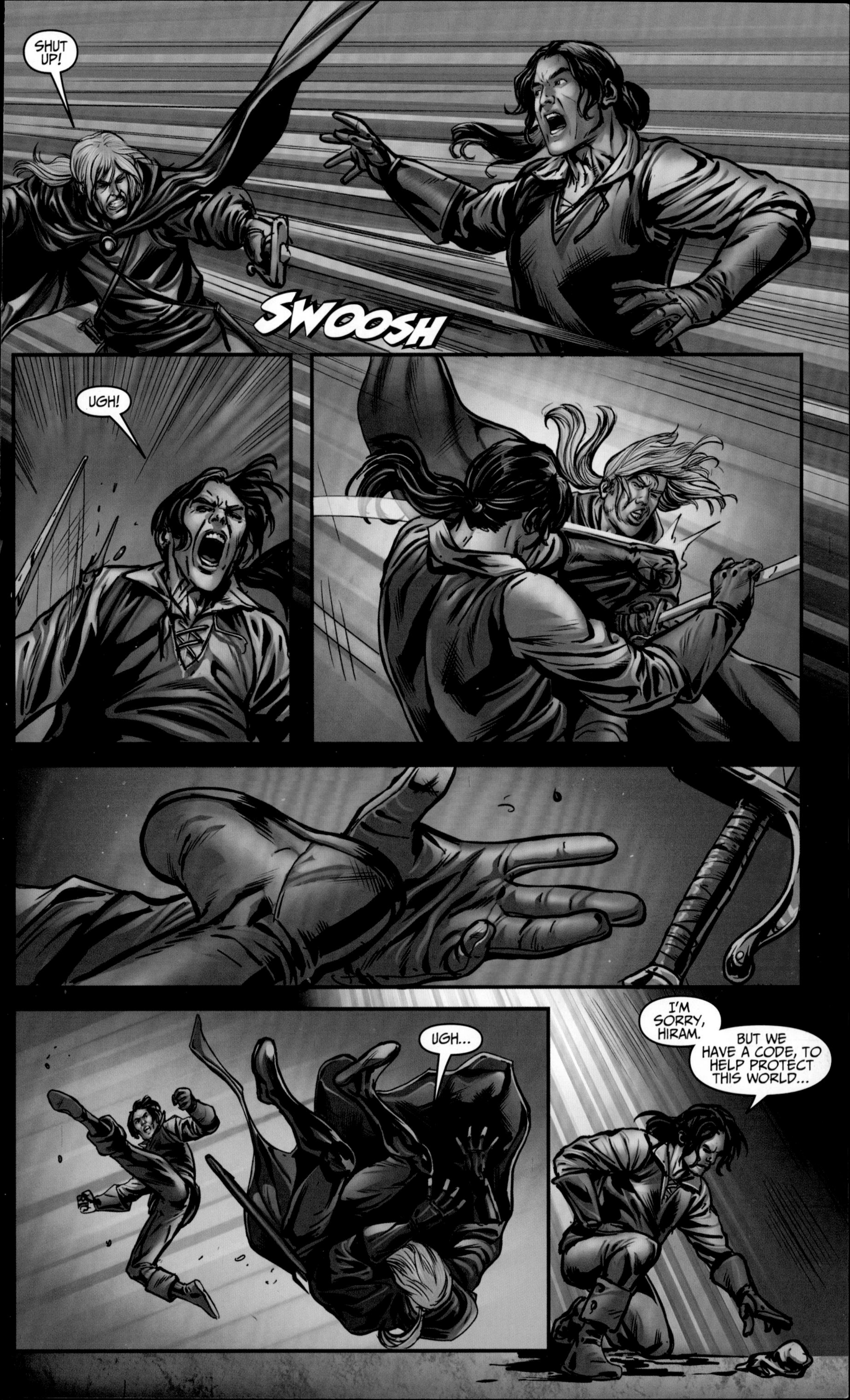
SHUT UP!
SWOOSH
UGH!
UGH...
I'M SORRY, HIRAM.
BUT WE HAVE A CODE, TO HELP PROTECT THIS WORLD...

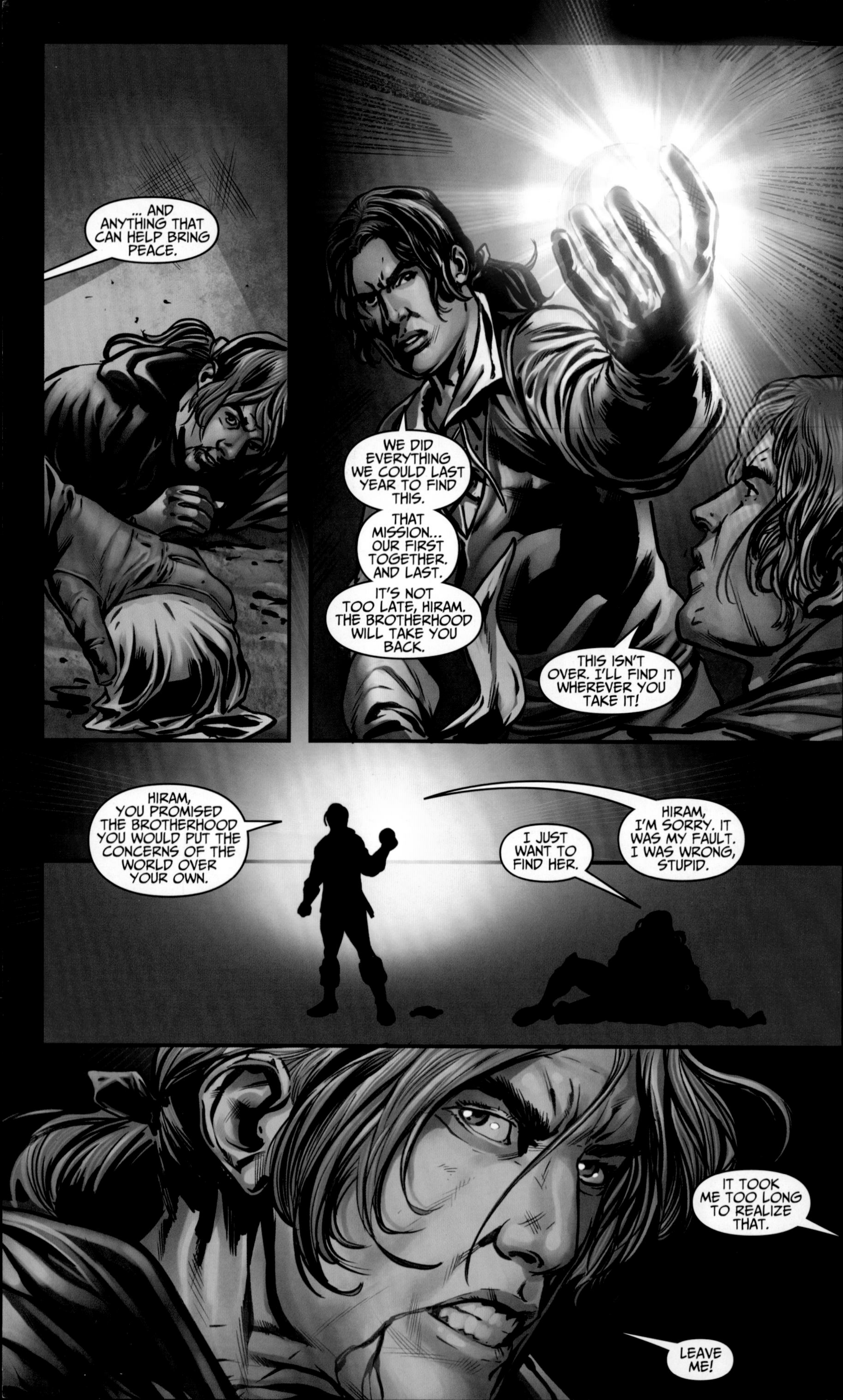

... AND ANYTHING THAT CAN HELP BRING PEACE.
WE DID EVERYTHING WE COULD LAST YEAR TO FIND THIS.
THAT MISSION... OUR FIRST TOGETHER. AND LAST.
IT'S NOT TOO LATE, HIRAM. THE BROTHERHOOD WILL TAKE YOU BACK.
THIS ISN'T OVER. I'LL FIND IT WHEREVER YOU TAKE IT!
HIRAM, YOU PROMISED THE BROTHERHOOD YOU WOULD PUT THE CONCERNS OF THE WORLD OVER YOUR OWN.
HIRAM, I'M SORRY. IT WAS MY FAULT. I WAS WRONG, STUPID.
I JUST WANT TO FIND HER.
IT TOOK ME TOO LONG TO REALIZE THAT.
LEAVE ME!

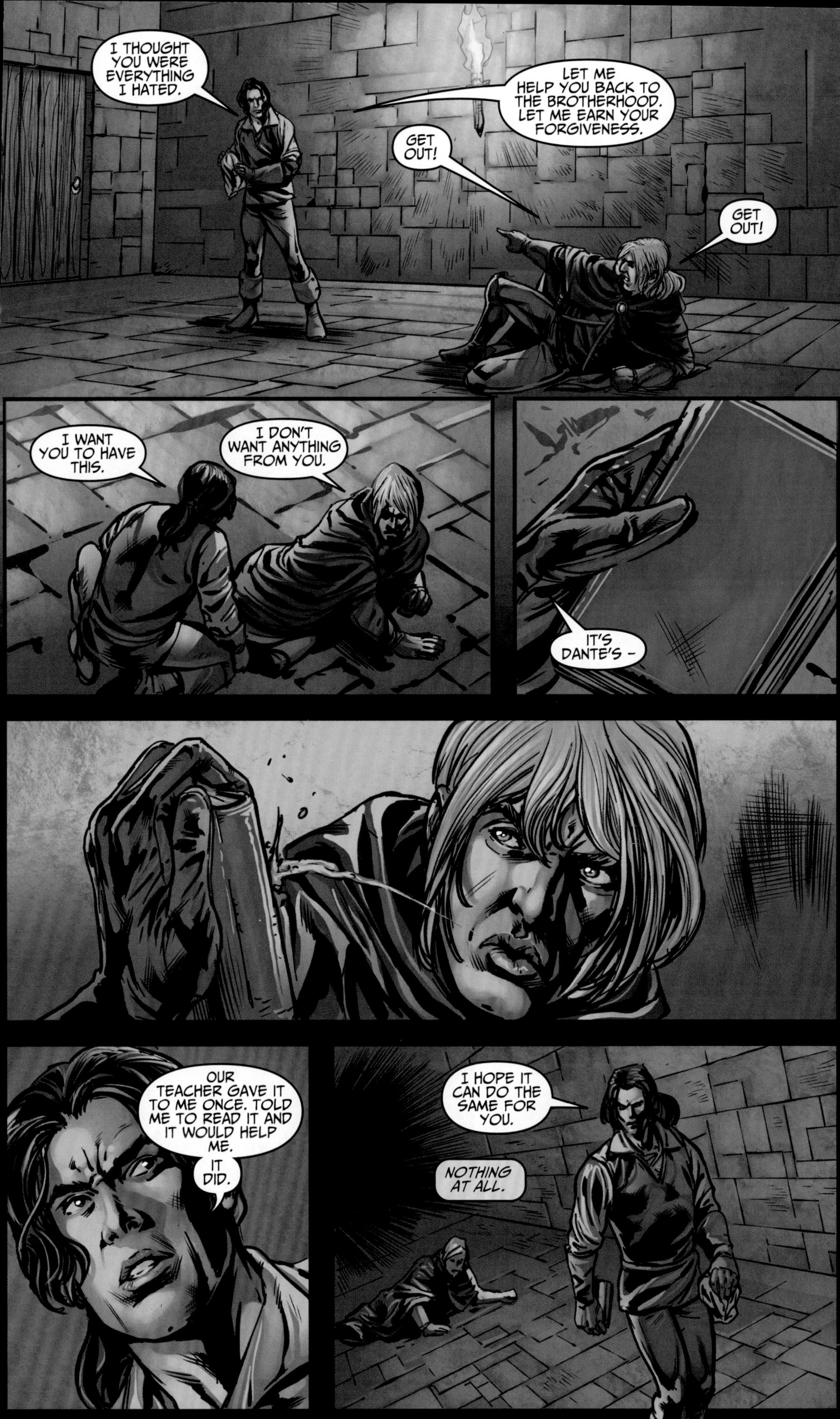
I THOUGHT YOU WERE EVERYTHING I HATED.
LET ME HELP YOU BACK TO THE BROTHERHOOD. LET ME EARN YOUR FORGIVENESS.
GET OUT!
GET OUT!
I WANT YOU TO HAVE THIS.
I DON'T WANT ANYTHING FROM YOU.
IT'S DANTE'S -
OUR TEACHER GAVE IT TO ME ONCE. TOLD ME TO READ IT AND IT WOULD HELP ME.
IT DID.
I HOPE IT CAN DO THE SAME FOR YOU.
NOTHING AT ALL.

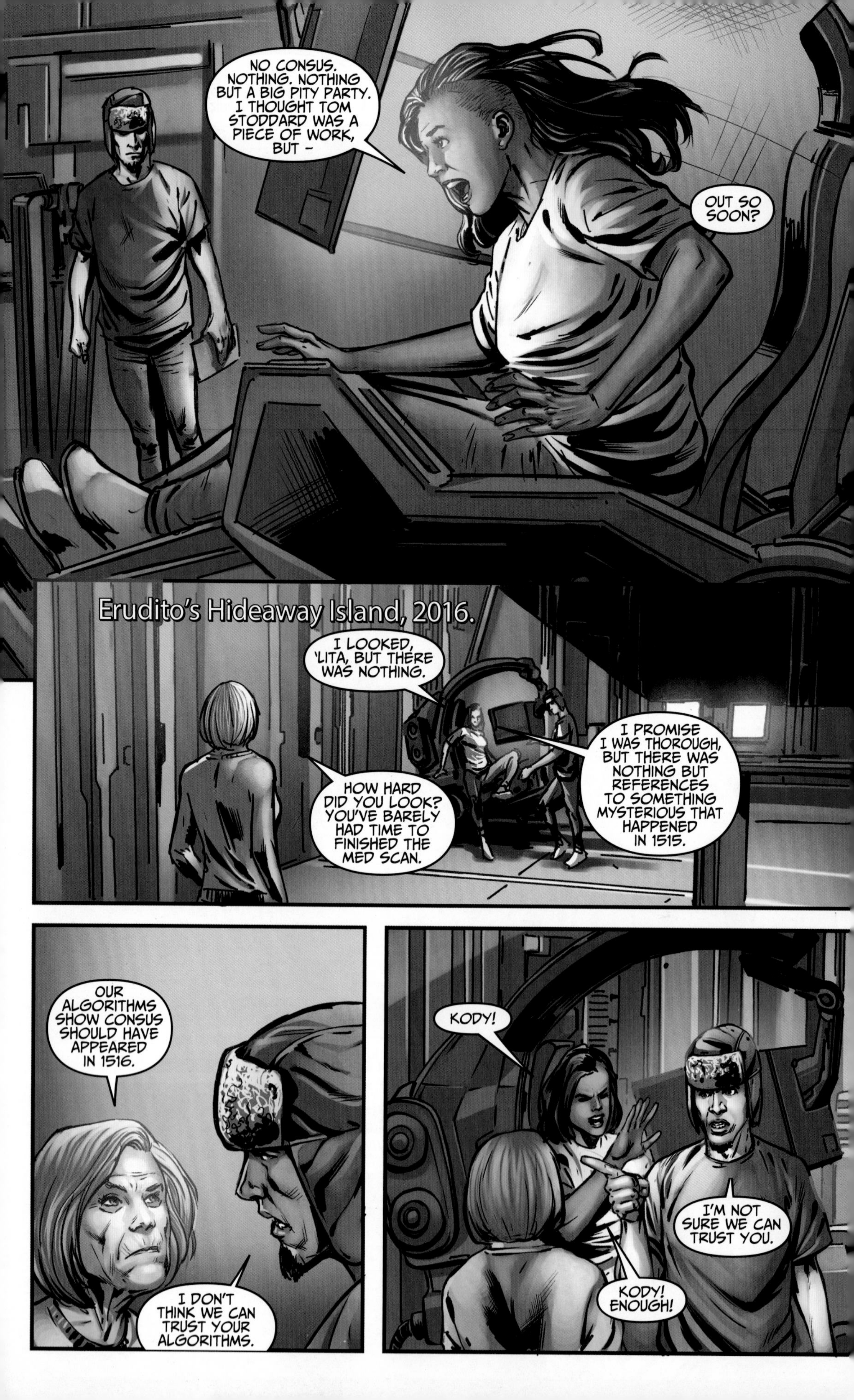
NO CONSUS. NOTHING. NOTHING BUT A BIG PITY PARTY. I THOUGHT TOM STODDARD WAS A PIECE OF WORK, BUT –
OUT SO SOON?
Erudito's Hideaway Island, 2016.
I LOOKED, 'LITA, BUT THERE WAS NOTHING.
HOW HARD DID YOU LOOK? YOU'VE BARELY HAD TIME TO FINISHED THE MED SCAN.
I PROMISE I WAS THOROUGH, BUT THERE WAS NOTHING BUT REFERENCES TO SOMETHING MYSTERIOUS THAT HAPPENED IN 1515.
OUR ALGORITHMS SHOW CONSUS SHOULD HAVE APPEARED IN 1516.
I DON'T THINK WE CAN TRUST YOUR ALGORITHMS.
KODY!
I'M NOT SURE WE CAN TRUST YOU.
KODY! ENOUGH!

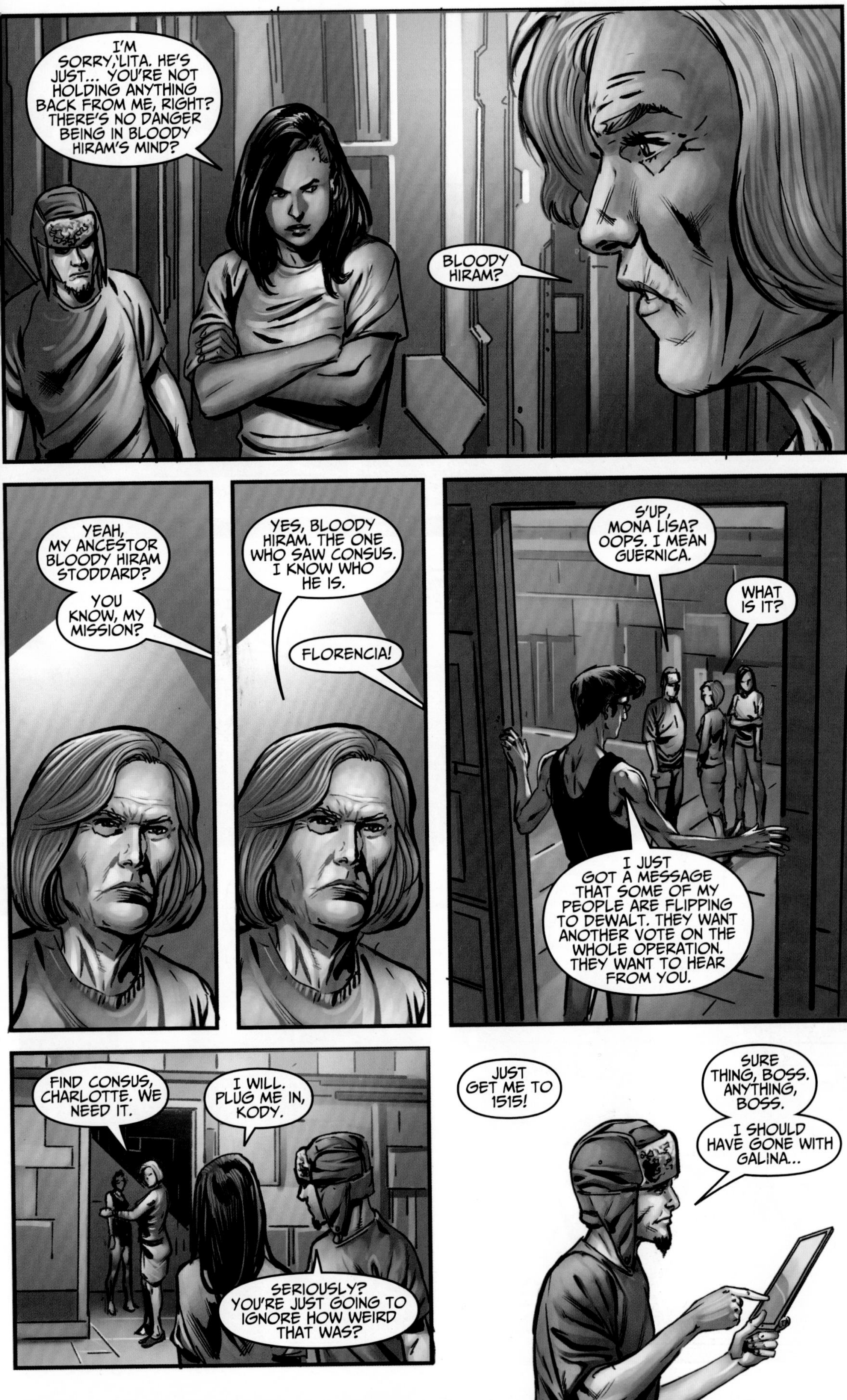
I'M SORRY, 'LITA. HE'S JUST... YOU'RE NOT HOLDING ANYTHING BACK FROM ME, RIGHT? THERE'S NO DANGER BEING IN BLOODY HIRAM'S MIND?
BLOODY HIRAM?
YEAH, MY ANCESTOR BLOODY HIRAM STODDARD?
YOU KNOW, MY MISSION?
YES, BLOODY HIRAM. THE ONE WHO SAW CONSUS. I KNOW WHO HE IS.
FLORENCIA!
S'UP, MONA LISA? OOPS. I MEAN GUERNICA.
WHAT IS IT?
I JUST GOT A MESSAGE THAT SOME OF MY PEOPLE ARE FLIPPING TO DEWALT. THEY WANT ANOTHER VOTE ON THE WHOLE OPERATION. THEY WANT TO HEAR FROM YOU.
FIND CONSUS, CHARLOTTE. WE NEED IT.
I WILL. PLUG ME IN, KODY.
SERIOUSLY? YOU'RE JUST GOING TO IGNORE HOW WEIRD THAT WAS?
JUST GET ME TO 1515!
SURE THING, BOSS. ANYTHING, BOSS.
I SHOULD HAVE GONE WITH GALINA...

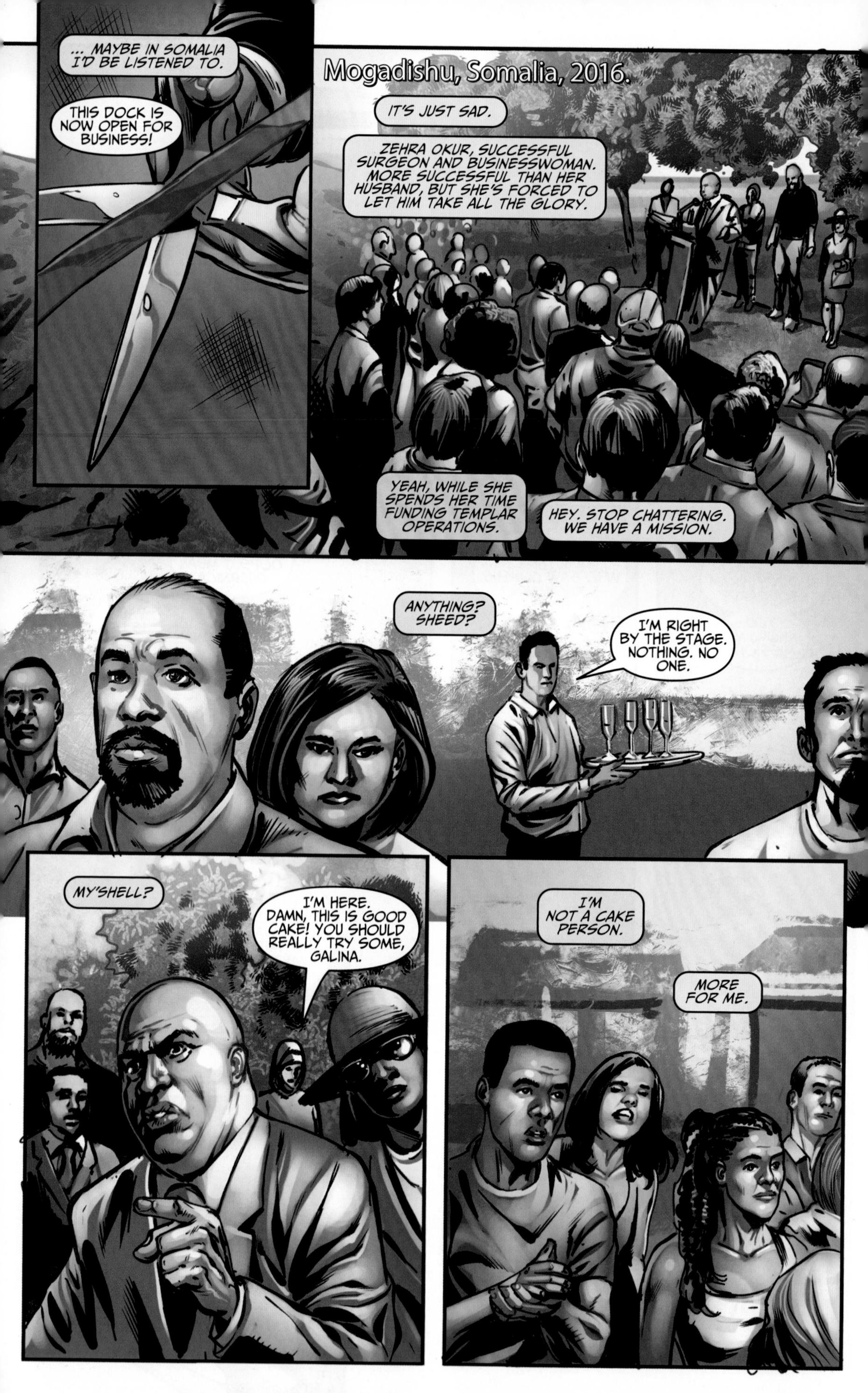
... MAYBE IN SOMALIA I'D BE LISTENED TO.
THIS DOCK IS NOW OPEN FOR BUSINESS!
Mogadishu, Somalia, 2016.
IT'S JUST SAD.
ZEHRA OKUR, SUCCESSFUL SURGEON AND BUSINESSWOMAN. MORE SUCCESSFUL THAN HER HUSBAND, BUT SHE'S FORCED TO LET HIM TAKE ALL THE GLORY.
YEAH, WHILE SHE SPENDS HER TIME FUNDING TEMPLAR OPERATIONS.
HEY. STOP CHATTERING. WE HAVE A MISSION.
ANYTHING? SHEED?
I'M RIGHT BY THE STAGE. NOTHING. NO ONE.
MY'SHELL?
I'M HERE. DAMN, THIS IS GOOD CAKE! YOU SHOULD REALLY TRY SOME, GALINA.
I'M NOT A CAKE PERSON.
MORE FOR ME.

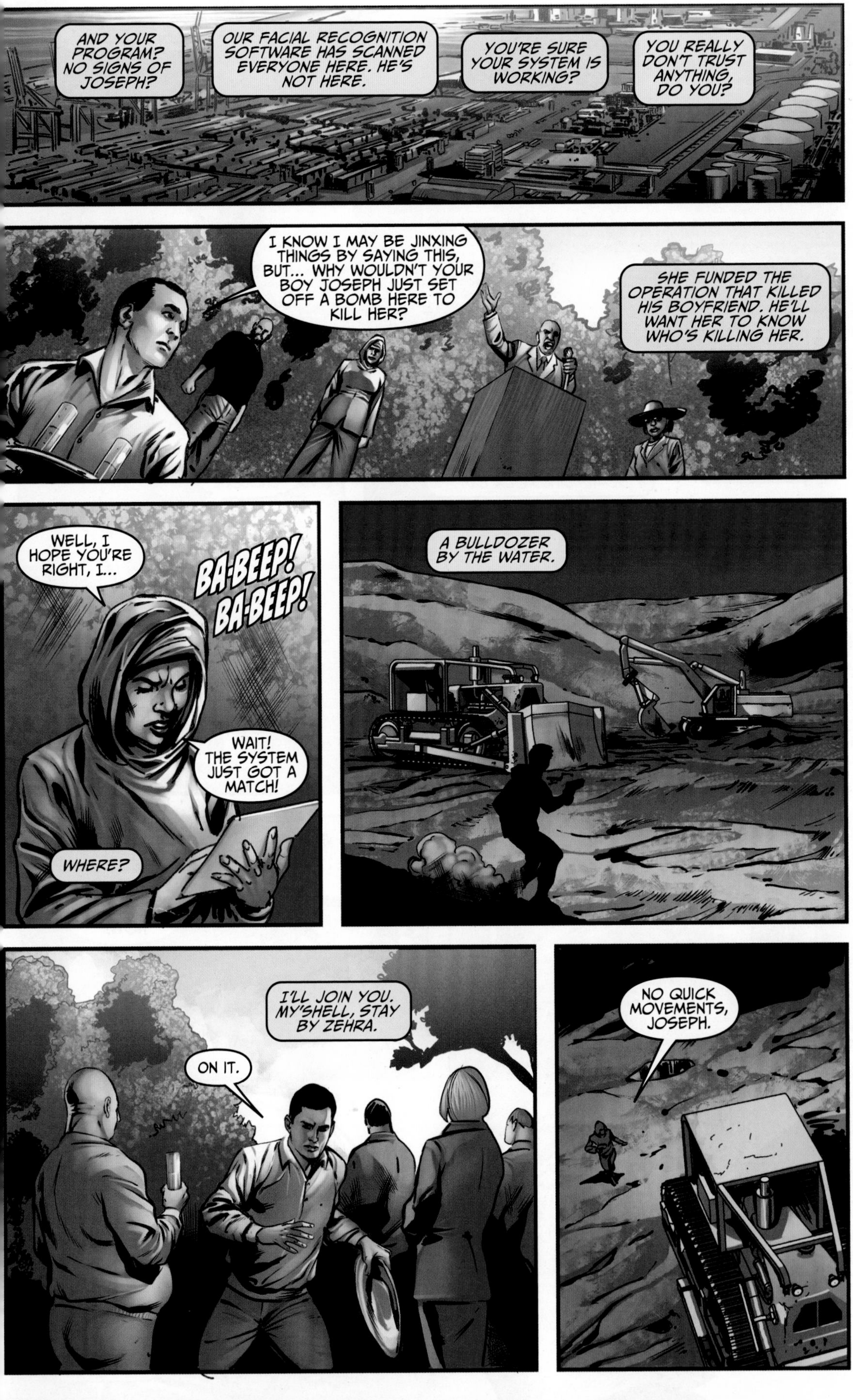
AND YOUR PROGRAM? NO SIGNS OF JOSEPH?
OUR FACIAL RECOGNITION SOFTWARE HAS SCANNED EVERYONE HERE. HE'S NOT HERE.
YOU'RE SURE YOUR SYSTEM IS WORKING?
YOU REALLY DON'T TRUST ANYTHING, DO YOU?
I KNOW I MAY BE JINXING THINGS BY SAYING THIS, BUT... WHY WOULDN'T YOUR BOY JOSEPH JUST SET OFF A BOMB HERE TO KILL HER?
SHE FUNDED THE OPERATION THAT KILLED HIS BOYFRIEND. HE'LL WANT HER TO KNOW WHO'S KILLING HER.
WELL, I HOPE YOU'RE RIGHT, I...
BA-BEEP! BA-BEEP!
WAIT! THE SYSTEM JUST GOT A MATCH!
WHERE?
A BULLDOZER BY THE WATER.
I'LL JOIN YOU. MY'SHELL, STAY BY ZEHRA.
ON IT.
NO QUICK MOVEMENTS, JOSEPH.

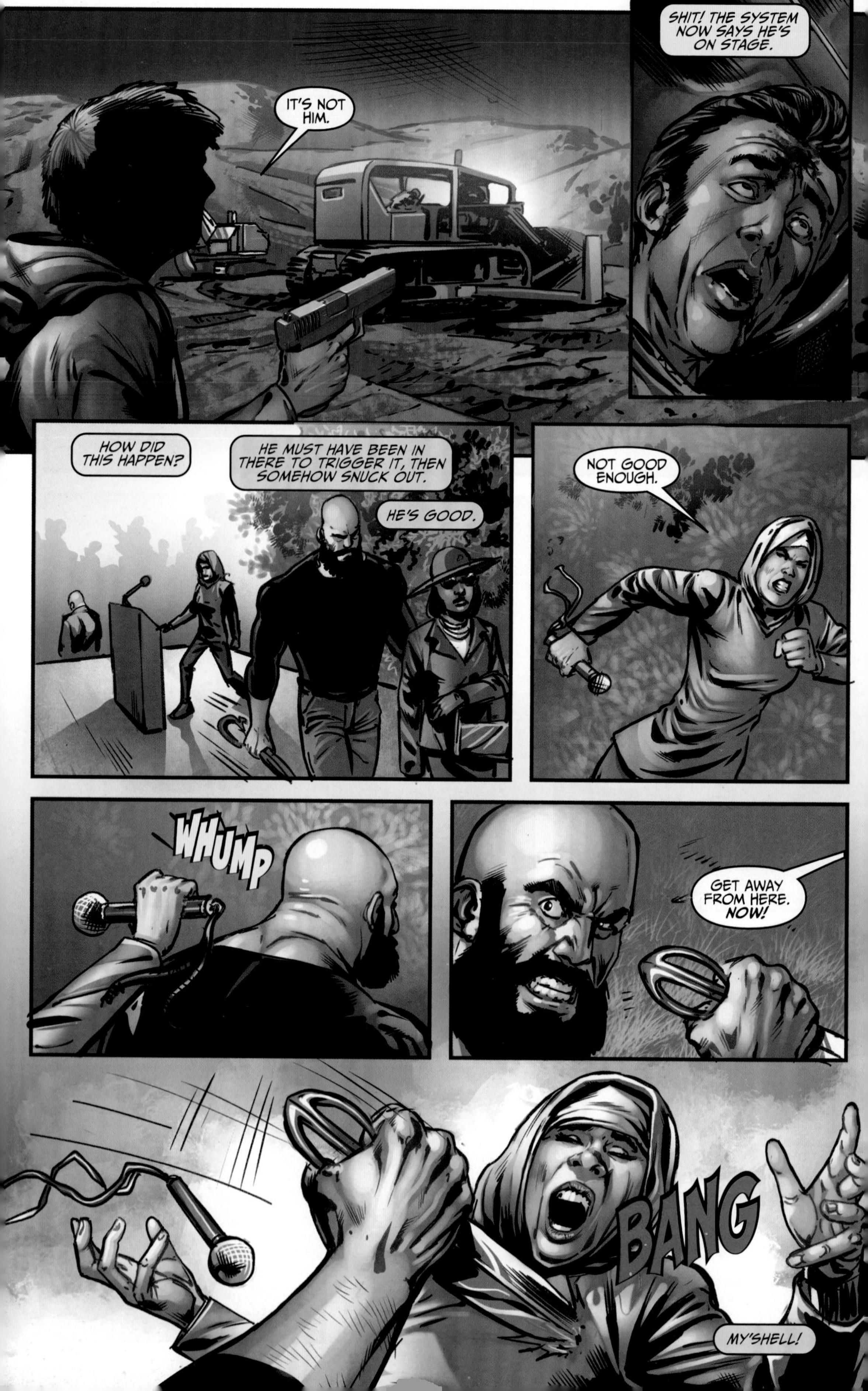
IT'S NOT HIM.
SHIT! THE SYSTEM NOW SAYS HE'S ON STAGE.
HOW DID THIS HAPPEN?
HE MUST HAVE BEEN IN THERE TO TRIGGER IT, THEN SOMEHOW SNUCK OUT.
HE'S GOOD.
NOT GOOD ENOUGH.
WHUMP
GET AWAY FROM HERE. NOW!
BANG
MY'SHELL!

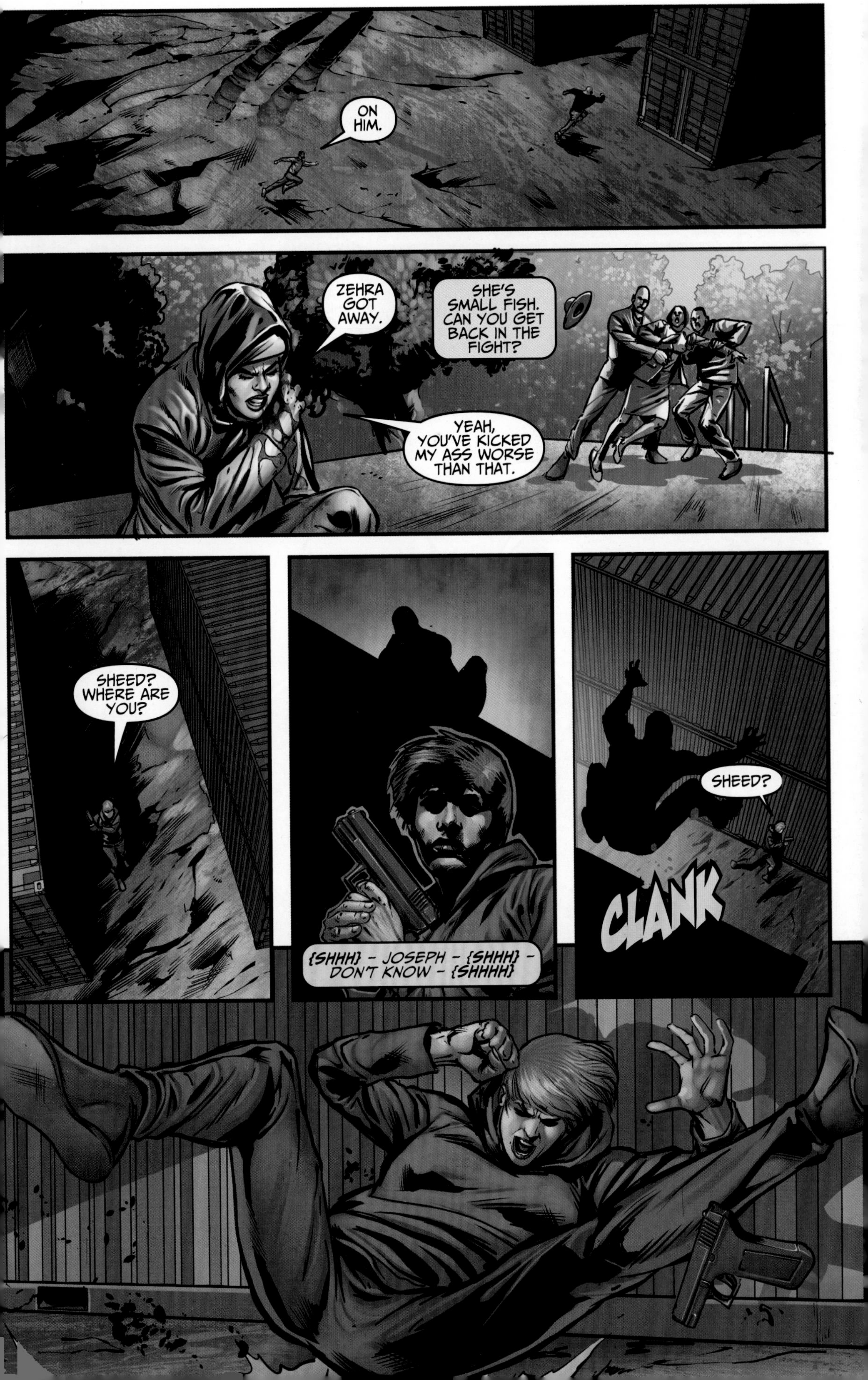
ON HIM.
ZEHRA GOT AWAY.
SHE'S SMALL FISH. CAN YOU GET BACK IN THE FIGHT?
YEAH, YOU'VE KICKED MY ASS WORSE THAN THAT.
SHEED? WHERE ARE YOU?
{SHHH} - JOSEPH - {SHHH} - DON'T KNOW - {SHHHH}
SHEED?
CLANK

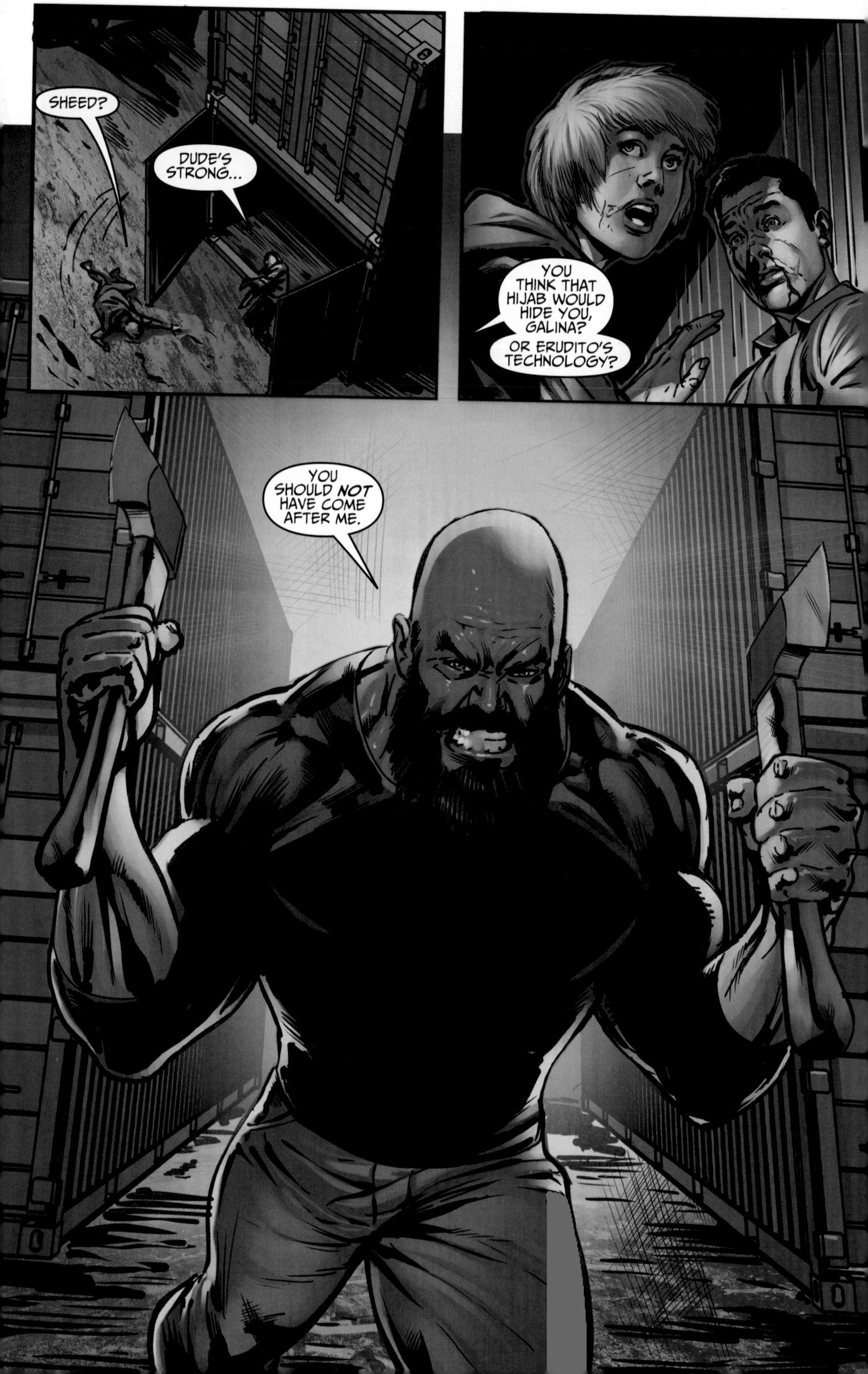
SHEED?
DUDE'S STRONG...
YOU THINK THAT HIJAB WOULD HIDE YOU, GALINA?
OR ERUDITO'S TECHNOLOGY?
YOU SHOULD NOT HAVE COME AFTER ME.

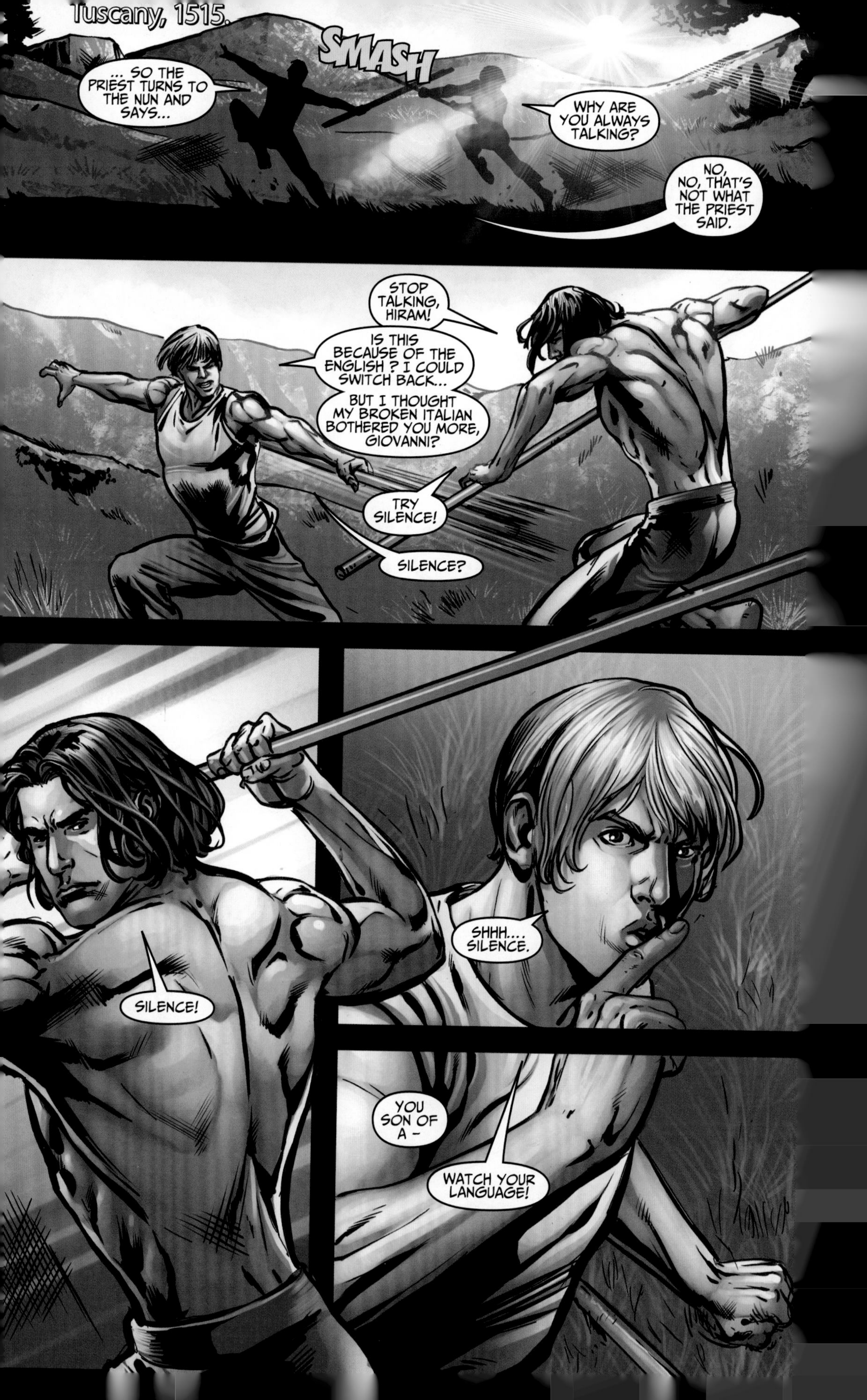
Tuscany, 1515.
SMASH
... SO THE PRIEST TURNS TO THE NUN AND SAYS...
WHY ARE YOU ALWAYS TALKING?
NO, NO, THAT'S NOT WHAT THE PRIEST SAID.
STOP TALKING, HIRAM!
IS THIS BECAUSE OF THE ENGLISH ? I COULD SWITCH BACK...
BUT I THOUGHT MY BROKEN ITALIAN BOTHERED YOU MORE, GIOVANNI?
TRY SILENCE!
SILENCE?
SHHH.... SILENCE.
SILENCE!
YOU SON OF A –
WATCH YOUR LANGUAGE!

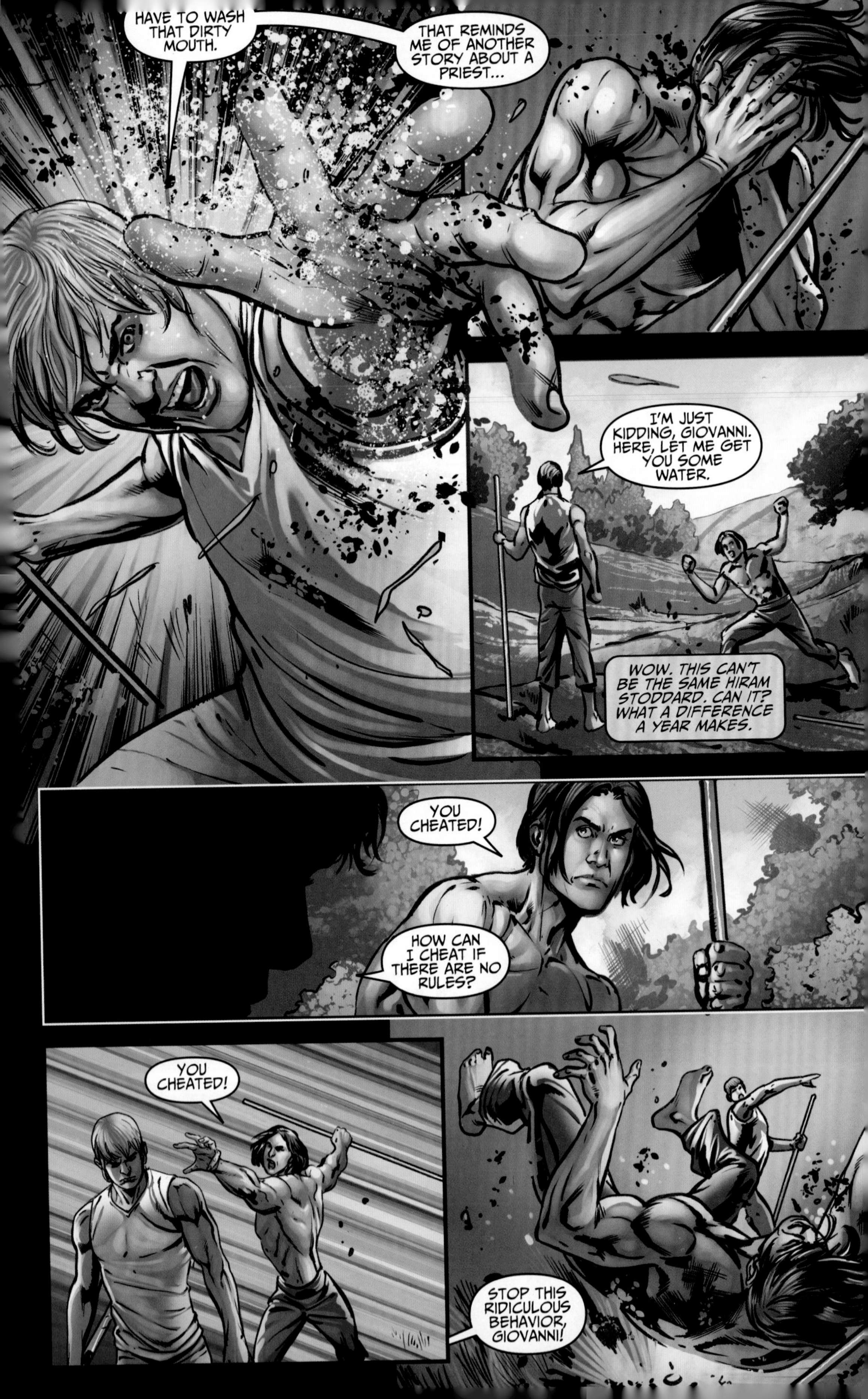
HAVE TO WASH THAT DIRTY MOUTH.
THAT REMINDS ME OF ANOTHER STORY ABOUT A PRIEST...
I'M JUST KIDDING, GIOVANNI. HERE, LET ME GET YOU SOME WATER.
WOW. THIS CAN'T BE THE SAME HIRAM STODDARD. CAN IT? WHAT A DIFFERENCE A YEAR MAKES.
YOU CHEATED!
HOW CAN I CHEAT IF THERE ARE NO RULES?
YOU CHEATED!
STOP THIS RIDICULOUS BEHAVIOR, GIOVANNI!

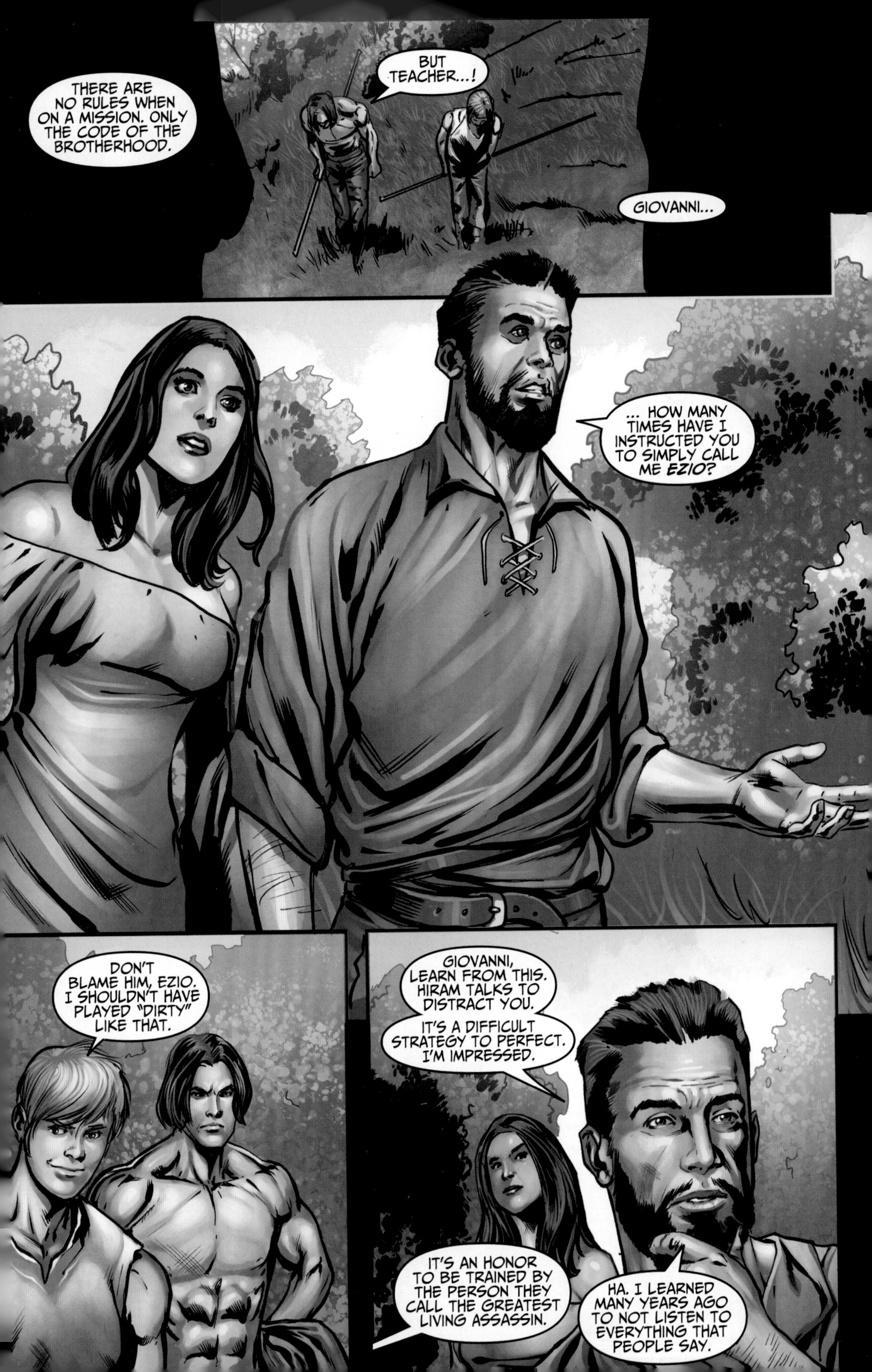
THERE ARE NO RULES WHEN ON A MISSION. ONLY THE CODE OF THE BROTHERHOOD.
BUT TEACHER...!
GIOVANNI...
... HOW MANY TIMES HAVE I INSTRUCTED YOU TO SIMPLY CALL ME EZIO?
DON'T BLAME HIM, EZIO. I SHOULDN'T HAVE PLAYED "DIRTY" LIKE THAT.
GIOVANNI, LEARN FROM THIS. HIRAM TALKS TO DISTRACT YOU.
IT'S A DIFFICULT STRATEGY TO PERFECT. I'M IMPRESSED.
IT'S AN HONOR TO BE TRAINED BY THE PERSON THEY CALL THE GREATEST LIVING ASSASSIN.
HA. I LEARNED MANY YEARS AGO TO NOT LISTEN TO EVERYTHING THAT PEOPLE SAY.

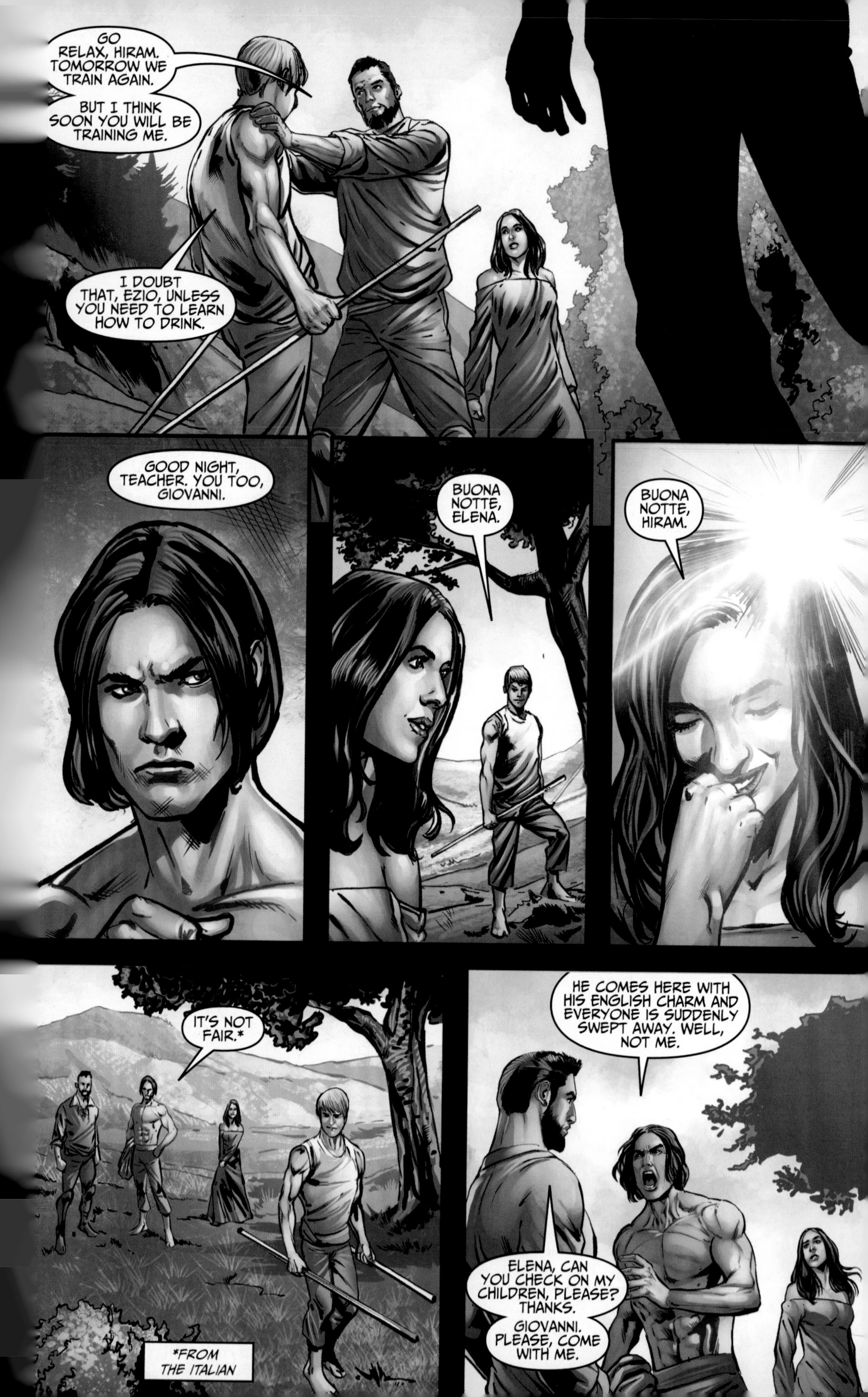
GO RELAX, HIRAM. TOMORROW WE TRAIN AGAIN.
BUT I THINK SOON YOU WILL BE TRAINING ME.
I DOUBT THAT, EZIO, UNLESS YOU NEED TO LEARN HOW TO DRINK.
GOOD NIGHT, TEACHER. YOU TOO, GIOVANNI.
BUONA NOTTE, ELENA.
BUONA NOTTE, HIRAM.
IT'S NOT FAIR.*
*FROM THE ITALIAN
HE COMES HERE WITH HIS ENGLISH CHARM AND EVERYONE IS SUDDENLY SWEPT AWAY. WELL, NOT ME.
ELENA, CAN YOU CHECK ON MY CHILDREN, PLEASE? THANKS.
GIOVANNI. PLEASE, COME WITH ME.

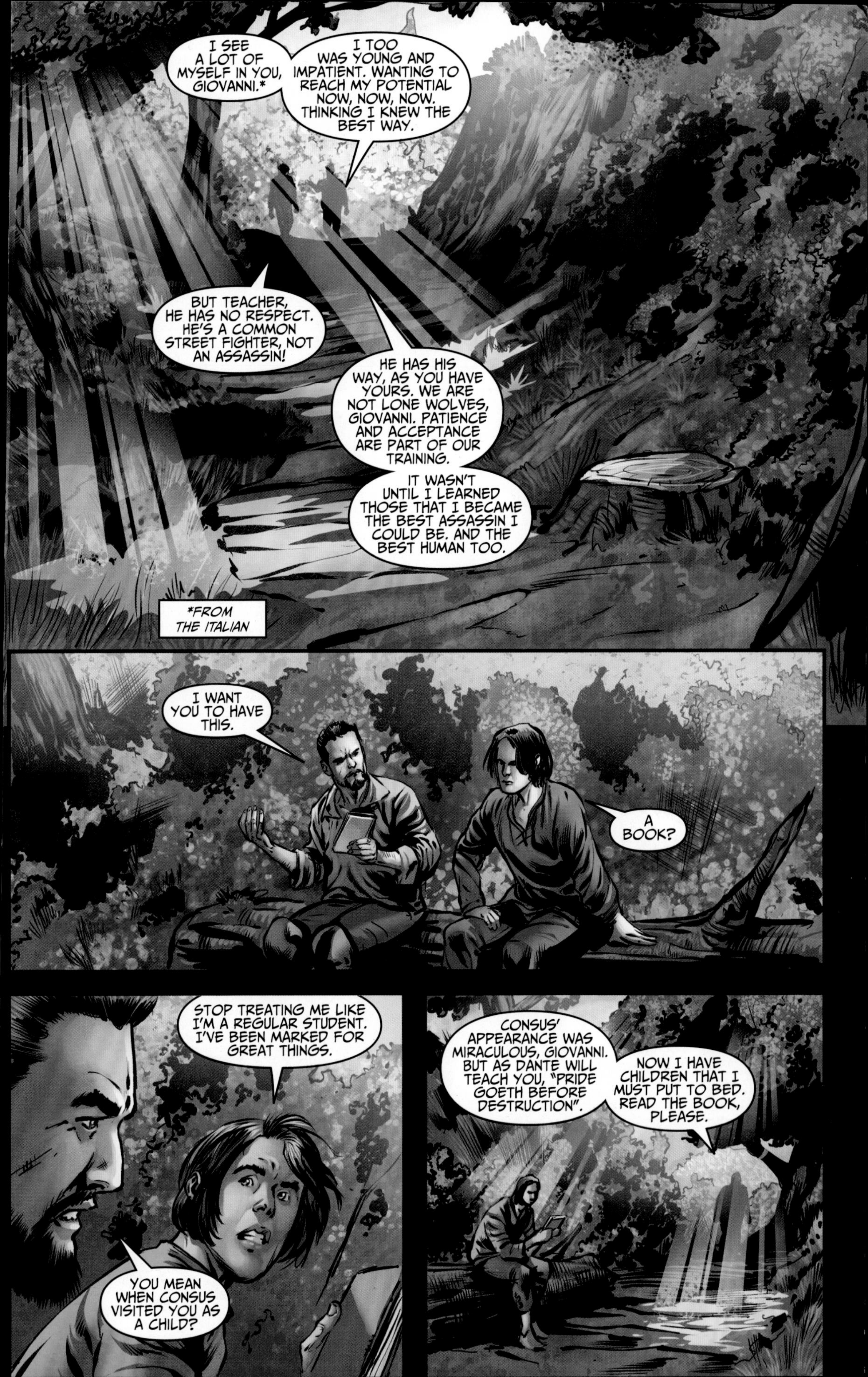
I SEE A LOT OF MYSELF IN YOU, GIOVANNI.*
I TOO WAS YOUNG AND IMPATIENT. WANTING TO REACH MY POTENTIAL NOW, NOW, NOW. THINKING I KNEW THE BEST WAY.
BUT TEACHER, HE HAS NO RESPECT. HE'S A COMMON STREET FIGHTER, NOT AN ASSASSIN!
HE HAS HIS WAY, AS YOU HAVE YOURS. WE ARE NOT LONE WOLVES, GIOVANNI. PATIENCE AND ACCEPTANCE ARE PART OF OUR TRAINING.
IT WASN'T UNTIL I LEARNED THOSE THAT I BECAME THE BEST ASSASSIN I COULD BE. AND THE BEST HUMAN TOO.
*FROM THE ITALIAN
I WANT YOU TO HAVE THIS.
A BOOK?
STOP TREATING ME LIKE I'M A REGULAR STUDENT. I'VE BEEN MARKED FOR GREAT THINGS.
YOU MEAN WHEN CONSUS VISITED YOU AS A CHILD?
CONSUS' APPEARANCE WAS MIRACULOUS, GIOVANNI. BUT AS DANTE WILL TEACH YOU, "PRIDE GOETH BEFORE DESTRUCTION".
NOW I HAVE CHILDREN THAT I MUST PUT TO BED. READ THE BOOK, PLEASE.

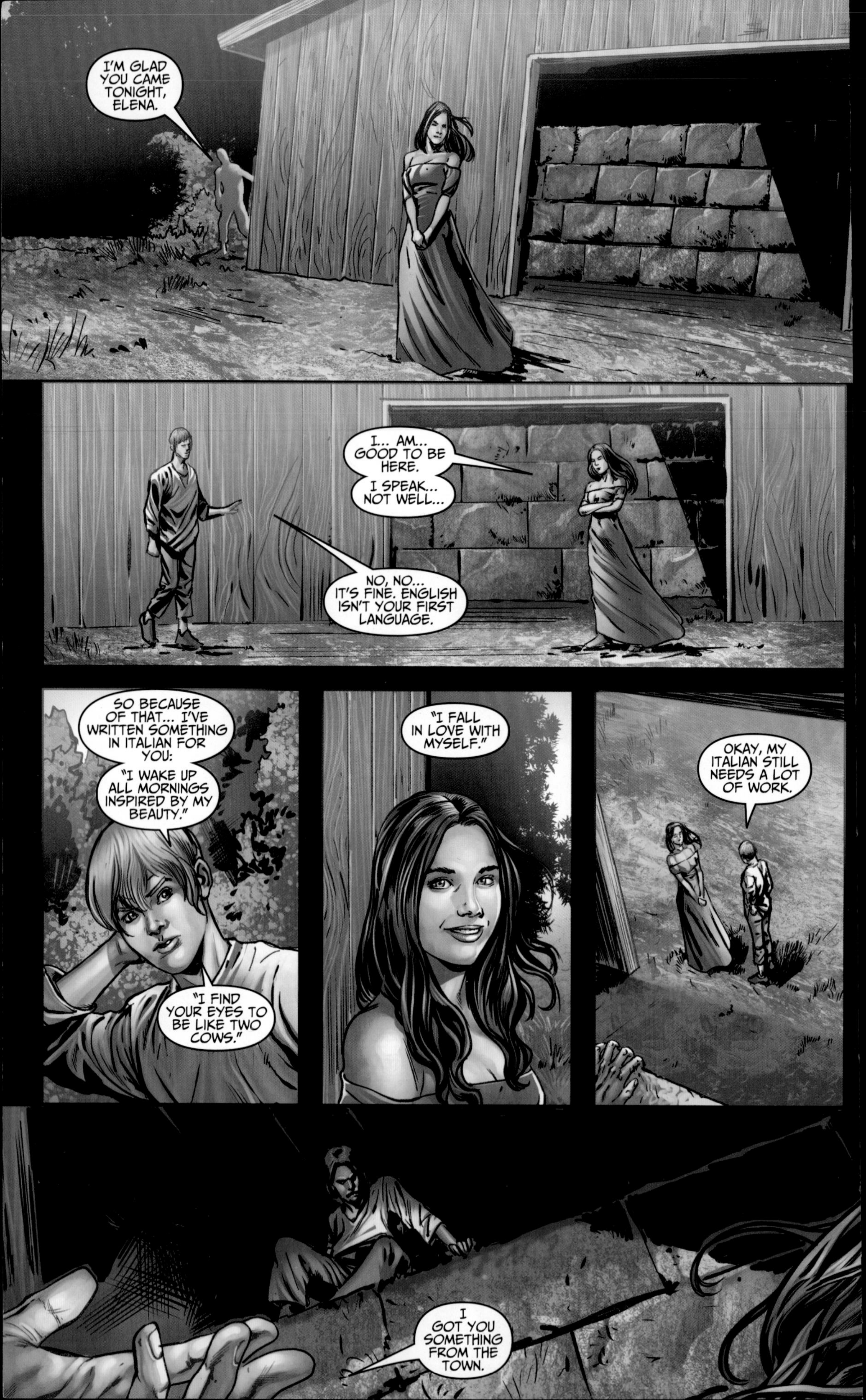
I'M GLAD YOU CAME TONIGHT, ELENA.
I... AM... GOOD TO BE HERE.
I SPEAK... NOT WELL...
NO, NO... IT'S FINE. ENGLISH ISN'T YOUR FIRST LANGUAGE.
SO BECAUSE OF THAT... I'VE WRITTEN SOMETHING IN ITALIAN FOR YOU:
"I WAKE UP ALL MORNINGS INSPIRED BY MY BEAUTY."
"I FIND YOUR EYES TO BE LIKE TWO COWS."
"I FALL IN LOVE WITH MYSELF."
OKAY, MY ITALIAN STILL NEEDS A LOT OF WORK.
I GOT YOU SOMETHING FROM THE TOWN.

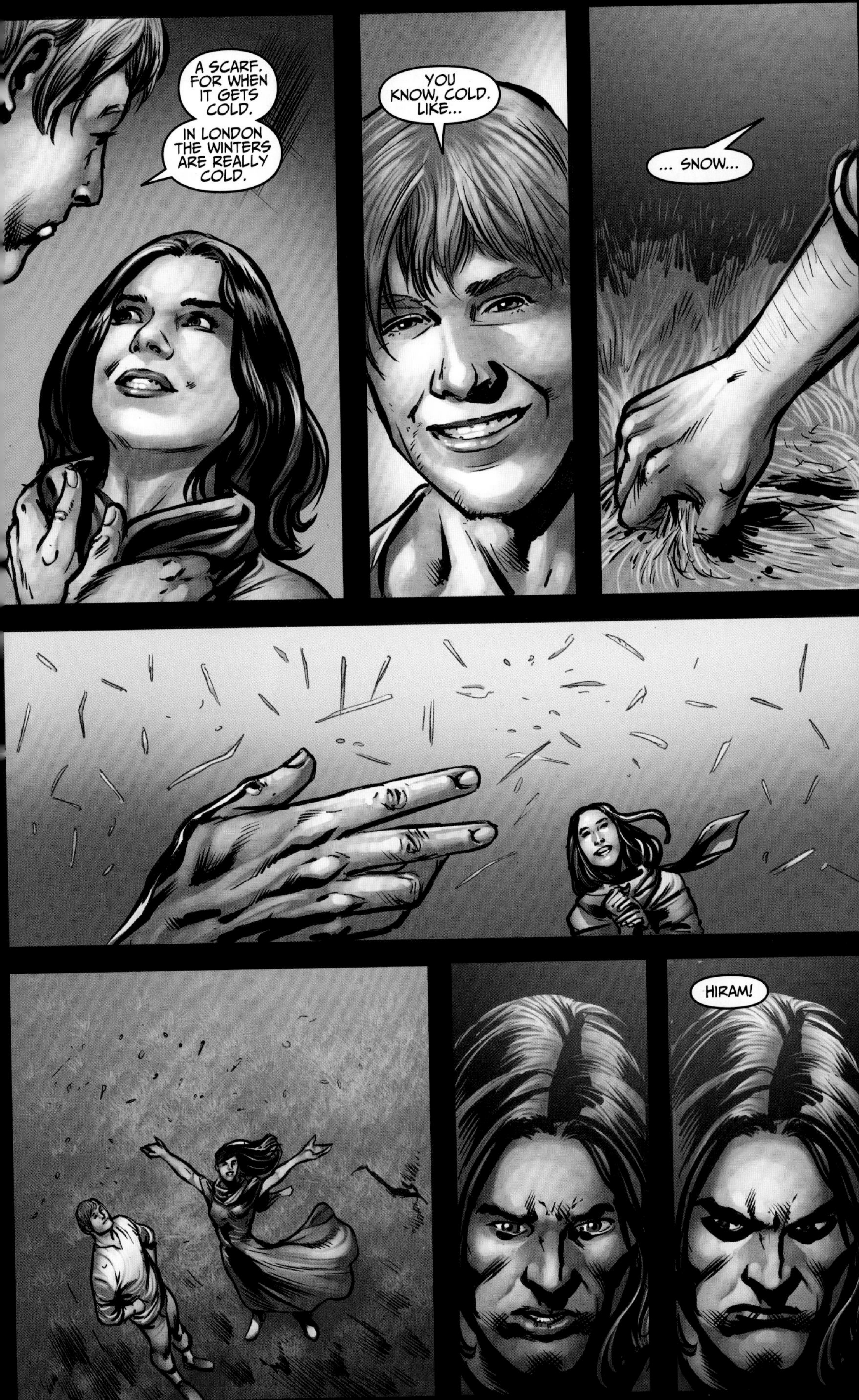
A SCARF. FOR WHEN IT GETS COLD.
IN LONDON THE WINTERS ARE REALLY COLD.
YOU KNOW, COLD. LIKE...
... SNOW...
HIRAM!

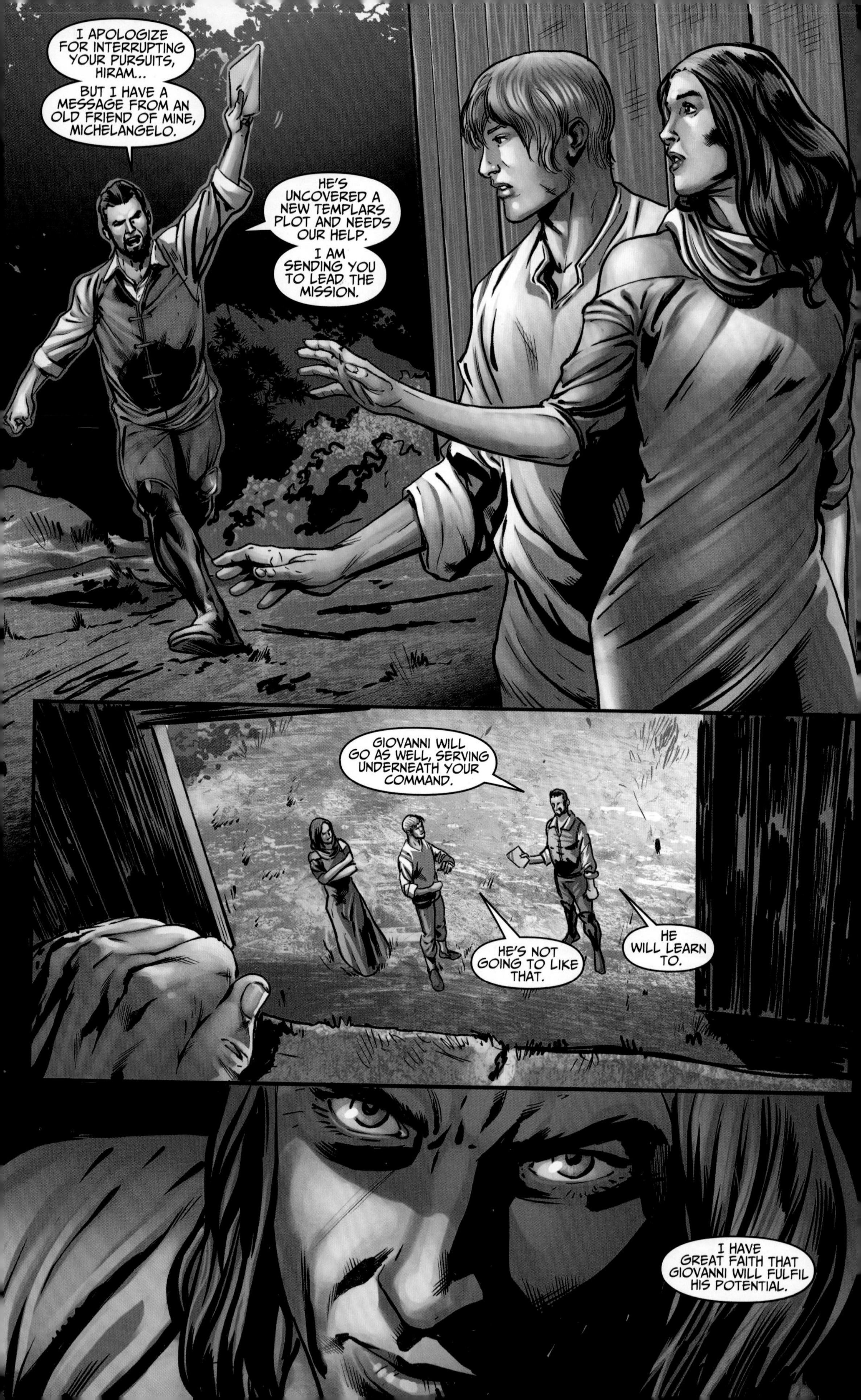
I APOLOGIZE FOR INTERRUPTING YOUR PURSUITS, HIRAM...
BUT I HAVE A MESSAGE FROM AN OLD FRIEND OF MINE, MICHELANGELO.
HE'S UNCOVERED A NEW TEMPLARS PLOT AND NEEDS OUR HELP.
I AM SENDING YOU TO LEAD THE MISSION.
GIOVANNI WILL GO AS WELL, SERVING UNDERNEATH YOUR COMMAND.
HE'S NOT GOING TO LIKE THAT.
HE WILL LEARN TO.
I HAVE GREAT FAITH THAT GIOVANNI WILL FULFIL HIS POTENTIAL.

CHAPTER
THIRTEEN

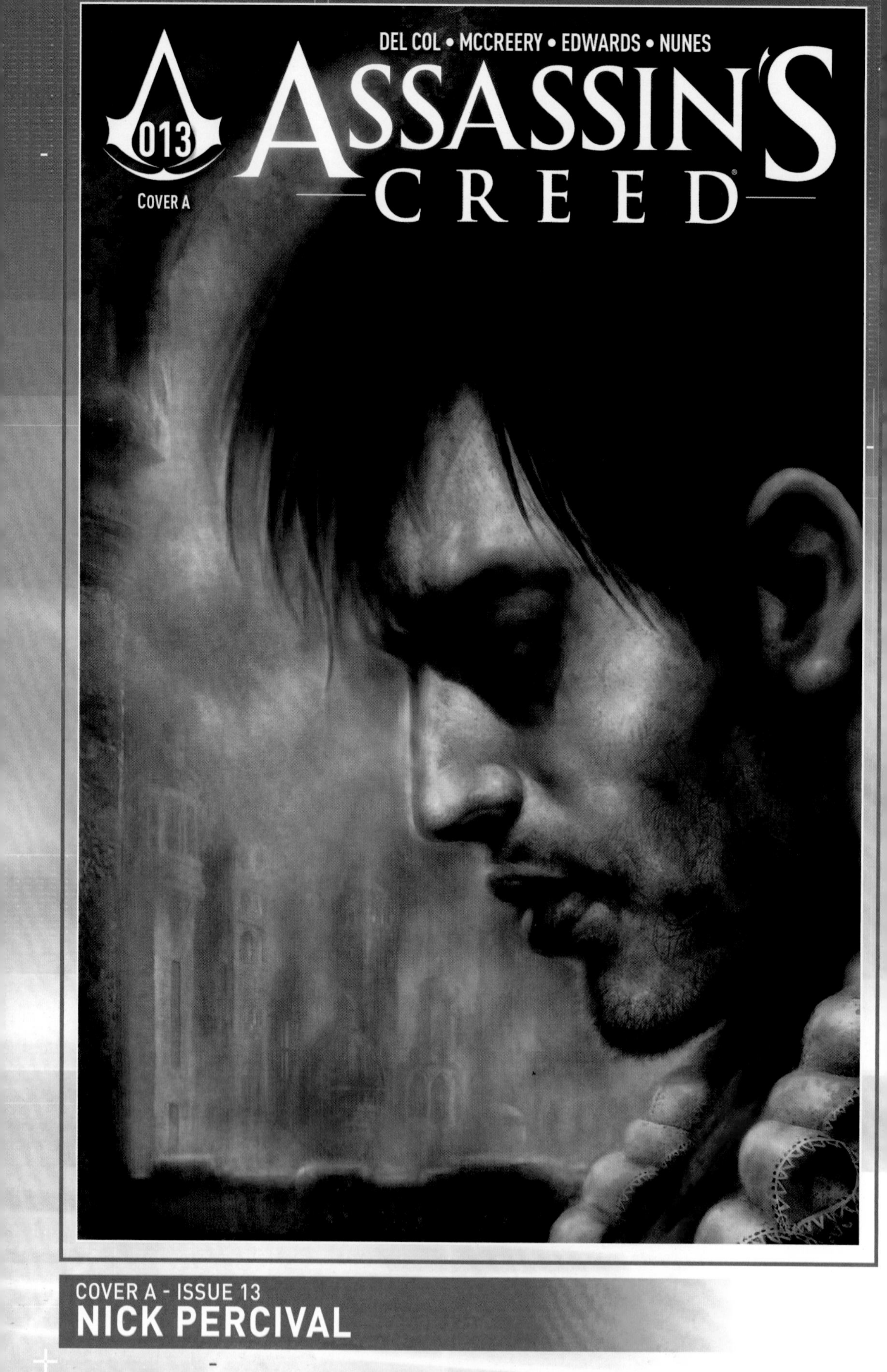
DEL COL • MCCREERY • EDWARDS • NUNES
013
COVER A
ASSASSIN'S
CREED

COVER A - ISSUE 13
NICK PERCIVAL

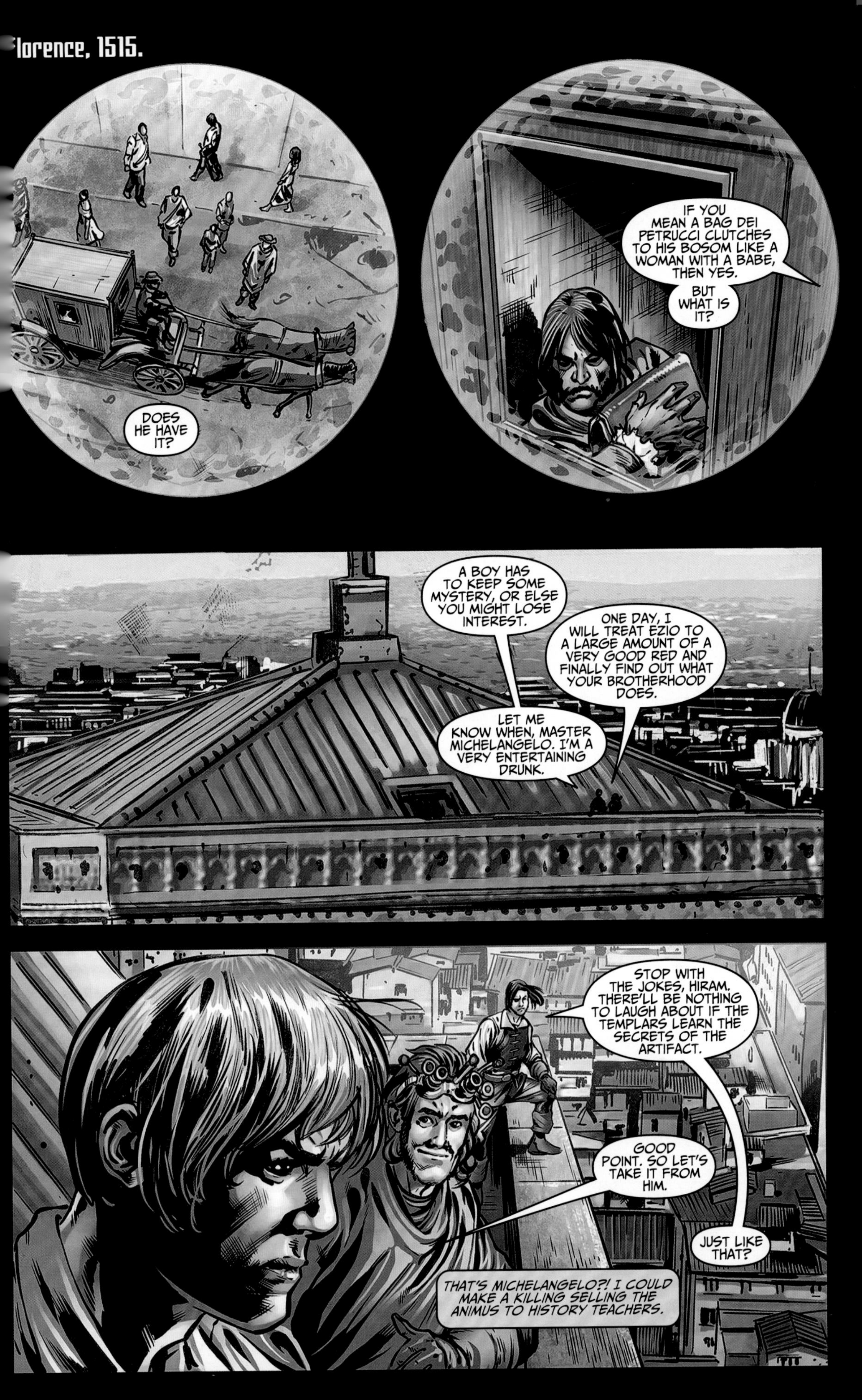
lorence, 1515.
DOES HE HAVE IT?
IF YOU MEAN A BAG DEI PETRUCCI CLUTCHES TO HIS BOSOM LIKE A WOMAN WITH A BABE, THEN YES.
BUT WHAT IS IT?
A BOY HAS TO KEEP SOME MYSTERY, OR ELSE YOU MIGHT LOSE INTEREST.
ONE DAY, I WILL TREAT EZIO TO A LARGE AMOUNT OF A VERY GOOD RED AND FINALLY FIND OUT WHAT YOUR BROTHERHOOD DOES.
LET ME KNOW WHEN, MASTER MICHELANGELO. I'M A VERY ENTERTAINING DRUNK.
STOP WITH THE JOKES, HIRAM. THERE'LL BE NOTHING TO LAUGH ABOUT IF THE TEMPLARS LEARN THE SECRETS OF THE ARTIFACT.
GOOD POINT. SO LET'S TAKE IT FROM HIM.
JUST LIKE THAT?
THAT'S MICHELANGELO?! I COULD MAKE A KILLING SELLING THE ANIMUS TO HISTORY TEACHERS.

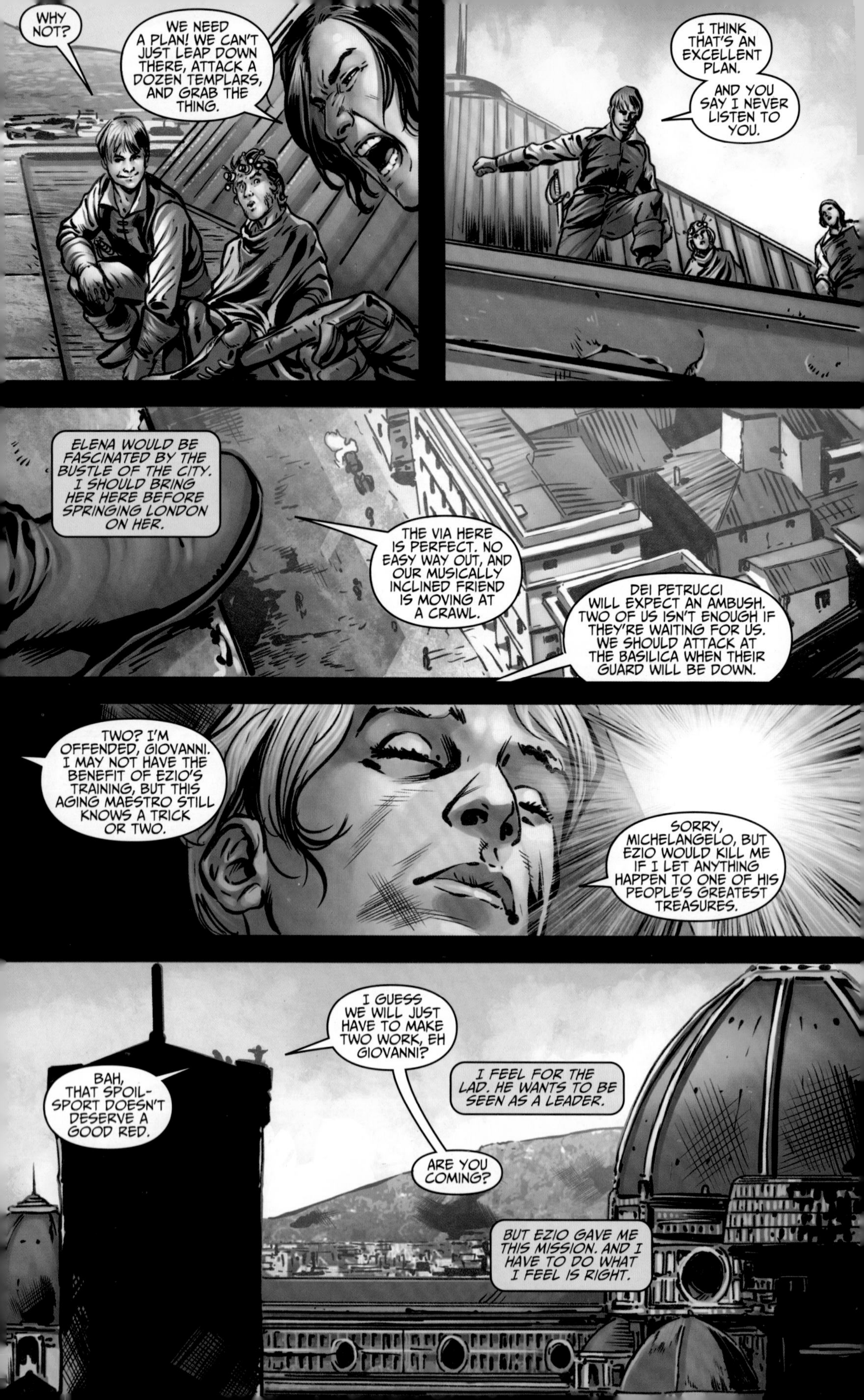
WHY NOT?
WE NEED A PLAN! WE CAN'T JUST LEAP DOWN THERE, ATTACK A DOZEN TEMPLARS, AND GRAB THE THING.
I THINK THAT'S AN EXCELLENT PLAN.
AND YOU SAY I NEVER LISTEN TO YOU.
ELENA WOULD BE FASCINATED BY THE BUSTLE OF THE CITY. I SHOULD BRING HER HERE BEFORE SPRINGING LONDON ON HER.
THE VIA HERE IS PERFECT. NO EASY WAY OUT, AND OUR MUSICALLY INCLINED FRIEND IS MOVING AT A CRAWL.
DEI PETRUCCI WILL EXPECT AN AMBUSH. TWO OF US ISN'T ENOUGH IF THEY'RE WAITING FOR US. WE SHOULD ATTACK AT THE BASILICA WHEN THEIR GUARD WILL BE DOWN.
TWO? I'M OFFENDED, GIOVANNI. I MAY NOT HAVE THE BENEFIT OF EZIO'S TRAINING, BUT THIS AGING MAESTRO STILL KNOWS A TRICK OR TWO.
SORRY, MICHELANGELO, BUT EZIO WOULD KILL ME IF I LET ANYTHING HAPPEN TO ONE OF HIS PEOPLE'S GREATEST TREASURES.
BAH, THAT SPOIL-SPORT DOESN'T DESERVE A GOOD RED.
I GUESS WE WILL JUST HAVE TO MAKE TWO WORK, EH GIOVANNI?
ARE YOU COMING?
I FEEL FOR THE LAD. HE WANTS TO BE SEEN AS A LEADER.
BUT EZIO GAVE ME THIS MISSION. AND I HAVE TO DO WHAT I FEEL IS RIGHT.

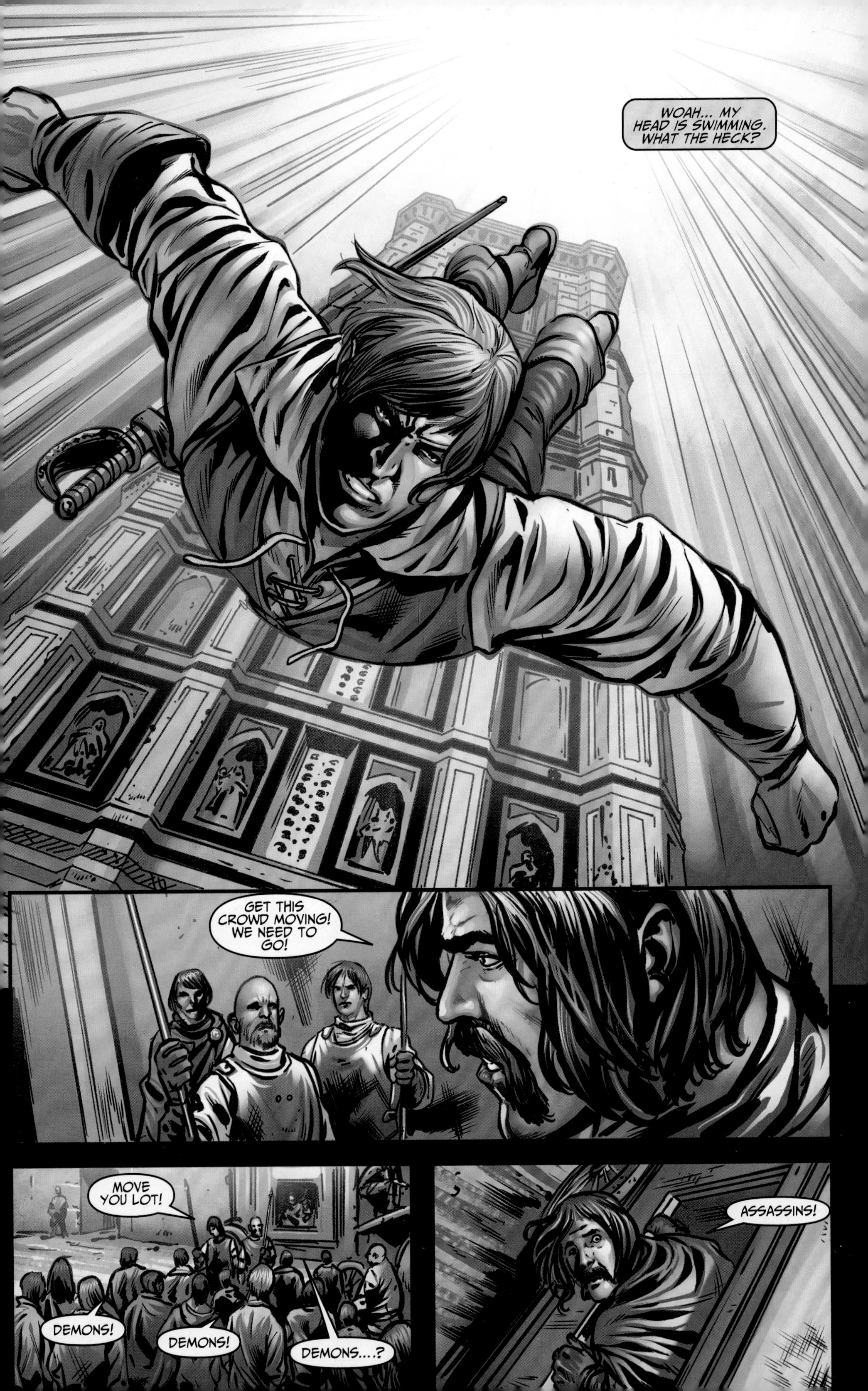
WOAH... MY HEAD IS SWIMMING. WHAT THE HECK?
GET THIS CROWD MOVING! WE NEED TO GO!
MOVE YOU LOT!
DEMONS!
DEMONS!
DEMONS....?
ASSASSINS!

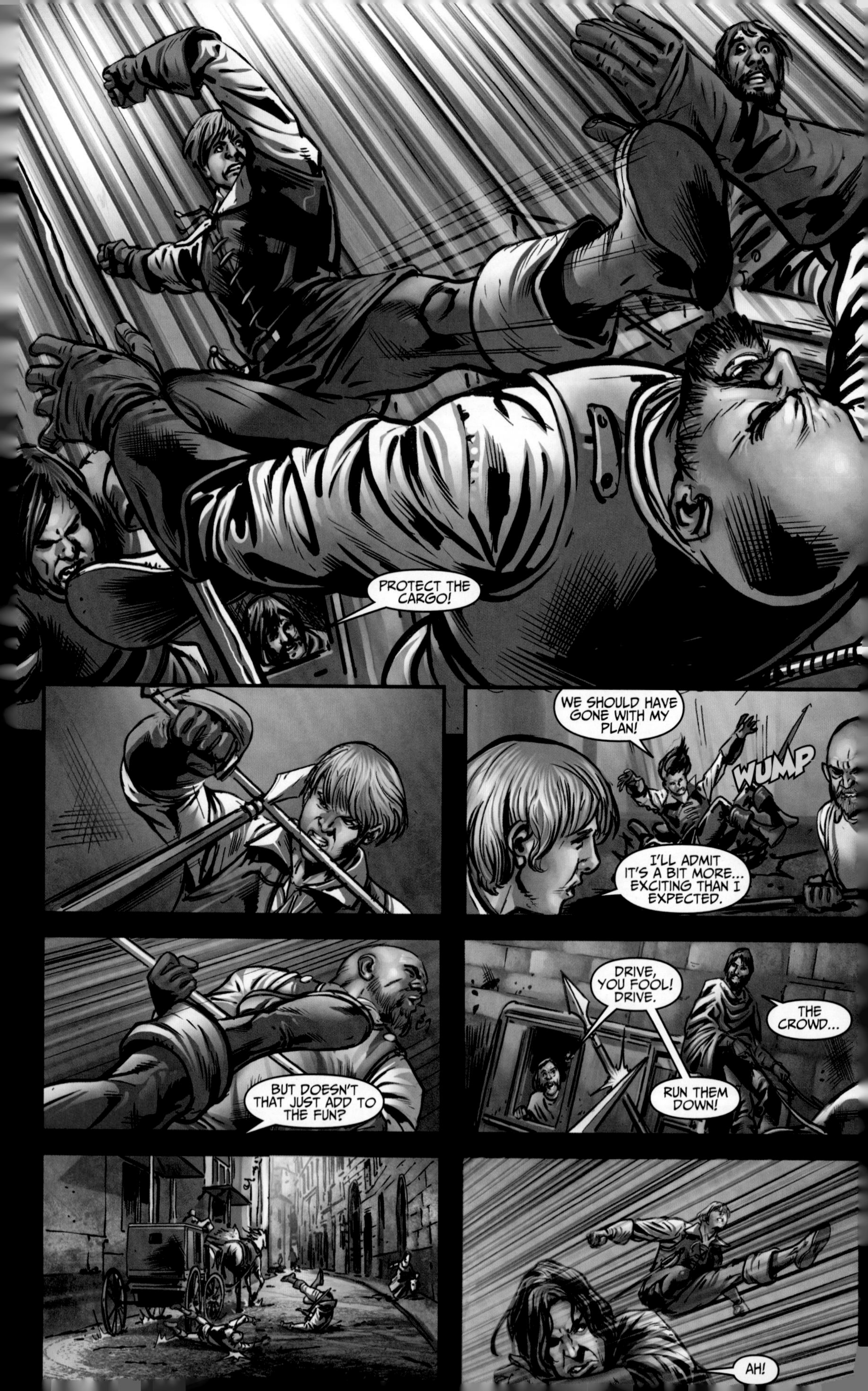
PROTECT THE CARGO!
WE SHOULD HAVE GONE WITH MY PLAN!
WUMP
I'LL ADMIT IT'S A BIT MORE... EXCITING THAN I EXPECTED.
BUT DOESN'T THAT JUST ADD TO THE FUN?
DRIVE, YOU FOOL! DRIVE.
THE CROWD...
RUN THEM DOWN!
AH!

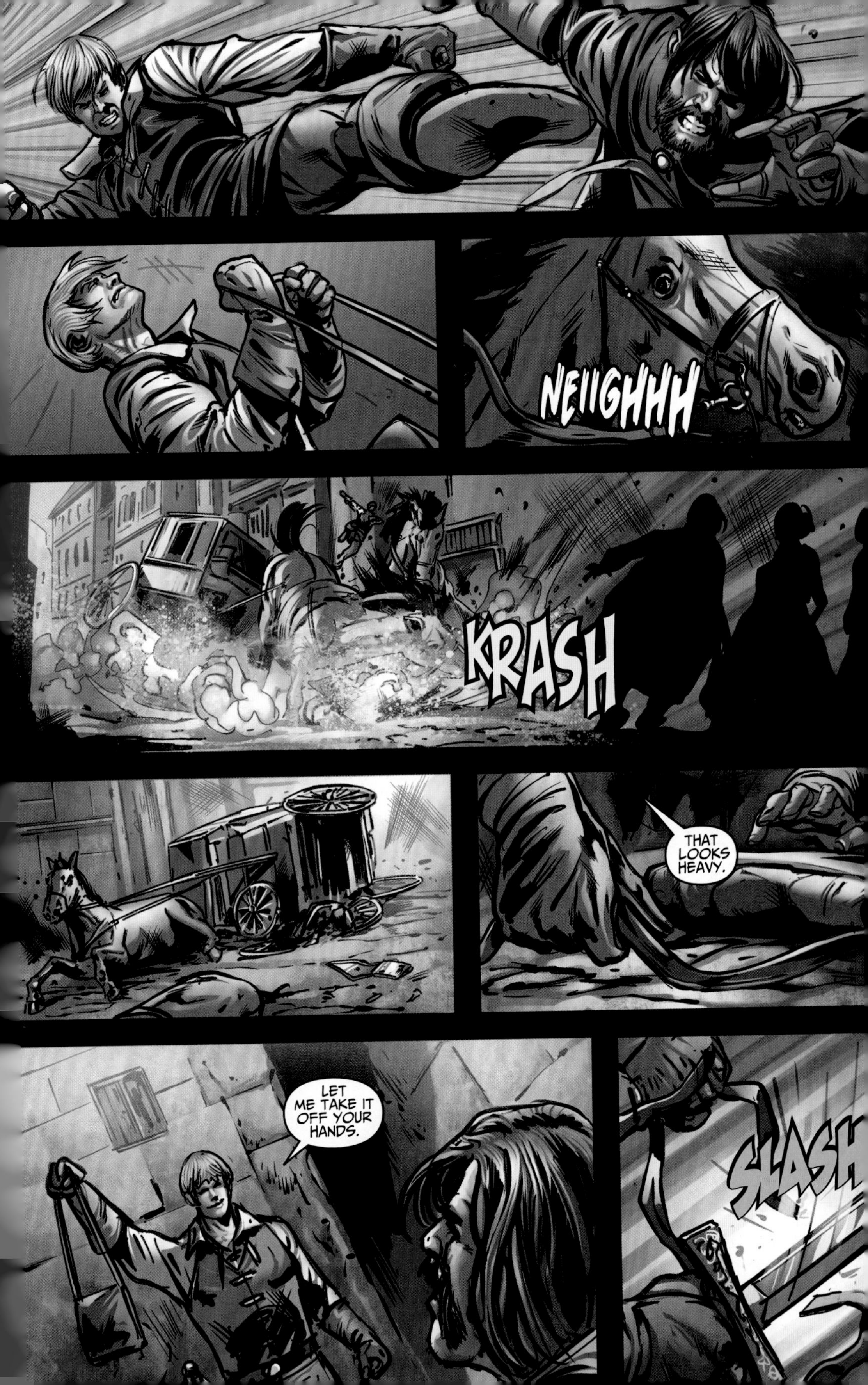
NEIIGHHH
KRASH
THAT LOOKS HEAVY.
LET ME TAKE IT OFF YOUR HANDS.
SLASH

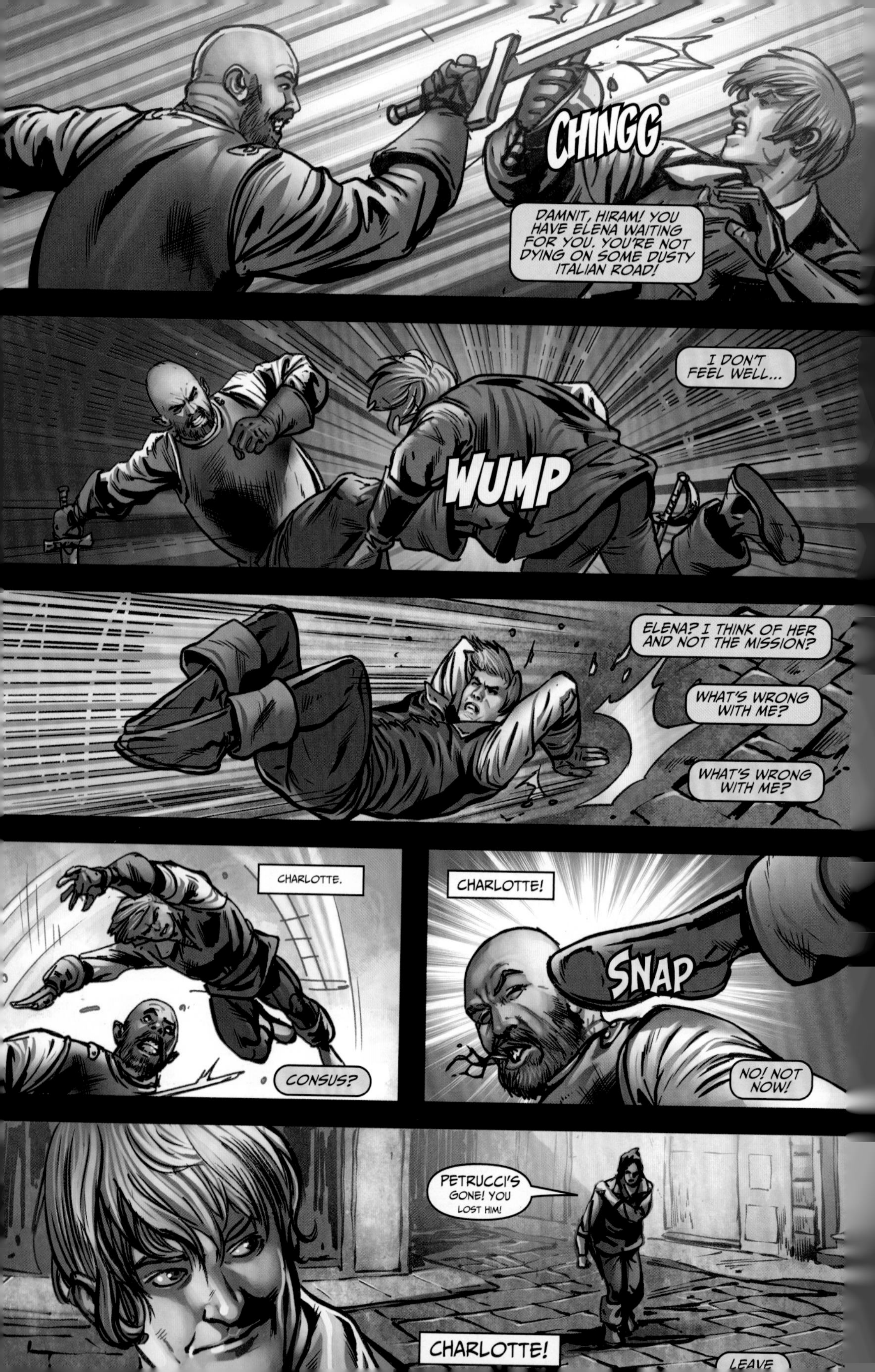
CHINGG
DAMNIT, HIRAM! YOU HAVE ELENA WAITING FOR YOU. YOU'RE NOT DYING ON SOME DUSTY ITALIAN ROAD!
I DON'T FEEL WELL...
WUMP
ELENA? I THINK OF HER AND NOT THE MISSION?
WHAT'S WRONG WITH ME?
WHAT'S WRONG WITH ME?
CHARLOTTE.
CONSUS?
CHARLOTTE!
SNAP
NO! NOT NOW!
PETRUCCI'S GONE! YOU LOST HIM!
CHARLOTTE!
LEAVE

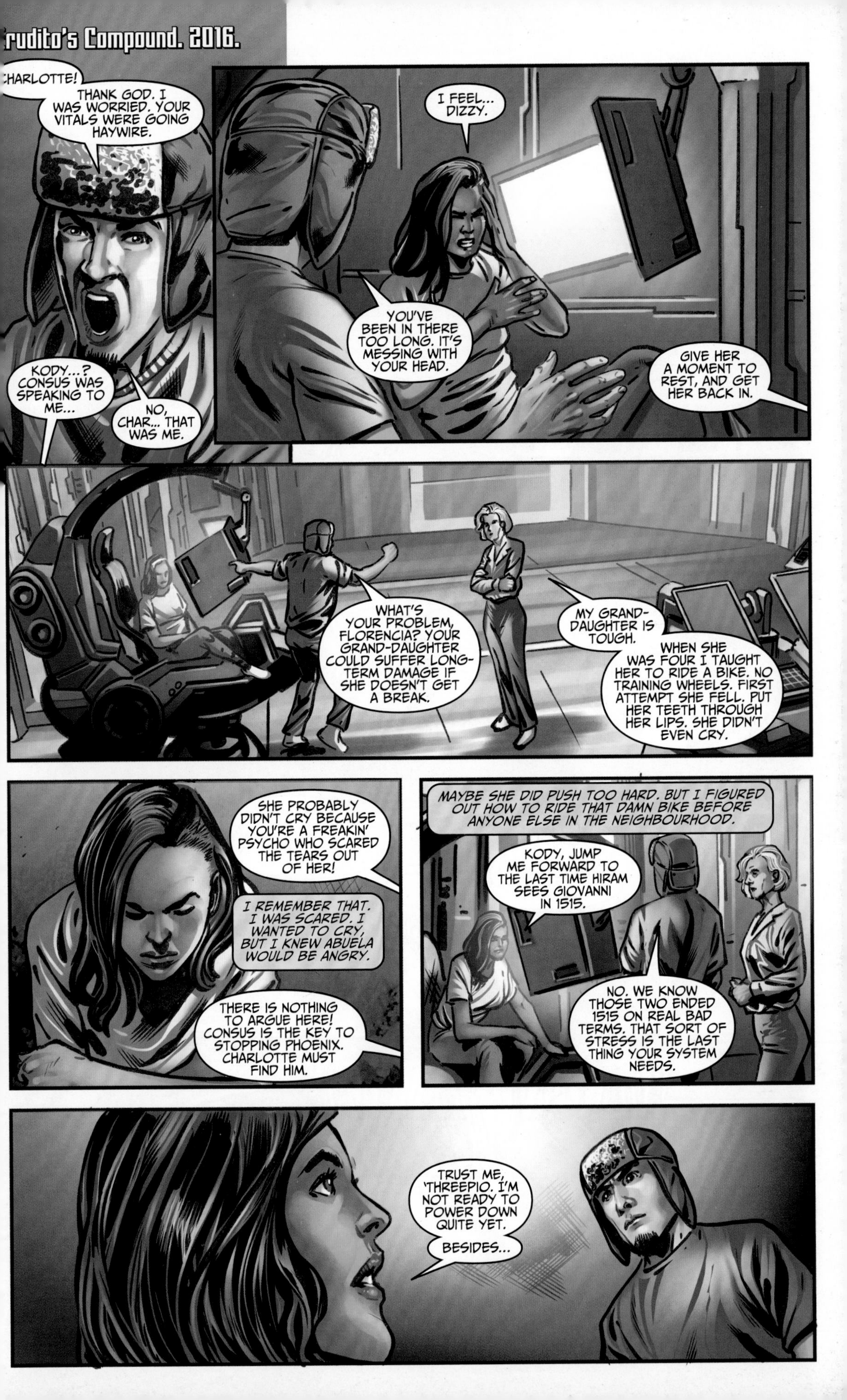

Erudito's Compound. 2016.
CHARLOTTE!
THANK GOD. I WAS WORRIED. YOUR VITALS WERE GOING HAYWIRE.
I FEEL... DIZZY.
YOU'VE BEEN IN THERE TOO LONG. IT'S MESSING WITH YOUR HEAD.
KODY...? CONSUS WAS SPEAKING TO ME...
NO, CHAR... THAT WAS ME.
GIVE HER A MOMENT TO REST, AND GET HER BACK IN.
WHAT'S YOUR PROBLEM, FLORENCIA? YOUR GRAND-DAUGHTER COULD SUFFER LONG-TERM DAMAGE IF SHE DOESN'T GET A BREAK.
MY GRAND-DAUGHTER IS TOUGH.
WHEN SHE WAS FOUR I TAUGHT HER TO RIDE A BIKE. NO TRAINING WHEELS. FIRST ATTEMPT SHE FELL. PUT HER TEETH THROUGH HER LIPS. SHE DIDN'T EVEN CRY.
SHE PROBABLY DIDN'T CRY BECAUSE YOU'RE A FREAKIN' PSYCHO WHO SCARED THE TEARS OUT OF HER!
I REMEMBER THAT. I WAS SCARED. I WANTED TO CRY, BUT I KNEW ABUELA WOULD BE ANGRY.
THERE IS NOTHING TO ARGUE HERE! CONSUS IS THE KEY TO STOPPING PHOENIX. CHARLOTTE MUST FIND HIM.
MAYBE SHE DID PUSH TOO HARD. BUT I FIGURED OUT HOW TO RIDE THAT DAMN BIKE BEFORE ANYONE ELSE IN THE NEIGHBOURHOOD.
KODY, JUMP ME FORWARD TO THE LAST TIME HIRAM SEES GIOVANNI IN 1515.
NO. WE KNOW THOSE TWO ENDED 1515 ON REAL BAD TERMS. THAT SORT OF STRESS IS THE LAST THING YOUR SYSTEM NEEDS.
TRUST ME, 'THREEPIO. I'M NOT READY TO POWER DOWN QUITE YET.
BESIDES...

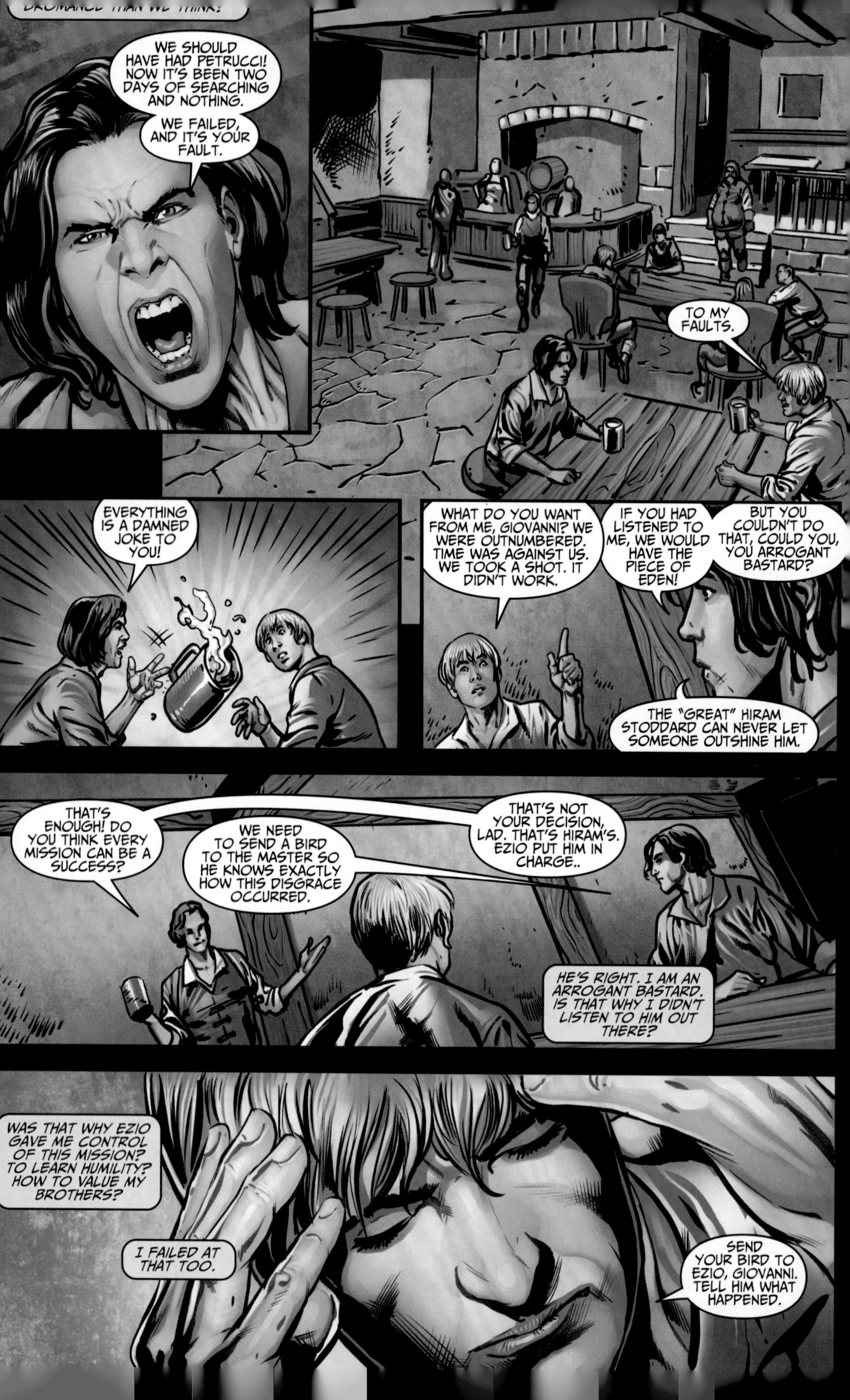

WE SHOULD HAVE HAD PETRUCCI! NOW IT'S BEEN TWO DAYS OF SEARCHING AND NOTHING.
WE FAILED, AND IT'S YOUR FAULT.
TO MY FAULTS.
EVERYTHING IS A DAMNED JOKE TO YOU!
WHAT DO YOU WANT FROM ME, GIOVANNI? WE WERE OUTNUMBERED. TIME WAS AGAINST US. WE TOOK A SHOT. IT DIDN'T WORK.
IF YOU HAD LISTENED TO ME, WE WOULD HAVE THE PIECE OF EDEN!
BUT YOU COULDN'T DO THAT, COULD YOU, YOU ARROGANT BASTARD?
THE "GREAT" HIRAM STODDARD CAN NEVER LET SOMEONE OUTSHINE HIM.
THAT'S ENOUGH! DO YOU THINK EVERY MISSION CAN BE A SUCCESS?
WE NEED TO SEND A BIRD TO THE MASTER SO HE KNOWS EXACTLY HOW THIS DISGRACE OCCURRED.
THAT'S NOT YOUR DECISION, LAD. THAT'S HIRAM'S. EZIO PUT HIM IN CHARGE..
HE'S RIGHT. I AM AN ARROGANT BASTARD. IS THAT WHY I DIDN'T LISTEN TO HIM OUT THERE?
WAS THAT WHY EZIO GAVE ME CONTROL OF THIS MISSION? TO LEARN HUMILITY? HOW TO VALUE MY BROTHERS?
I FAILED AT THAT TOO.
SEND YOUR BIRD TO EZIO, GIOVANNI. TELL HIM WHAT HAPPENED.

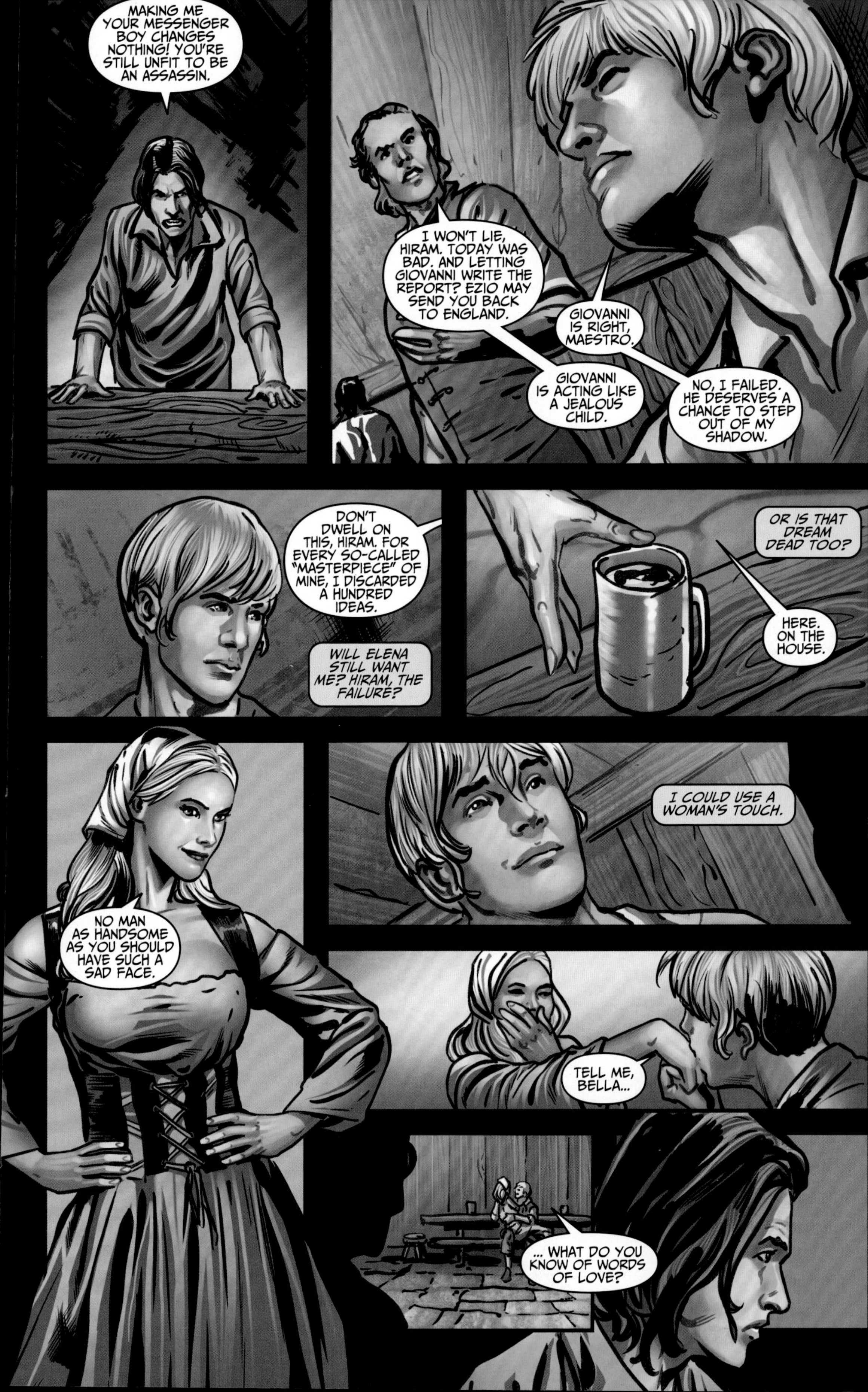
MAKING ME YOUR MESSENGER BOY CHANGES NOTHING! YOU'RE STILL UNFIT TO BE AN ASSASSIN.
I WON'T LIE, HIRAM. TODAY WAS BAD. AND LETTING GIOVANNI WRITE THE REPORT? EZIO MAY SEND YOU BACK TO ENGLAND.
GIOVANNI IS RIGHT, MAESTRO.
GIOVANNI IS ACTING LIKE A JEALOUS CHILD.
NO, I FAILED. HE DESERVES A CHANCE TO STEP OUT OF MY SHADOW.
DON'T DWELL ON THIS, HIRAM. FOR EVERY SO-CALLED "MASTERPIECE" OF MINE, I DISCARDED A HUNDRED IDEAS.
WILL ELENA STILL WANT ME? HIRAM, THE FAILURE?
OR IS THAT DREAM DEAD TOO?
HERE. ON THE HOUSE.
NO MAN AS HANDSOME AS YOU SHOULD HAVE SUCH A SAD FACE.
I COULD USE A WOMAN'S TOUCH.
TELL ME, BELLA...
... WHAT DO YOU KNOW OF WORDS OF LOVE?

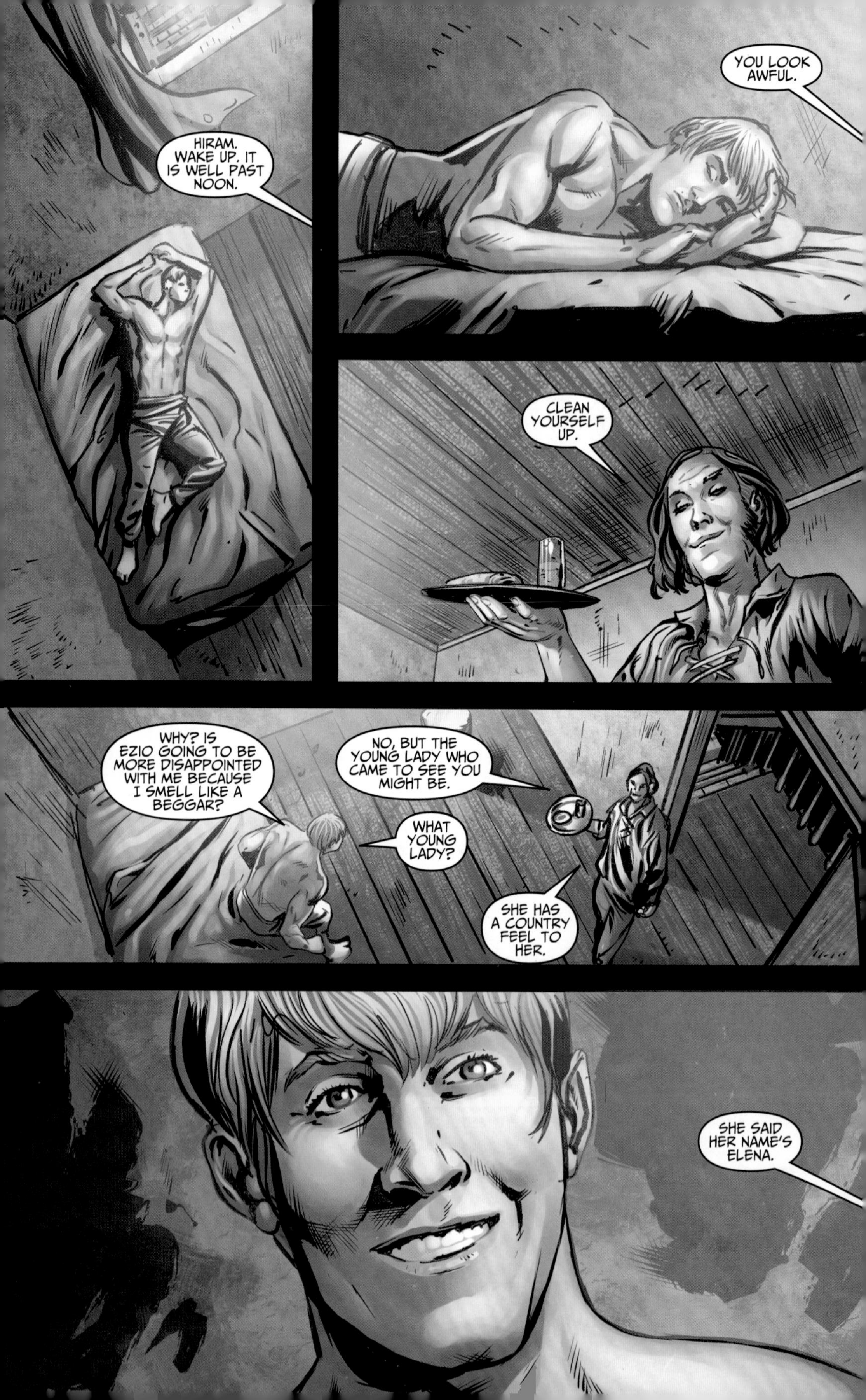
HIRAM. WAKE UP. IT IS WELL PAST NOON.
YOU LOOK AWFUL.
CLEAN YOURSELF UP.
WHY? IS EZIO GOING TO BE MORE DISAPPOINTED WITH ME BECAUSE I SMELL LIKE A BEGGAR?
NO, BUT THE YOUNG LADY WHO CAME TO SEE YOU MIGHT BE.
WHAT YOUNG LADY?
SHE HAS A COUNTRY FEEL TO HER.
SHE SAID HER NAME'S ELENA.

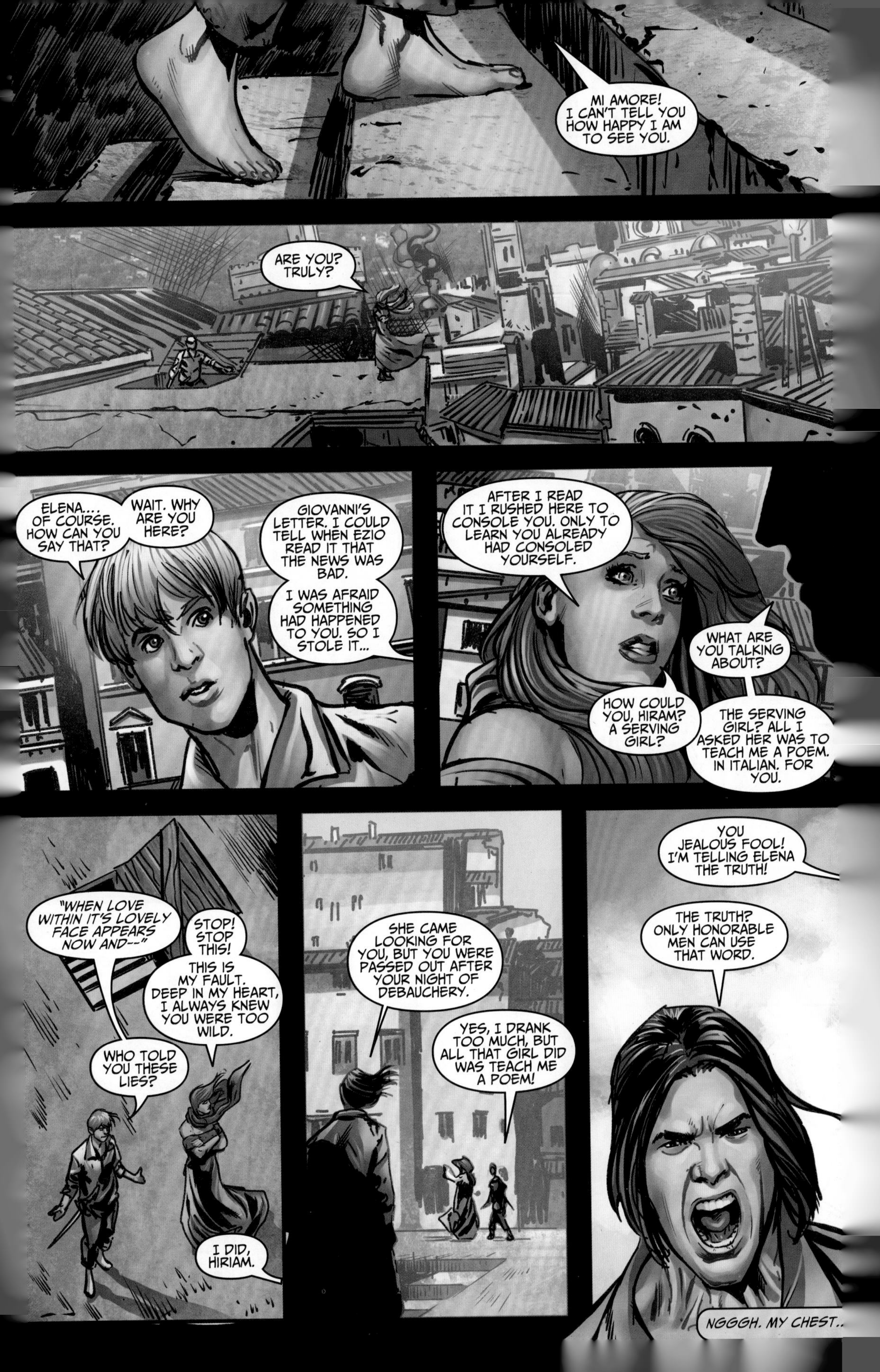
MI AMORE! I CAN'T TELL YOU HOW HAPPY I AM TO SEE YOU.
ARE YOU? TRULY?
ELENA.... OF COURSE. HOW CAN YOU SAY THAT?
WAIT. WHY ARE YOU HERE?
GIOVANNI'S LETTER. I COULD TELL WHEN EZIO READ IT THAT THE NEWS WAS BAD.
I WAS AFRAID SOMETHING HAD HAPPENED TO YOU. SO I STOLE IT...
AFTER I READ IT I RUSHED HERE TO CONSOLE YOU. ONLY TO LEARN YOU ALREADY HAD CONSOLED YOURSELF.
WHAT ARE YOU TALKING ABOUT?
HOW COULD YOU, HIRAM? A SERVING GIRL?
THE SERVING GIRL? ALL I ASKED HER WAS TO TEACH ME A POEM. IN ITALIAN. FOR YOU.
"WHEN LOVE WITHIN IT'S LOVELY FACE APPEARS NOW AND--"
STOP! STOP THIS!
THIS IS MY FAULT. DEEP IN MY HEART, I ALWAYS KNEW YOU WERE TOO WILD.
WHO TOLD YOU THESE LIES?
I DID, HIRIAM.
SHE CAME LOOKING FOR YOU, BUT YOU WERE PASSED OUT AFTER YOUR NIGHT OF DEBAUCHERY.
YES, I DRANK TOO MUCH, BUT ALL THAT GIRL DID WAS TEACH ME A POEM!
YOU JEALOUS FOOL! I'M TELLING ELENA THE TRUTH!
THE TRUTH? ONLY HONORABLE MEN CAN USE THAT WORD.
NGGGH. MY CHEST..

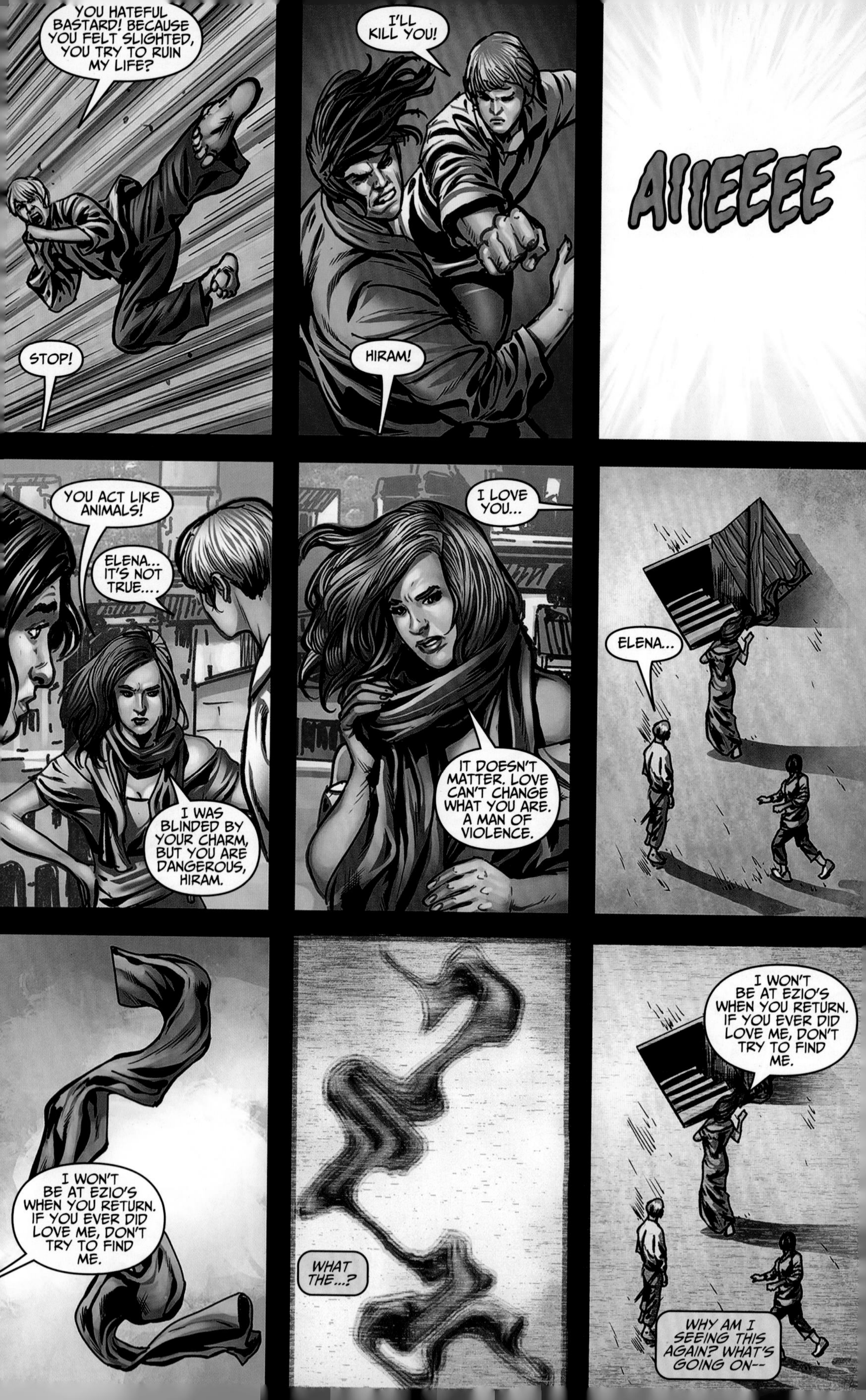
YOU HATEFUL BASTARD! BECAUSE YOU FELT SLIGHTED, YOU TRY TO RUIN MY LIFE?
STOP!
I'LL KILL YOU!
HIRAM!
AIIEEEE
YOU ACT LIKE ANIMALS!
ELENA... IT'S NOT TRUE....
I WAS BLINDED BY YOUR CHARM, BUT YOU ARE DANGEROUS, HIRAM.
I LOVE YOU...
IT DOESN'T MATTER. LOVE CAN'T CHANGE WHAT YOU ARE. A MAN OF VIOLENCE.
ELENA...
I WON'T BE AT EZIO'S WHEN YOU RETURN. IF YOU EVER DID LOVE ME, DON'T TRY TO FIND ME.
WHAT THE...?
I WON'T BE AT EZIO'S WHEN YOU RETURN. IF YOU EVER DID LOVE ME, DON'T TRY TO FIND ME.
WHY AM I SEEING THIS AGAIN? WHAT'S GOING ON--

YOU SAW THAT, RIGHT? WHAT'S GOING ON?

I THINK... I THINK WE'RE DEALING WITH A FALSE MEMORY.

YOU KNEW ABOUT THIS, DIDN'T YOU?

WE... SUSPECTED... IT WAS A POSSIBILITY. FROM WHAT WE'VE LEARNED OF CONSUS IT MADE SENSE THAT "HE" COULD ERASE GIOVANNI'S MEMORY...

... BUT IF, AS I SUSPECTED, OUR ANCESTOR WITNESSED GIOVANNI'S POSSESSION, WHY DIDN'T HE SAY SOMETHING?

BECAUSE HIRAM DOESN'T REMEMBER WHAT REALLY HAPPENED. LIKE WHEN SOMEONE WAS ABUSED AS A KID?

YOU MIGHT BE RIGHT.

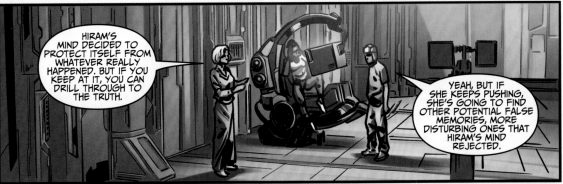

HIRAM'S MIND DECIDED TO PROTECT ITSELF FROM WHATEVER REALLY HAPPENED. BUT IF YOU KEEP AT IT, YOU CAN DRILL THROUGH TO THE TRUTH.

YEAH, BUT IF SHE KEEPS PUSHING, SHE'S GOING TO FIND OTHER POTENTIAL FALSE MEMORIES, MORE DISTURBING ONES THAT HIRAM'S MIND REJECTED.

CHARLOTTE, LISTEN TO ME. YOU'VE PUSHED TOO FAR, ABSORBED TOO MUCH STRESS FROM HIRAM ALREADY. THESE FALSE MEMORIES ARE GOING TO RAMP THAT UP LIKE CRAZY.

IF IT BECOMES TOO MUCH, YOUR BRAIN COULD SHUT DOWN TO PROTECT ITSELF. LIKE... FOREVER....

I DON'T WANT YOUR BRAIN TO DO THAT.

KODY. YOU KNOW I HAVE TO DO THIS.

BUT FOR YOU? I'LL TAKE A BREAK BEFORE I GO BACK IN.

CHARLOTTE, WE DON'T KNOW HOW CLOSE THE TEMPLARS ARE TO UNLEASHING PHOENIX.

I'M NOT GOING TO MAKE THE MISTAKE HIRAM MADE, RUSHING INTO THINGS.

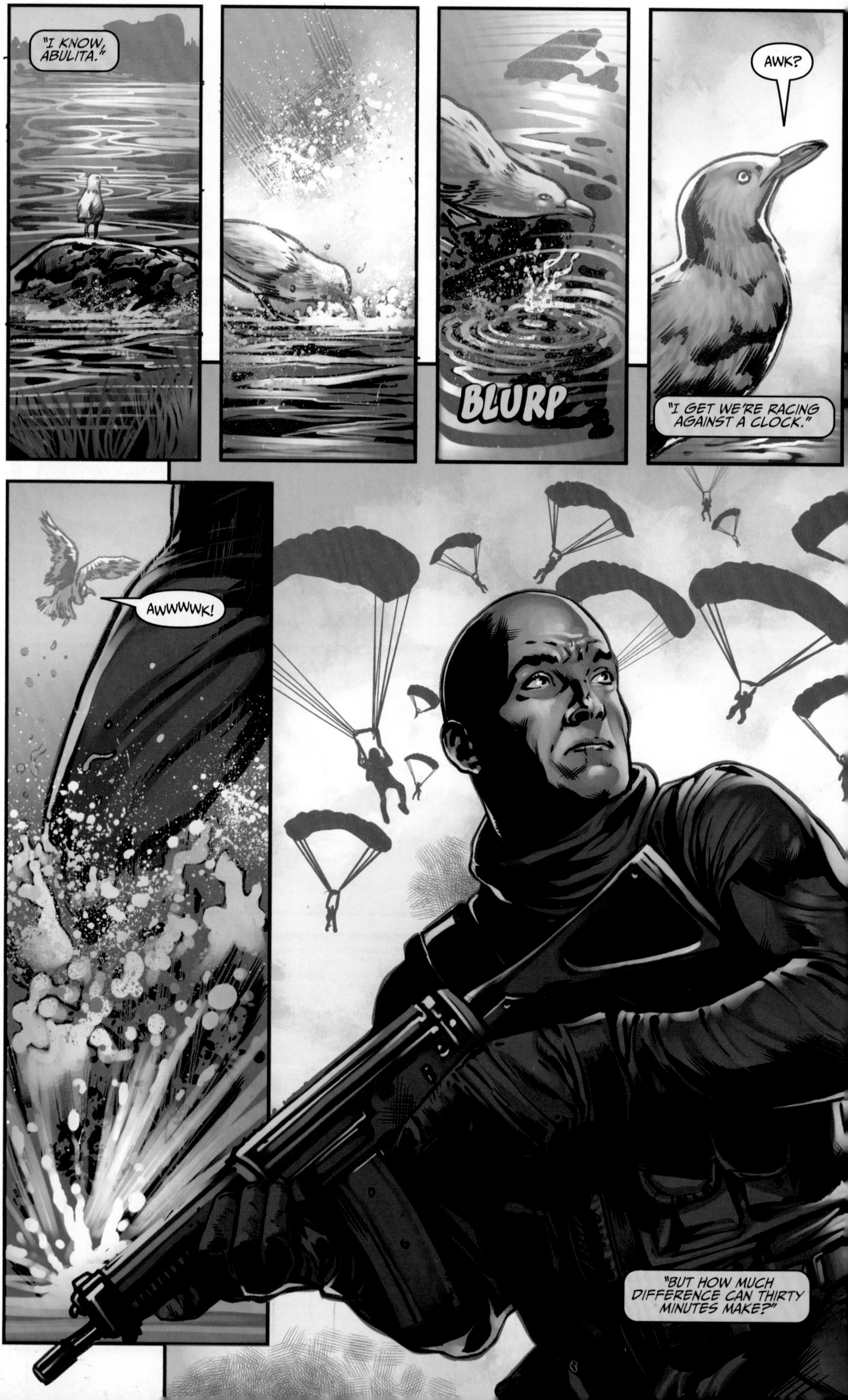
"I KNOW, ABULITA."
BLURP
AWK?
"I GET WE'RE RACING AGAINST A CLOCK."
AWWWWK!
"BUT HOW MUCH DIFFERENCE CAN THIRTY MINUTES MAKE?"

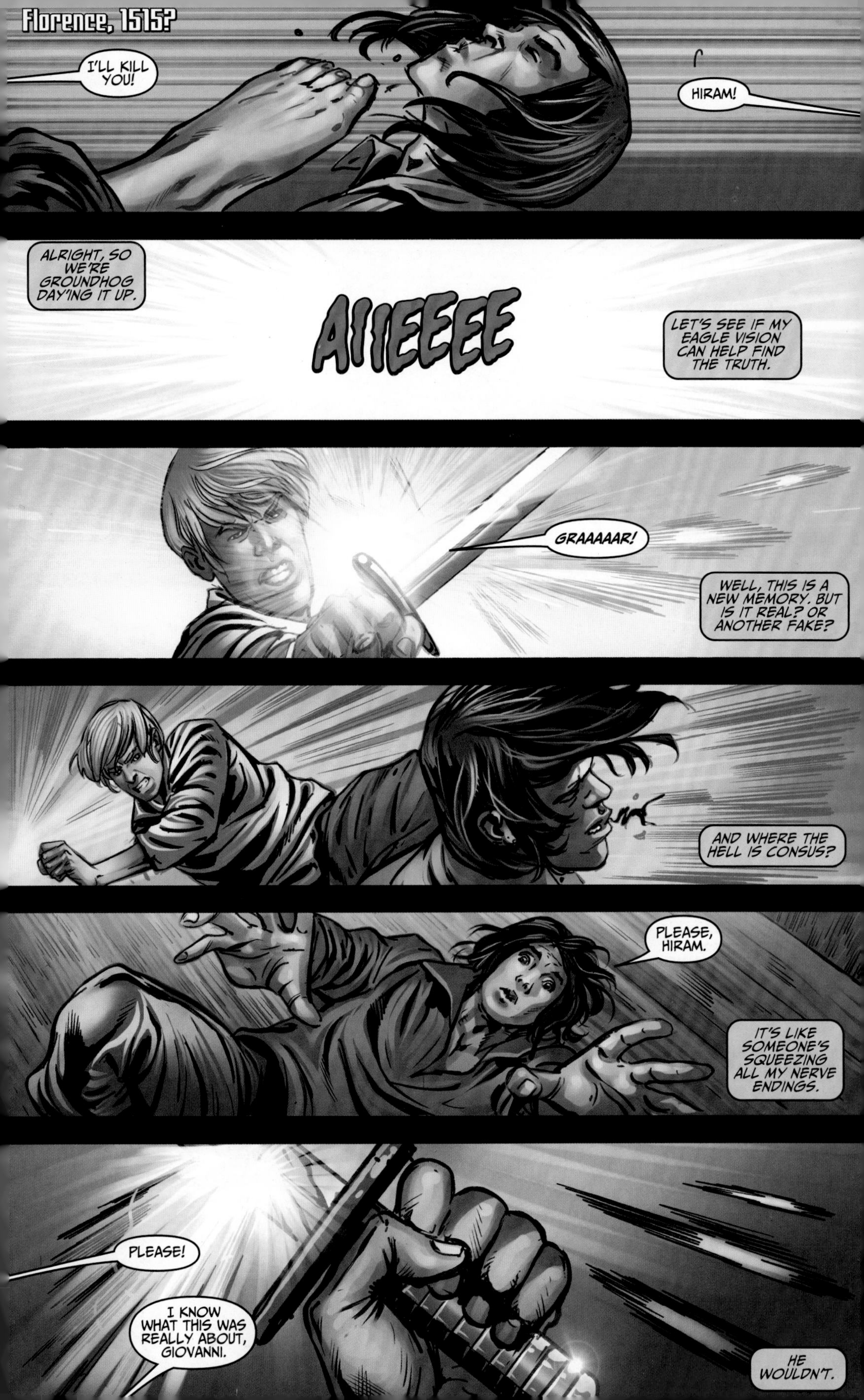
Florence, 1515?
I'LL KILL YOU!
HIRAM!
ALRIGHT, SO WE'RE GROUNDHOG DAY'ING IT UP.
AIIEEEE
LET'S SEE IF MY EAGLE VISION CAN HELP FIND THE TRUTH.
GRAAAAAR!
WELL, THIS IS A NEW MEMORY. BUT IS IT REAL? OR ANOTHER FAKE?
AND WHERE THE HELL IS CONSUS?
PLEASE, HIRAM.
IT'S LIKE SOMEONE'S SQUEEZING ALL MY NERVE ENDINGS.
PLEASE!
I KNOW WHAT THIS WAS REALLY ABOUT, GIOVANNI.
HE WOULDN'T.

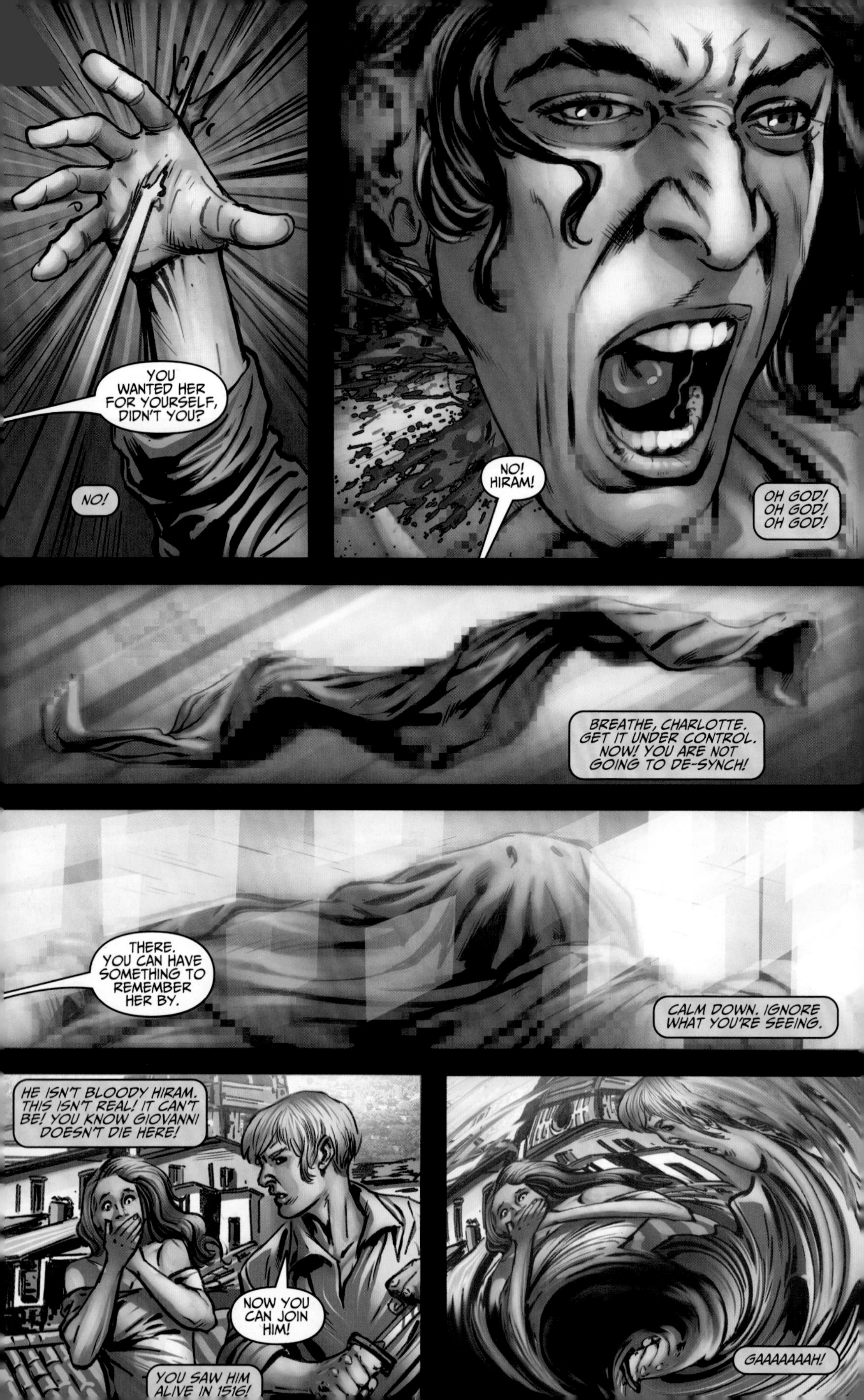
YOU WANTED HER FOR YOURSELF, DIDN'T YOU?
NO!
NO! HIRAM!
OH GOD! OH GOD! OH GOD!
BREATHE, CHARLOTTE. GET IT UNDER CONTROL. NOW! YOU ARE NOT GOING TO DE-SYNCH!
THERE. YOU CAN HAVE SOMETHING TO REMEMBER HER BY.
CALM DOWN. IGNORE WHAT YOU'RE SEEING.
HE ISN'T BLOODY HIRAM. THIS ISN'T REAL! IT CAN'T BE! YOU KNOW GIOVANNI DOESN'T DIE HERE!
NOW YOU CAN JOIN HIM!
YOU SAW HIM ALIVE IN 1516!
GAAAAAAAH!

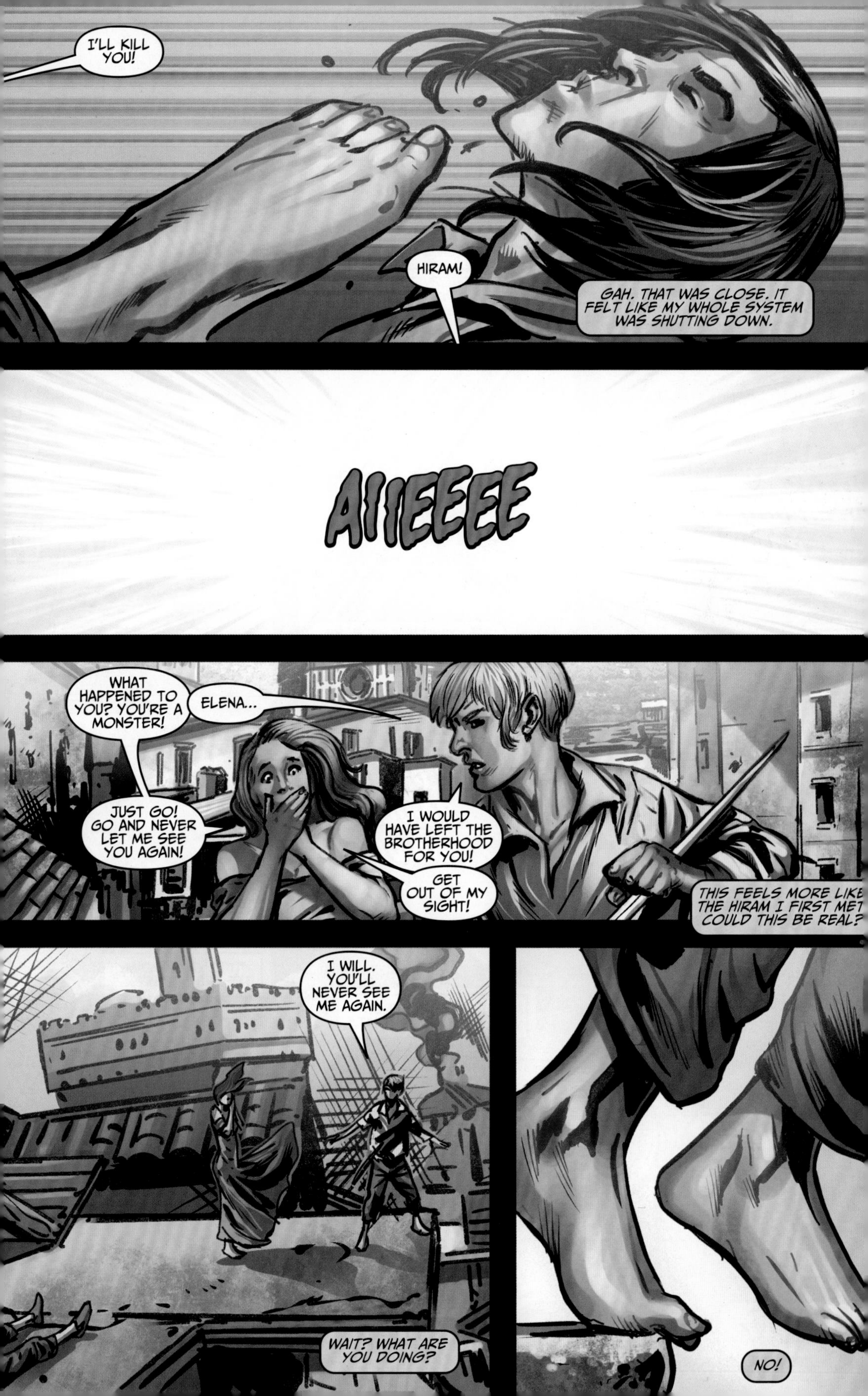
I'LL KILL YOU!
HIRAM!
GAH. THAT WAS CLOSE. IT FELT LIKE MY WHOLE SYSTEM WAS SHUTTING DOWN.
AIIEEEE
WHAT HAPPENED TO YOU? YOU'RE A MONSTER!
ELENA...
JUST GO! GO AND NEVER LET ME SEE YOU AGAIN!
I WOULD HAVE LEFT THE BROTHERHOOD FOR YOU!
GET OUT OF MY SIGHT!
THIS FEELS MORE LIKE THE HIRAM I FIRST MET. COULD THIS BE REAL?
I WILL. YOU'LL NEVER SEE ME AGAIN.
WAIT? WHAT ARE YOU DOING?
NO!

THIS ISN'T REAL, CHAR!

HIRAM WOULDN'T HAVE KILLED HIMSELF BECAUSE OF ELENA!

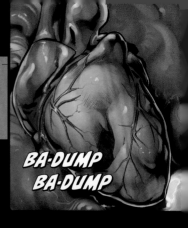

BA-DUMP BA-DUMP

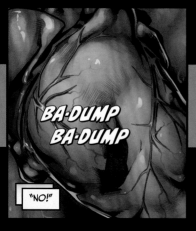

BA-DUMP BA-DUMP

"NO!"

HE COULDN'T HAVE! HE BECAME BLOODY HIRAM!

SHE'S TOO FAR GONE!

WHAT DO YOU MEAN?

THIS MEMORY ENDS WITH HIRAM DYING! FOR CHAR IT WILL FEEL LIKE SHE'S DYING!

BA-DUMP BA-DUMP BA-DUMP

"HER MIND WON'T LET HER EXPERIENCE THAT."

"IT'LL SHUT DOWN BEFORE SHE HITS!"

THINK, CHAR!

BA-DUMP BA-DUMP

THE SCARF... IT'S IN EVERY MEMORY.

IT'S THE KEY! IT HAS TO BE!

YOU CAN DO THIS! YOU MADE TOM TURN IN SALEM!

SHE'S CRASHING!

GET HER OUT!

"THE SHOCK WOULD KILL HER!"

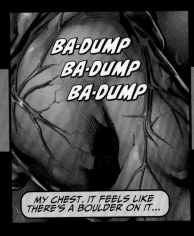

BA-DUMP
BA-DUMP
BA-DUMP

MY CHEST. IT FEELS LIKE THERE'S A BOULDER ON IT...

SHE CAN JUST ROLL WITH IT THOUGH, RIGHT? LET THE MEMORY PLAY OUT?

NO! NOT THIS ONE.

BA-DUMP
BA-DUMP
BA-DUMP

THE MIND DOESN'T WORK FROM NOTHING.

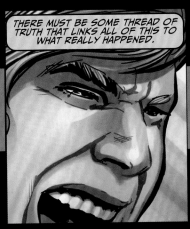

THERE MUST BE SOME THREAD OF TRUTH THAT LINKS ALL OF THIS TO WHAT REALLY HAPPENED.

BA-DUMP
BA-DUMP

MOVE HIS DAMNED HAND!

BA-DUMP
BA-DUMP

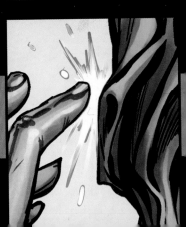

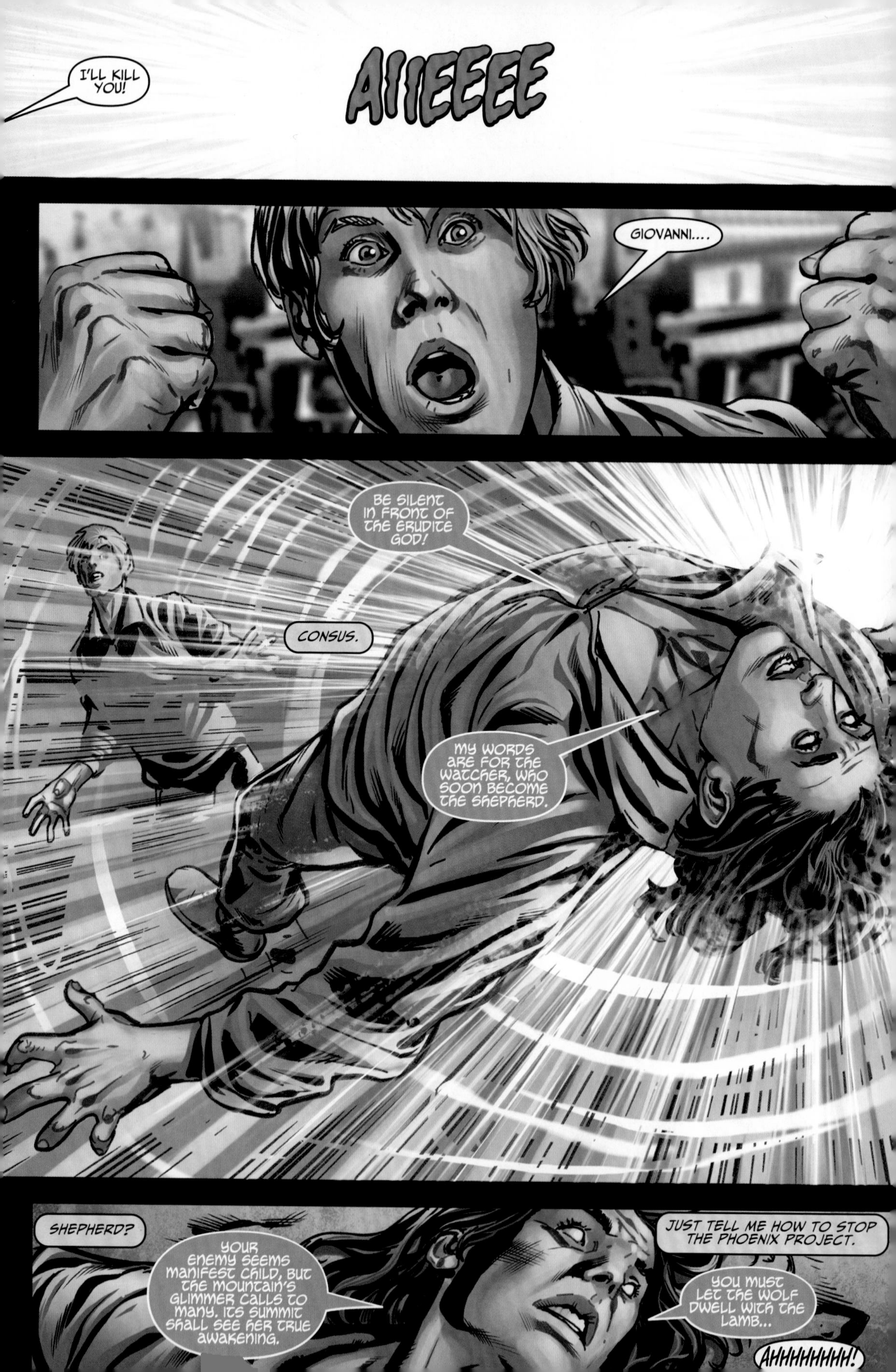

I'LL KILL YOU!
AIIEEEE
GIOVANNI....
BE SILENT IN FRONT OF THE ERUDITE GOD!
CONSUS.
MY WORDS ARE FOR THE WATCHER, WHO SOON BECOME THE SHEPHERD.
SHEPHERD?
YOUR ENEMY SEEMS MANIFEST CHILD, BUT THE MOUNTAIN'S GLIMMER CALLS TO MANY. ITS SUMMIT SHALL SEE HER TRUE AWAKENING.
JUST TELL ME HOW TO STOP THE PHOENIX PROJECT.
YOU MUST LET THE WOLF DWELL WITH THE LAMB...
AHHHHHHHH!

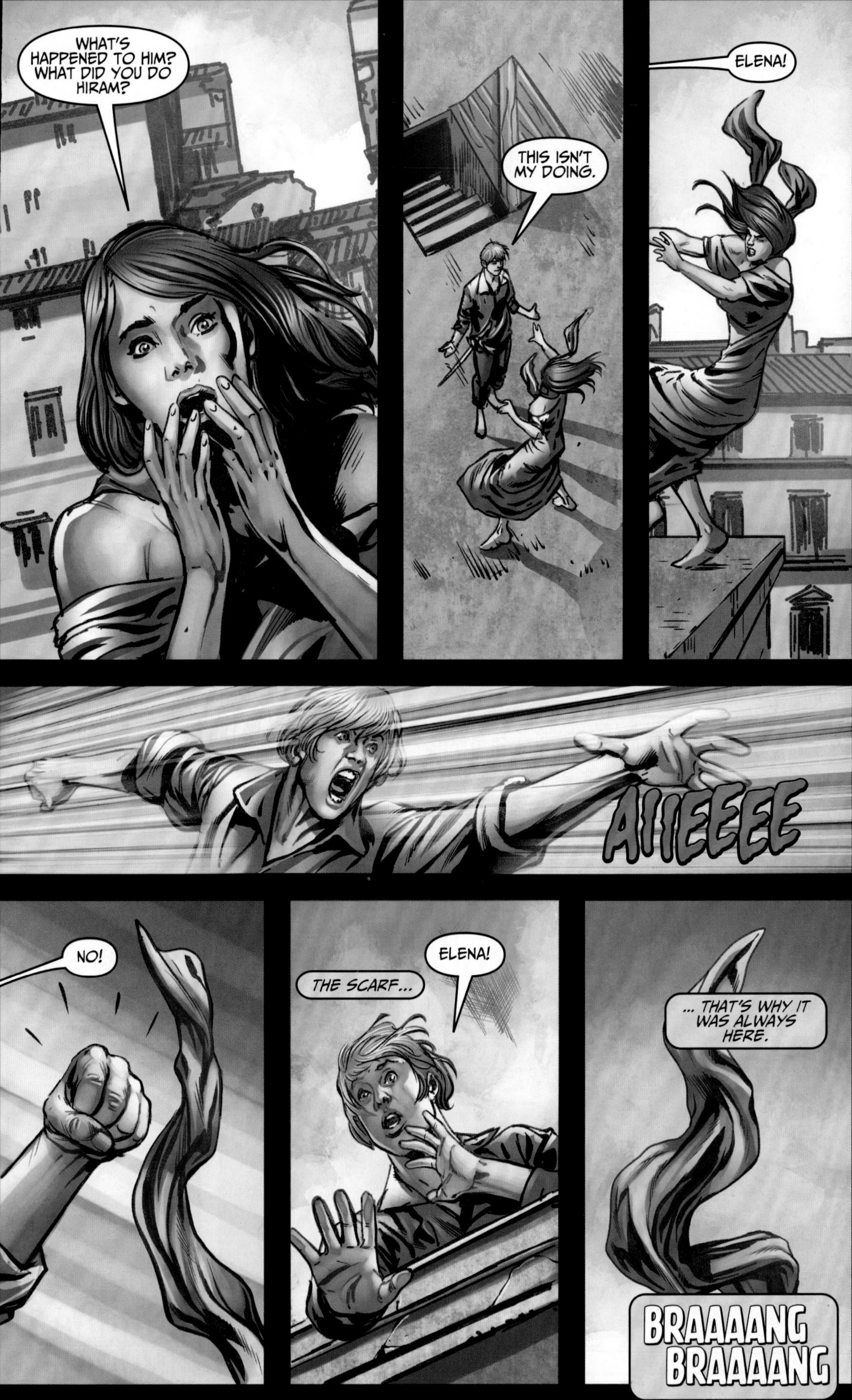
WHAT'S HAPPENED TO HIM? WHAT DID YOU DO HIRAM?
THIS ISN'T MY DOING.
ELENA!
AIIEEEE
NO!
THE SCARF...
ELENA!
... THAT'S WHY IT WAS ALWAYS HERE.
BRAAAANG BRAAAANG

KODY.... WHAT'S GOING ON?

THE TEMPLARS FOUND US SOMEHOW!

BRAAAAANG BRAAAANG

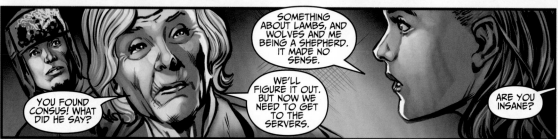

YOU FOUND CONSUS! WHAT DID HE SAY?

SOMETHING ABOUT LAMBS, AND WOLVES AND ME BEING A SHEPHERD. IT MADE NO SENSE.

WE'LL FIGURE IT OUT. BUT NOW WE NEED TO GET TO THE SERVERS.

ARE YOU INSANE?

PROTOCOL IS TO WIPE THEM REMOTELY ONCE EVERYONE IS SAFELY CLEAR OF THE COMPOUND. WE NEED TO GET TO THE BOATS!

BRAAAANG BRAAAANG

WHAT IF THE TEMPLARS GET TO THE SERVERS FIRST? EVERYTHING WE KNOW ABOUT PHOENIX IS ON THEM. THEY HAVE TO BE DESTROYED.

WE WON'T MAKE THE SERVER ROOM!

BRAAAANG BRAAAANG

CHAR, WE GOTTA GET OUT OF HERE! HOW MANY TIMES ARE YOU GOING TO RISK YOUR LIFE FOR THIS WOMAN?

FLORENCIA... THIS IS REALLY HEAVY...

EVERYTHING I'VE WORKED FOR WILL BE LOST!

I... I... CAN'T.

I GET IT NOW. HIRAM'S REAL MISTAKE WAS TURNING HIS BACK ON GIO, HIS FAMILY. I IGNORED FLORENCIA BEFORE, AND GAVE THE TEMPLARS TIME TO GET HERE.

IF YOU GUYS WANT TO RUN AND HIDE IN THE BOATS BECAUSE YOU THINK THE WAR AGAINST THE TEMPLARS SHOULD BE SAFE, GO AHEAD.

BRAAAANG BRAAAANG

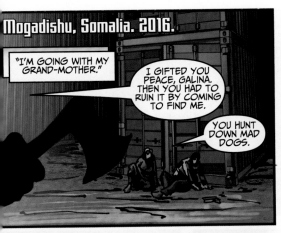

Mogadishu, Somalia. 2016.

"I'M GOING WITH MY GRAND-MOTHER."

I GIFTED YOU PEACE, GALINA. THEN YOU HAD TO RUIN IT BY COMING TO FIND ME.

YOU HUNT DOWN MAD DOGS.

YOU'RE LOYAL. I'LL GIVE YOU THAT.

BUT TO WHAT? ALL THE BROTHERHOOD DOES IS KILL. IT BUILDS NOTHING.

I SUPPOSE YOU PLANNED TO GIVE THAT GIRL A HUG TODAY, JOSEPH?

I DON'T WRAP MYSELF IN HIGH-MINDED RHETORIC AND SEND PEOPLE TO DIE.

THWOCK

DON'T MAKE ME PUT THE NEXT ONE INTO YOUR HEAD.

THAT LEG HASN'T HEALED ALL THE WAY. YOU'RE A STEP SLOWER.

EVEN THEN YOU WEREN'T FAST ENOUGH.

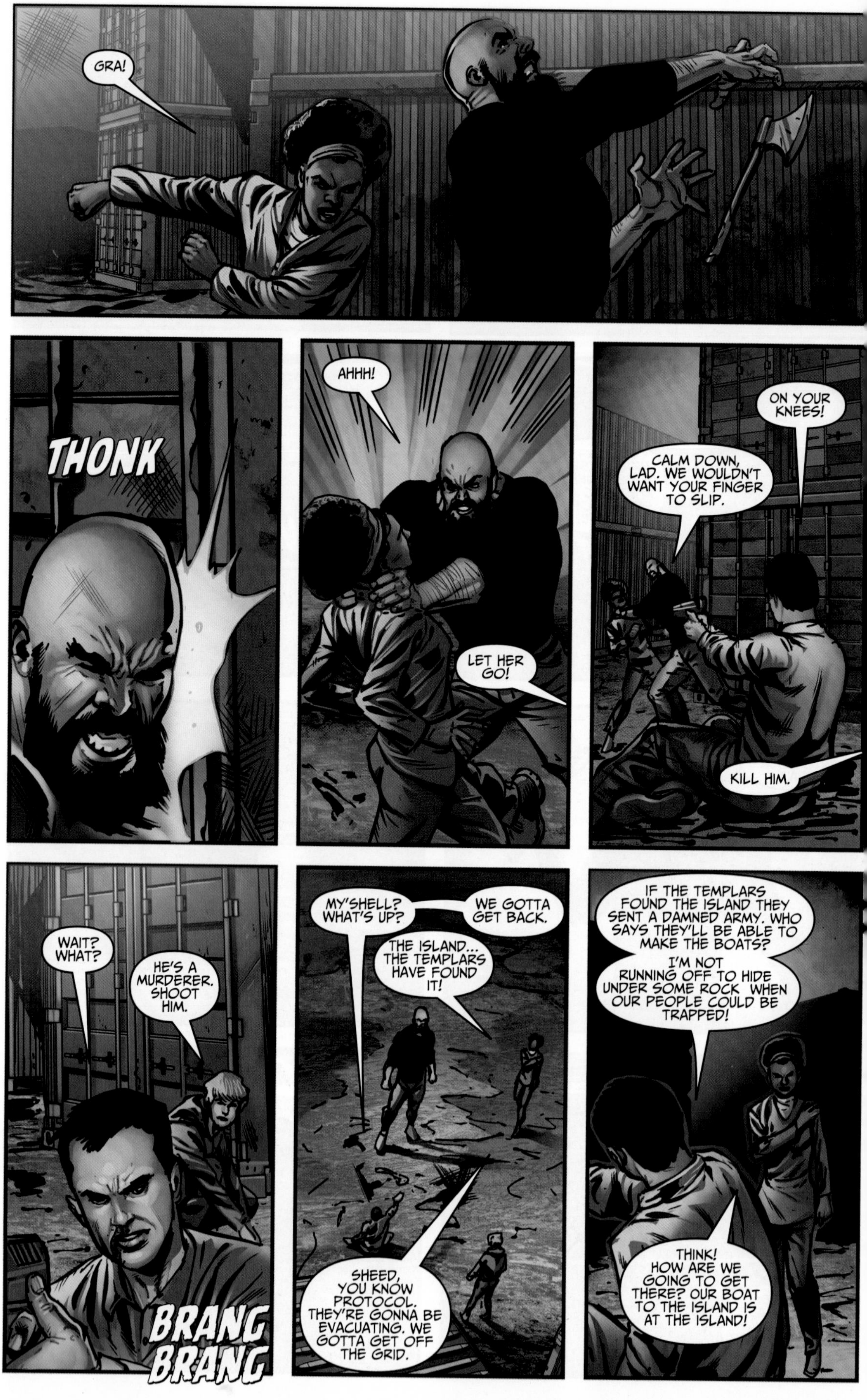
GRA!
THONK
AHHH!
LET HER GO!
ON YOUR KNEES!
CALM DOWN, LAD. WE WOULDN'T WANT YOUR FINGER TO SLIP.
KILL HIM.
WAIT? WHAT?
HE'S A MURDERER. SHOOT HIM.
BRANG
BRANG
MY'SHELL? WHAT'S UP?
WE GOTTA GET BACK.
THE ISLAND... THE TEMPLARS HAVE FOUND IT!
SHEED, YOU KNOW PROTOCOL. THEY'RE GONNA BE EVACUATING. WE GOTTA GET OFF THE GRID.
IF THE TEMPLARS FOUND THE ISLAND THEY SENT A DAMNED ARMY. WHO SAYS THEY'LL BE ABLE TO MAKE THE BOATS?
I'M NOT RUNNING OFF TO HIDE UNDER SOME ROCK WHEN OUR PEOPLE COULD BE TRAPPED!
THINK! HOW ARE WE GOING TO GET THERE? OUR BOAT TO THE ISLAND IS AT THE ISLAND!

I CAN GET YOU THERE. I HAVE A PLANE.

WHAT DO YOU MEAN, "YOU HAVE A PLANE?"

IT'S HOW I GOT HERE. I'M A PILOT.

SHEED, WE CAN'T TELL HIM WHERE THE COMPOUND IS!

WHAT DOES THAT MATTER, MY'SHELL? IF IT'S UNDER ATTACK THE SECRET'S ALREADY BLOWN.

I CAN GET YOU THERE. ALL I ASK IS IF CHARLOTTE WANTS TO COME WITH ME, YOU STAY OUT OF MY WAY.

FORGIVE ME, BUT YOU DON'T EXACTLY SEEM TO BE THE MENTOR TYPE...

... WHY DO YOU GIVE A RAT'S ASS WHAT HAPPENS TO HER?

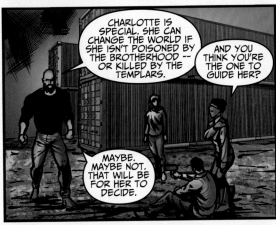

CHARLOTTE IS SPECIAL. SHE CAN CHANGE THE WORLD IF SHE ISN'T POISONED BY THE BROTHERHOOD -- OR KILLED BY THE TEMPLARS.

AND YOU THINK YOU'RE THE ONE TO GUIDE HER?

MAYBE. MAYBE NOT. THAT WILL BE FOR HER TO DECIDE.

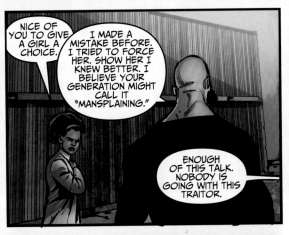

NICE OF YOU TO GIVE A GIRL A CHOICE.

I MADE A MISTAKE BEFORE. I TRIED TO FORCE HER. SHOW HER I KNEW BETTER. I BELIEVE YOUR GENERATION MIGHT CALL IT "MANSPLAINING."

ENOUGH OF THIS TALK. NOBODY IS GOING WITH THIS TRAITOR.

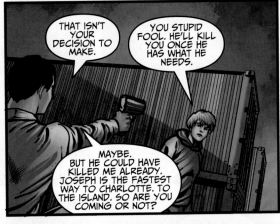

THAT ISN'T YOUR DECISION TO MAKE.

YOU STUPID FOOL. HE'LL KILL YOU ONCE HE HAS WHAT HE NEEDS.

MAYBE. BUT HE COULD HAVE KILLED ME ALREADY. JOSEPH IS THE FASTEST WAY TO CHARLOTTE. TO THE ISLAND. SO ARE YOU COMING OR NOT?

... YOU'RE RIGHT. GETTING TO CHARLOTTE IS OUR TOP PRIORITY.

BUT TELL YOUR PILOT THAT AFTER THIS IS FINISHED, REVENGE MOVES BACK UP THE LIST.

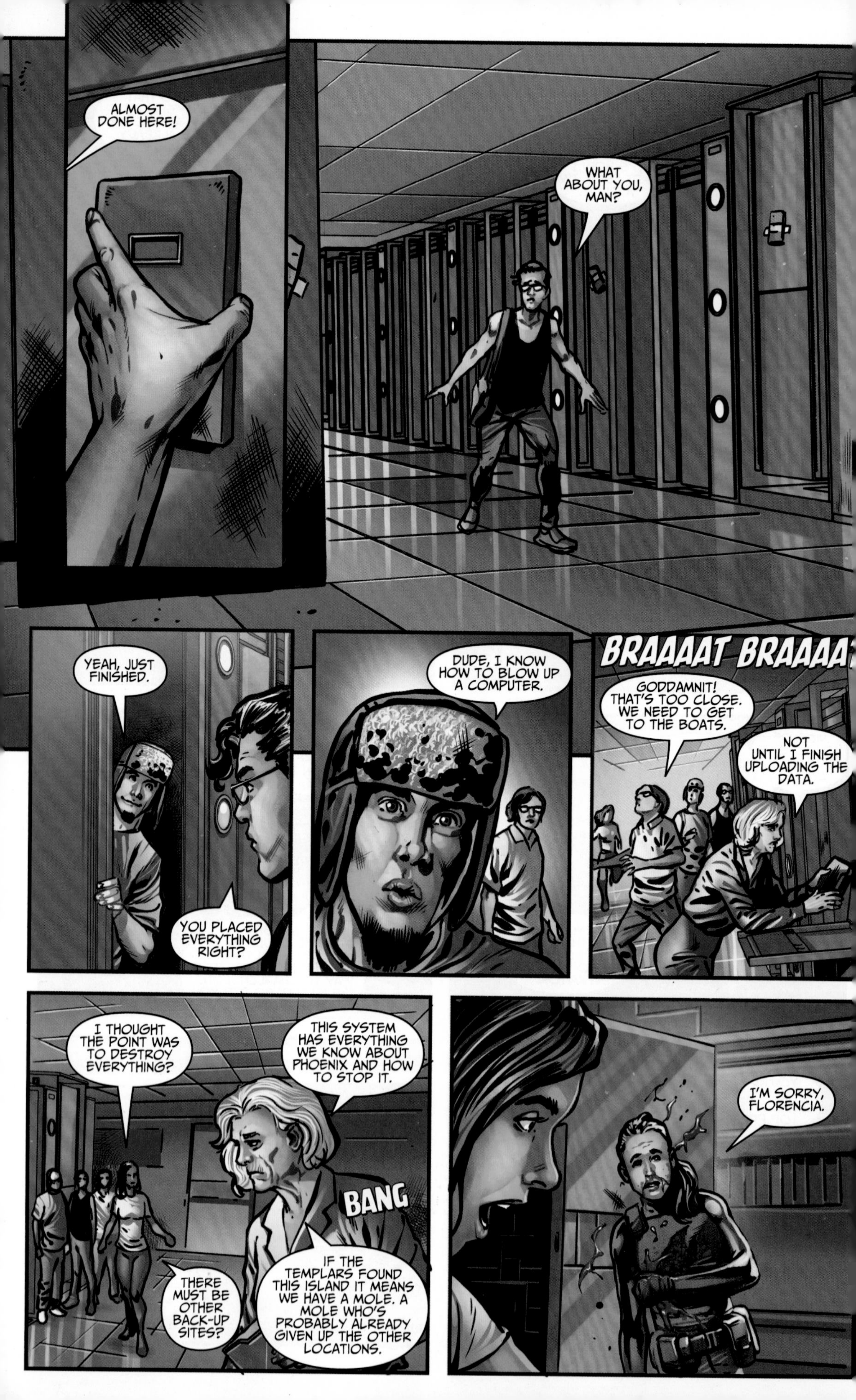
ALMOST DONE HERE!
WHAT ABOUT YOU, MAN?
YEAH, JUST FINISHED.
YOU PLACED EVERYTHING RIGHT?
DUDE, I KNOW HOW TO BLOW UP A COMPUTER.
BRAAAAT BRAAAAT
GODDAMNIT! THAT'S TOO CLOSE. WE NEED TO GET TO THE BOATS.
NOT UNTIL I FINISH UPLOADING THE DATA.
I THOUGHT THE POINT WAS TO DESTROY EVERYTHING?
THIS SYSTEM HAS EVERYTHING WE KNOW ABOUT PHOENIX AND HOW TO STOP IT.
THERE MUST BE OTHER BACK-UP SITES?
IF THE TEMPLARS FOUND THIS ISLAND IT MEANS WE HAVE A MOLE. A MOLE WHO'S PROBABLY ALREADY GIVEN UP THE OTHER LOCATIONS.
BANG
I'M SORRY, FLORENCIA.

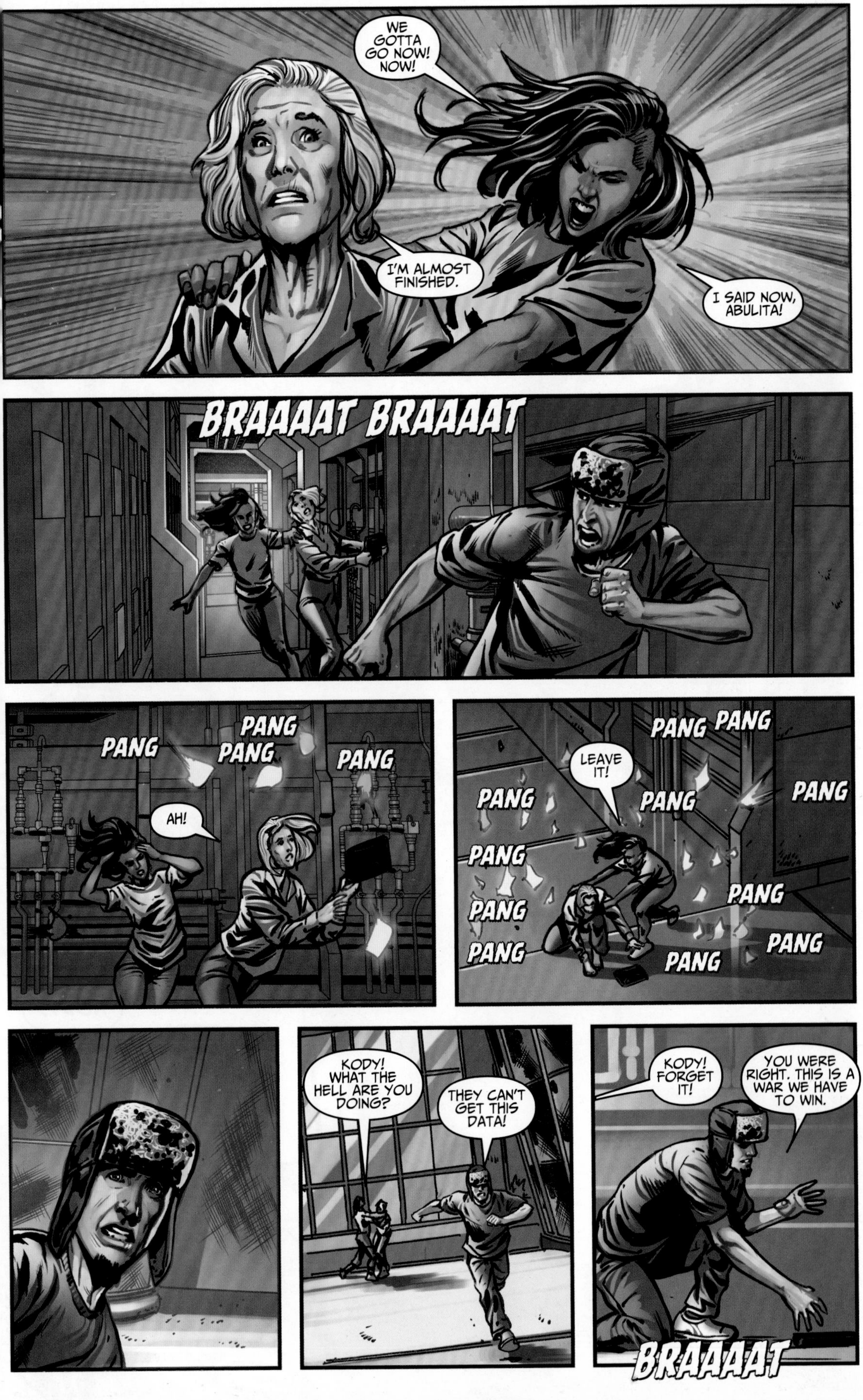
WE GOTTA GO NOW! NOW!
I'M ALMOST FINISHED.
I SAID NOW, ABULITA!
BRAAAAT BRAAAAT
PANG
PANG
PANG
PANG
AH!
PANG PANG
LEAVE IT!
PANG
PANG
PANG
PANG
PANG
PANG
PANG
PANG
PANG
KODY! WHAT THE HELL ARE YOU DOING?
THEY CAN'T GET THIS DATA!
KODY! FORGET IT!
YOU WERE RIGHT. THIS IS A WAR WE HAVE TO WIN.
BRAAAAT

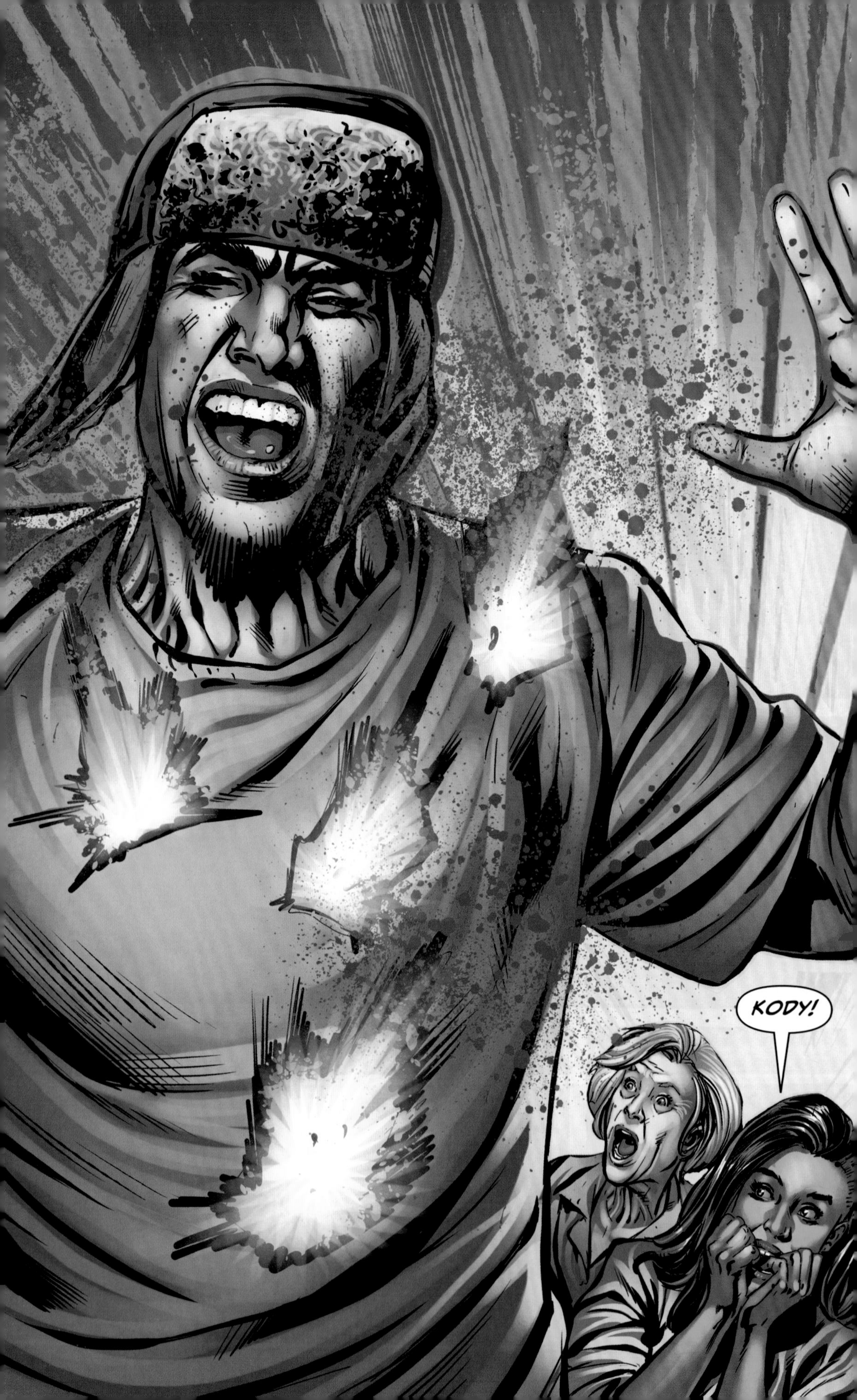
KODY!

CHAPTER
FOURTEEN

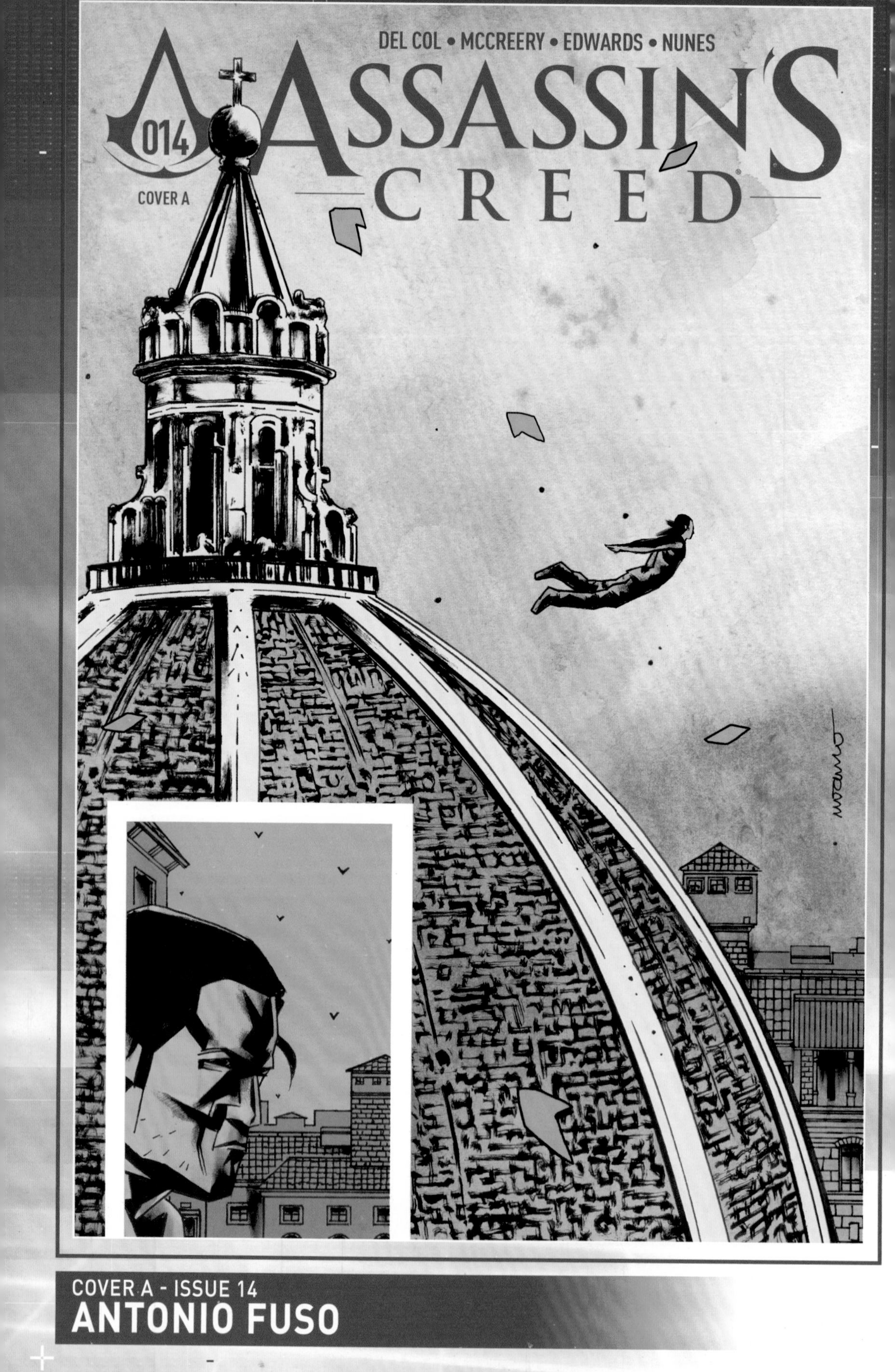
DEL COL • MCCREERY • EDWARDS • NUNES
ASSASSIN'S CREED
014
COVER A

COVER A - ISSUE 14
ANTONIO FUSO

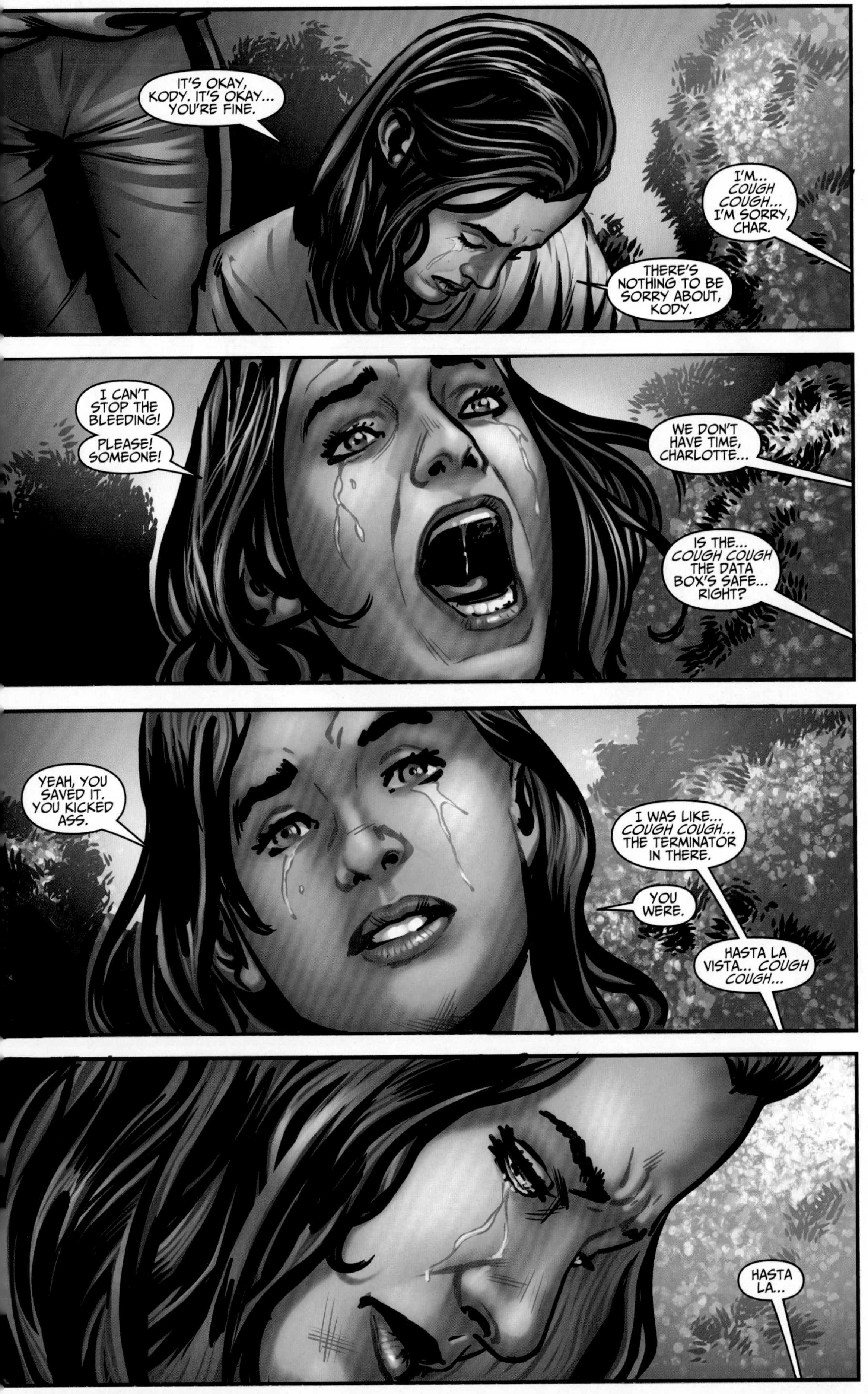

IT'S OKAY, KODY. IT'S OKAY... YOU'RE FINE.
I'M... COUGH COUGH... I'M SORRY, CHAR.
THERE'S NOTHING TO BE SORRY ABOUT, KODY.
I CAN'T STOP THE BLEEDING!
PLEASE! SOMEONE!
WE DON'T HAVE TIME, CHARLOTTE...
IS THE... COUGH COUGH THE DATA BOX'S SAFE... RIGHT?
YEAH, YOU SAVED IT. YOU KICKED ASS.
I WAS LIKE... COUGH COUGH... THE TERMINATOR IN THERE.
YOU WERE.
HASTA LA VISTA... COUGH COUGH...
HASTA LA...

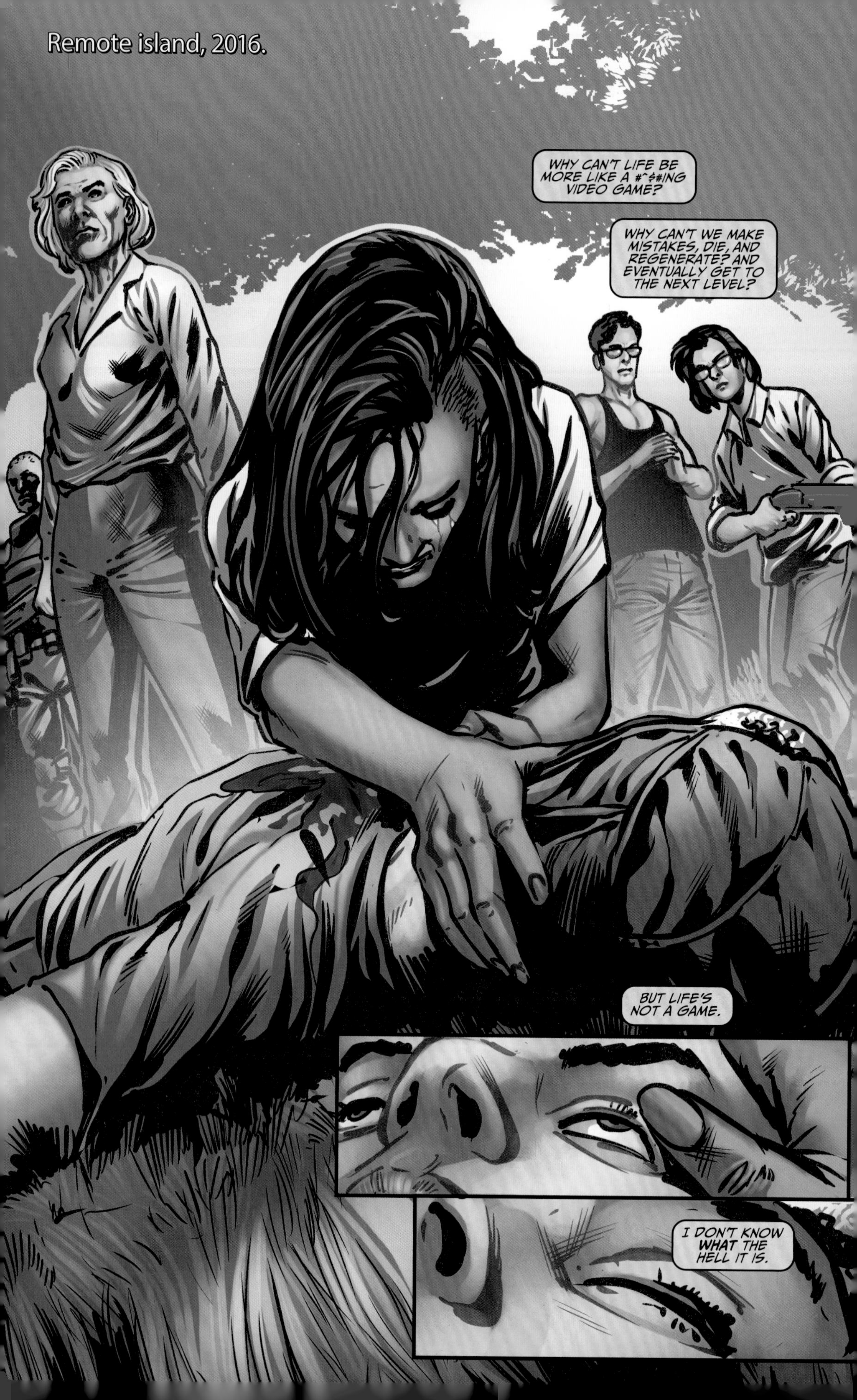
Remote island, 2016.
WHY CAN'T LIFE BE MORE LIKE A #^$#ING VIDEO GAME?
WHY CAN'T WE MAKE MISTAKES, DIE, AND REGENERATE? AND EVENTUALLY GET TO THE NEXT LEVEL?
BUT LIFE'S NOT A GAME.
I DON'T KNOW WHAT THE HELL IT IS.

HE WAS A GOOD SOLDIER. HE SAVED THE DATA. WE NEED TO HONOR HIS SACRIFICE AND GET MOVING SO THE TEMPLARS...

THE DATA?!

IT'S YOUR FAULT, 'LITA! IF WE WERE AT THE BOATS HE'D STILL BE ALIVE!

IF WE WEREN'T HERE HE'D STILL BE ALIVE!

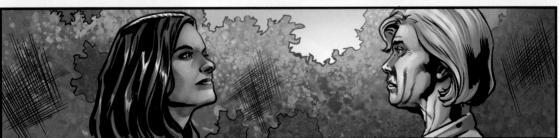

IF I HADN'T...

RRRRRRRRRRRR

IT'S MY FAULT. I DRAGGED HIM HERE.

IT'S NOT YOUR FAULT, PISHTACO. YOU DID WHAT YOU HAD TO. HE DID THE SAME.

UM, GUYS, THERE'S... SOMETHING COMING.

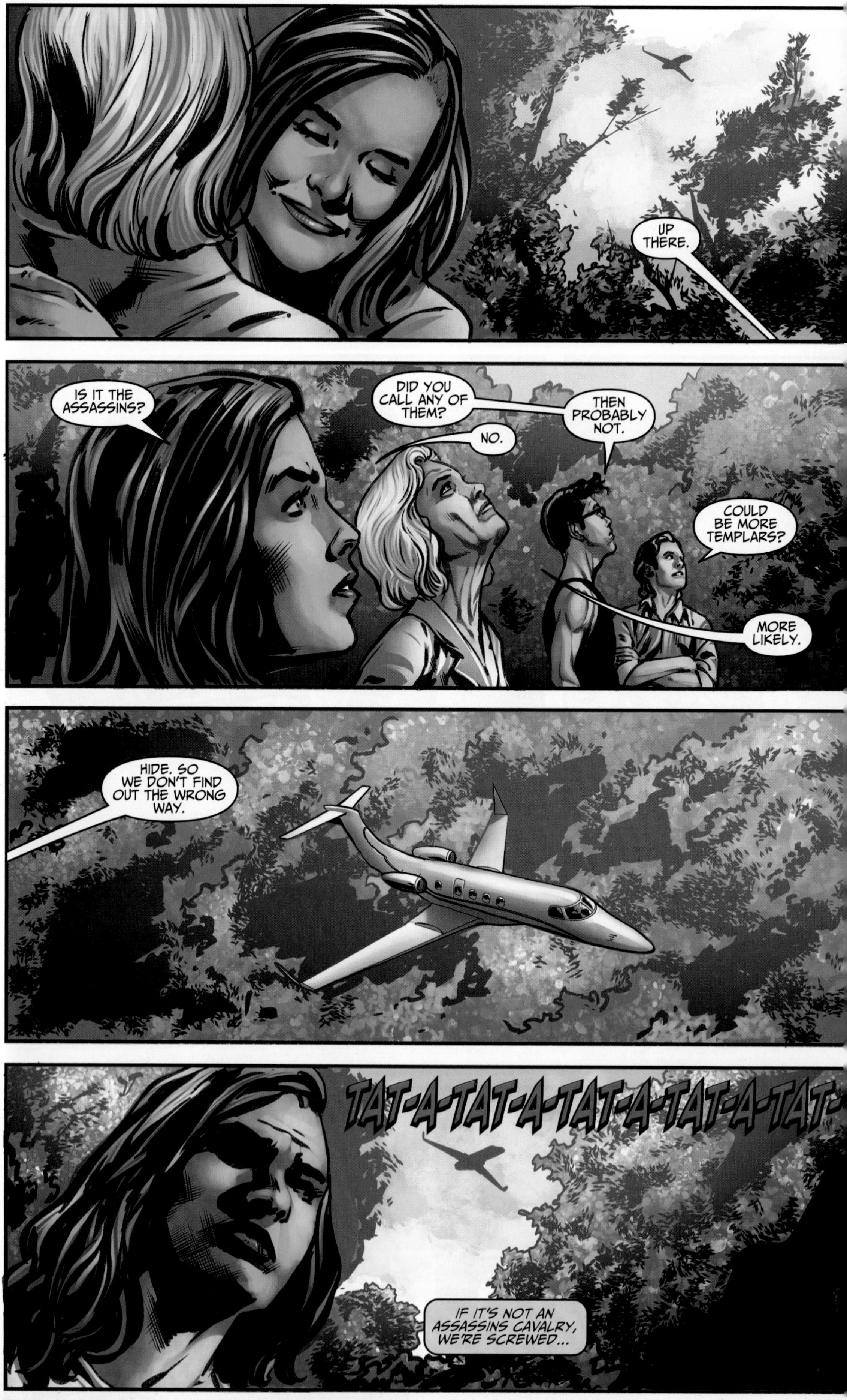
UP THERE.
IS IT THE ASSASSINS?
DID YOU CALL ANY OF THEM?
NO.
THEN PROBABLY NOT.
COULD BE MORE TEMPLARS?
MORE LIKELY.
HIDE. SO WE DON'T FIND OUT THE WRONG WAY.
TAT-A-TAT-A-TAT-A-TAT-A-TAT-
IF IT'S NOT AN ASSASSINS CAVALRY, WE'RE SCREWED...

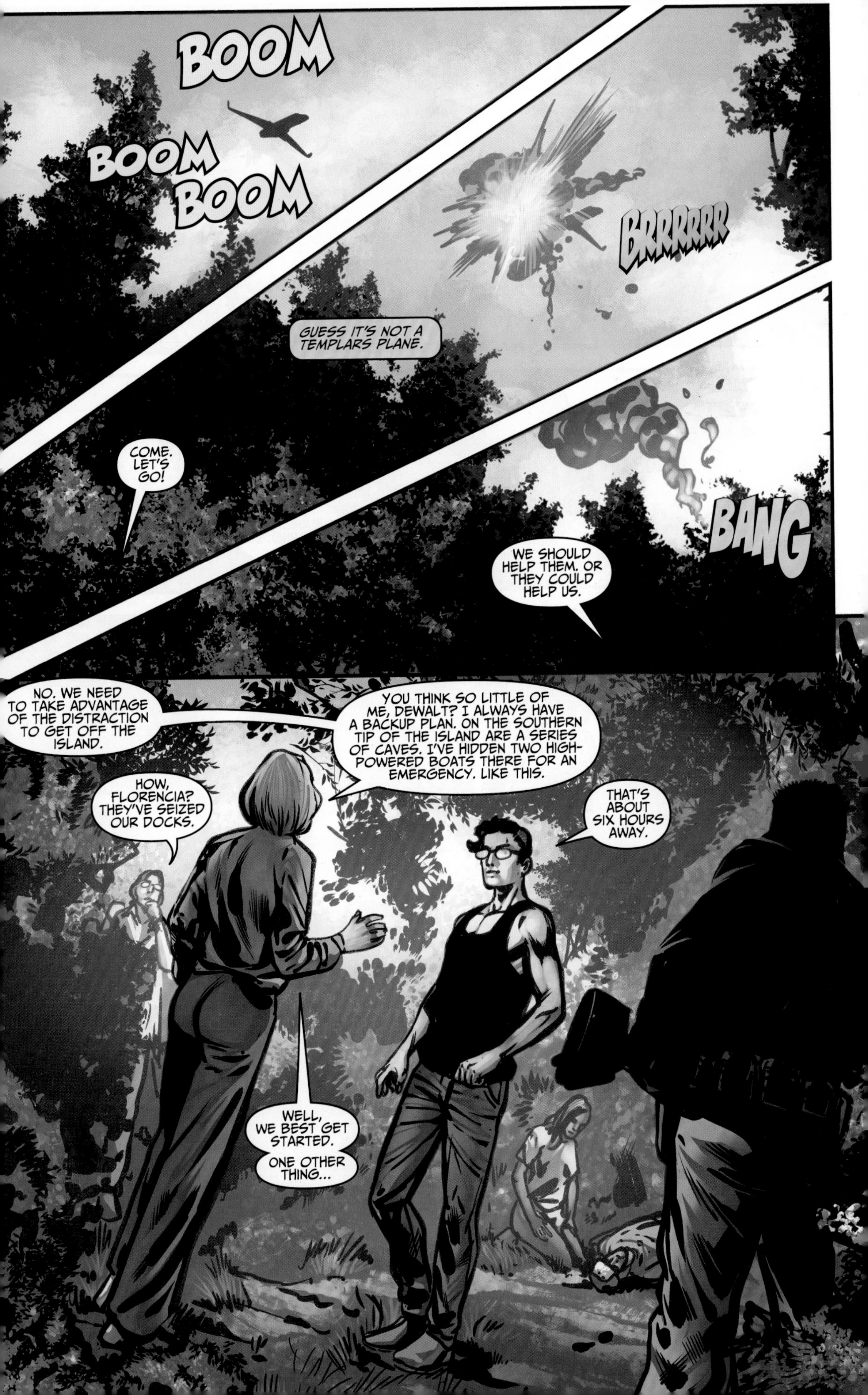
BOOM
BOOM
BOOM
BRRRRRR
GUESS IT'S NOT A TEMPLARS PLANE.
COME. LET'S GO!
BANG
WE SHOULD HELP THEM. OR THEY COULD HELP US.
NO. WE NEED TO TAKE ADVANTAGE OF THE DISTRACTION TO GET OFF THE ISLAND.
HOW, FLORENCIA? THEY'VE SEIZED OUR DOCKS.
YOU THINK SO LITTLE OF ME, DEWALT? I ALWAYS HAVE A BACKUP PLAN. ON THE SOUTHERN TIP OF THE ISLAND ARE A SERIES OF CAVES. I'VE HIDDEN TWO HIGH-POWERED BOATS THERE FOR AN EMERGENCY. LIKE THIS.
THAT'S ABOUT SIX HOURS AWAY.
WELL, WE BEST GET STARTED.
ONE OTHER THING...

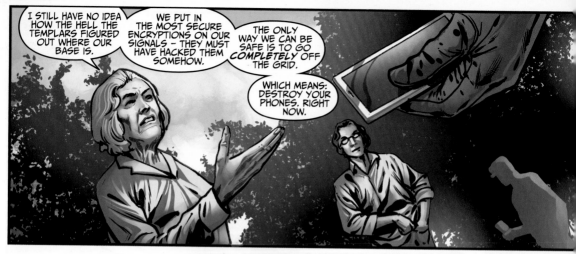

I STILL HAVE NO IDEA HOW THE HELL THE TEMPLARS FIGURED OUT WHERE OUR BASE IS.

WE PUT IN THE MOST SECURE ENCRYPTIONS ON OUR SIGNALS – THEY MUST HAVE HACKED THEM SOMEHOW.

THE ONLY WAY WE CAN BE SAFE IS TO GO COMPLETELY OFF THE GRID.

WHICH MEANS: DESTROY YOUR PHONES. RIGHT NOW.

GOOD. LET'S GET OUT OF HERE. NOW.

CHARLOTTE? ARE YOU –

YEAH, GUERNICA, I'M COMING. I JUST...

I DON'T WANT THEM TO FIND HIS BODY.

I'M SORRY, KODY.

YOU THOUGHT I WAS A LEADER, BUT...

I FAILED YOU.

I CAN'T FAIL THEM.

CHARLOTTE!

GOODBYE, KODY.

A QUESTION, MR. WHITTAKER: WHAT WOULD MAKE A TECH GEEK RACE INTO A FIELD OF FIRE?

SOMETHING HE THOUGHT WAS IMPORTANT.

LIKE DATA? PROJECT PHOENIX DATA?

YEAH, I'D SAY SO.

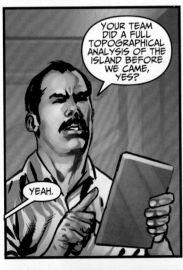

YOUR TEAM DID A FULL TOPOGRAPHICAL ANALYSIS OF THE ISLAND BEFORE WE CAME, YES?

YEAH.

IT SEEMS MS. DE LA CRUZ AND HER FRIENDS ARE HEADED WEST. WHAT COULD THEY BE AIMING FOR?

THERE'S NOT MUCH THERE. A BUNCH OF CLIFFS AND ROCKS. NOT MUCH... WAIT A MINUTE...

THERE'S A SERIES OF CAVES THERE, I BELIEVE.

BIG ENOUGH TO STORE SOMETHING?

LIKE A BOAT? YEAH.

TAKE THE EPSILON TEAM ON ONE OF THE BOATS AND GET THERE FIRST. LET'S SPRING A TRAP FOR THEM.

THANK YOU AGAIN, CHARLOTTE, FOR YOUR HELP.

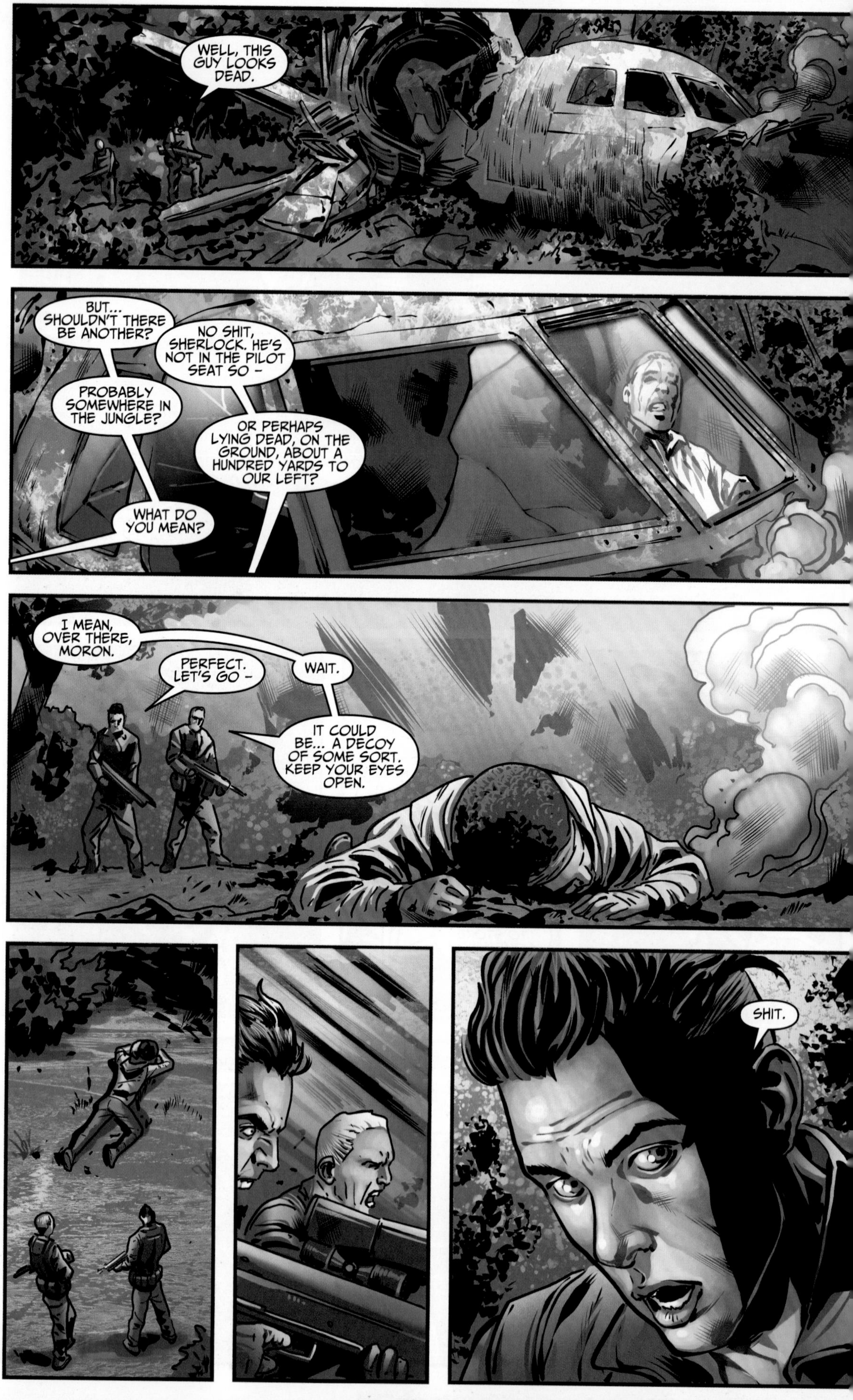
WELL, THIS GUY LOOKS DEAD.
BUT... SHOULDN'T THERE BE ANOTHER?
NO SHIT, SHERLOCK. HE'S NOT IN THE PILOT SEAT SO –
PROBABLY SOMEWHERE IN THE JUNGLE?
OR PERHAPS LYING DEAD, ON THE GROUND, ABOUT A HUNDRED YARDS TO OUR LEFT?
WHAT DO YOU MEAN?
I MEAN, OVER THERE, MORON.
PERFECT. LET'S GO –
WAIT.
IT COULD BE... A DECOY OF SOME SORT. KEEP YOUR EYES OPEN.
SHIT.

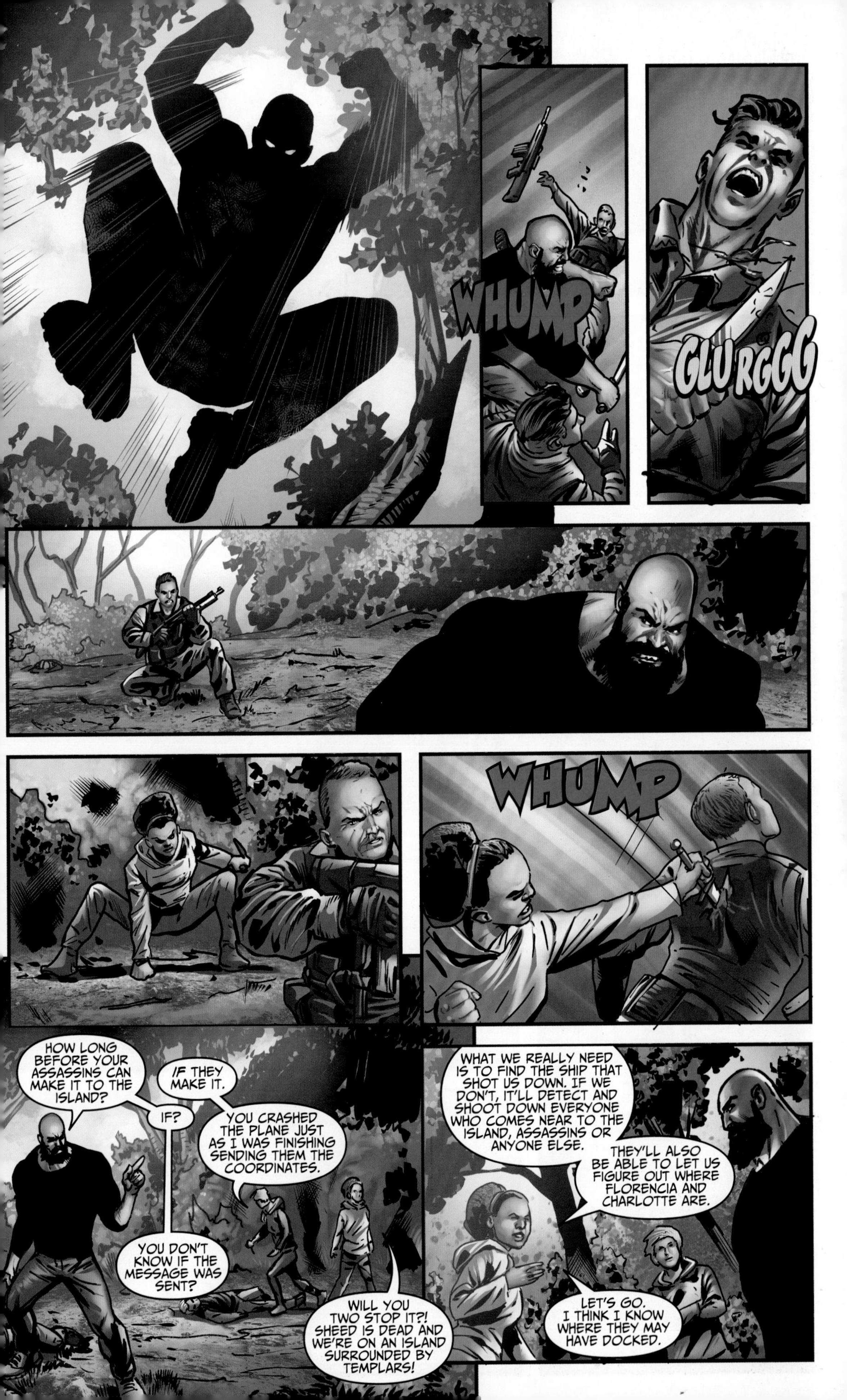
WHUMP
GLURGGG
WHUMP
HOW LONG BEFORE YOUR ASSASSINS CAN MAKE IT TO THE ISLAND?
IF THEY MAKE IT.
IF?
YOU CRASHED THE PLANE JUST AS I WAS FINISHING SENDING THEM THE COORDINATES.
YOU DON'T KNOW IF THE MESSAGE WAS SENT?
WILL YOU TWO STOP IT?! SHEED IS DEAD AND WE'RE ON AN ISLAND SURROUNDED BY TEMPLARS!
WHAT WE REALLY NEED IS TO FIND THE SHIP THAT SHOT US DOWN. IF WE DON'T, IT'LL DETECT AND SHOOT DOWN EVERYONE WHO COMES NEAR TO THE ISLAND, ASSASSINS OR ANYONE ELSE.
THEY'LL ALSO BE ABLE TO LET US FIGURE OUT WHERE FLORENCIA AND CHARLOTTE ARE.
LET'S GO. I THINK I KNOW WHERE THEY MAY HAVE DOCKED.

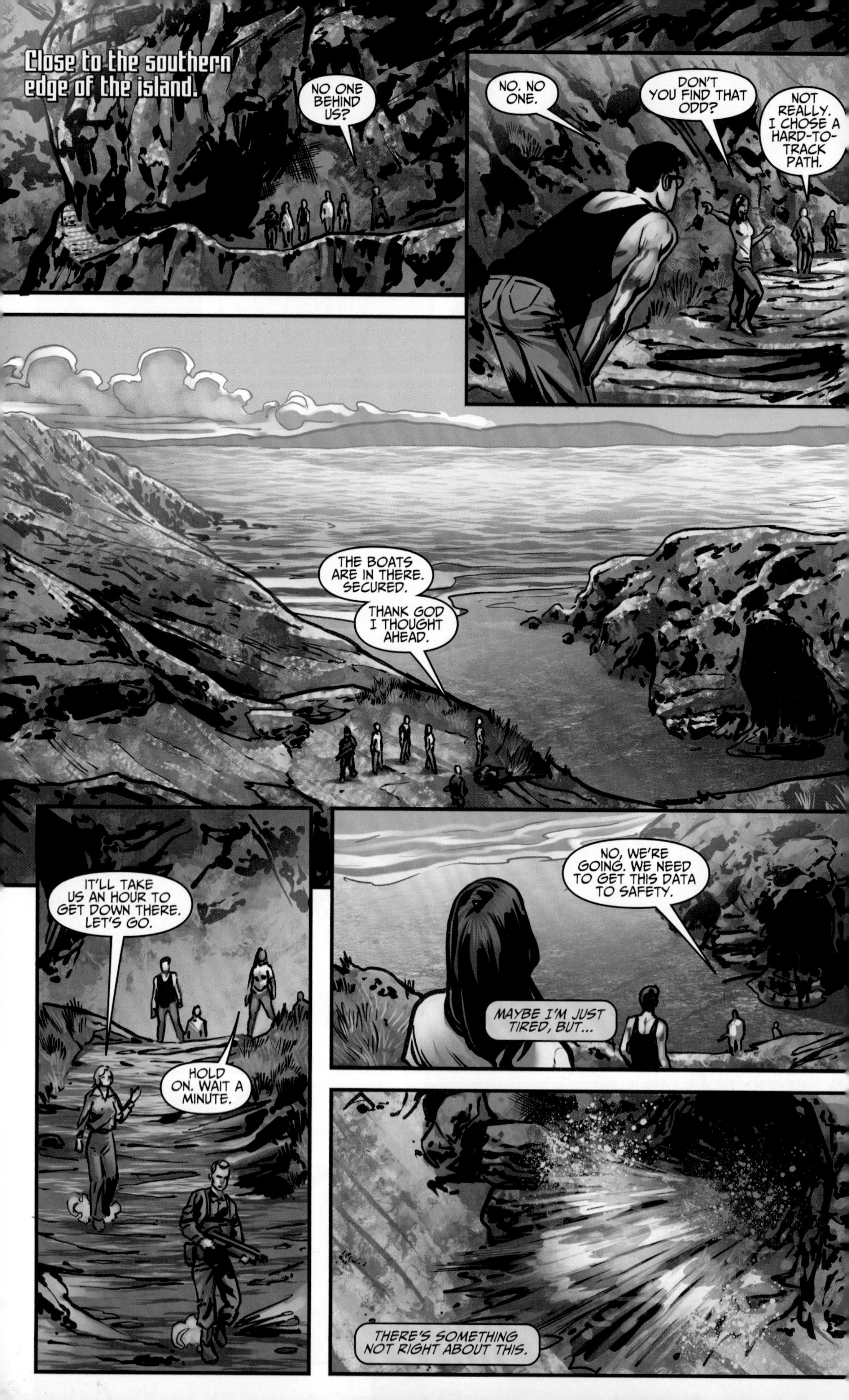
Close to the southern edge of the island.
NO ONE BEHIND US?
NO. NO ONE.
DON'T YOU FIND THAT ODD?
NOT REALLY. I CHOSE A HARD-TO-TRACK PATH.
THE BOATS ARE IN THERE. SECURED.
THANK GOD I THOUGHT AHEAD.
IT'LL TAKE US AN HOUR TO GET DOWN THERE. LET'S GO.
HOLD ON. WAIT A MINUTE.
NO, WE'RE GOING. WE NEED TO GET THIS DATA TO SAFETY.
MAYBE I'M JUST TIRED, BUT...
THERE'S SOMETHING NOT RIGHT ABOUT THIS.

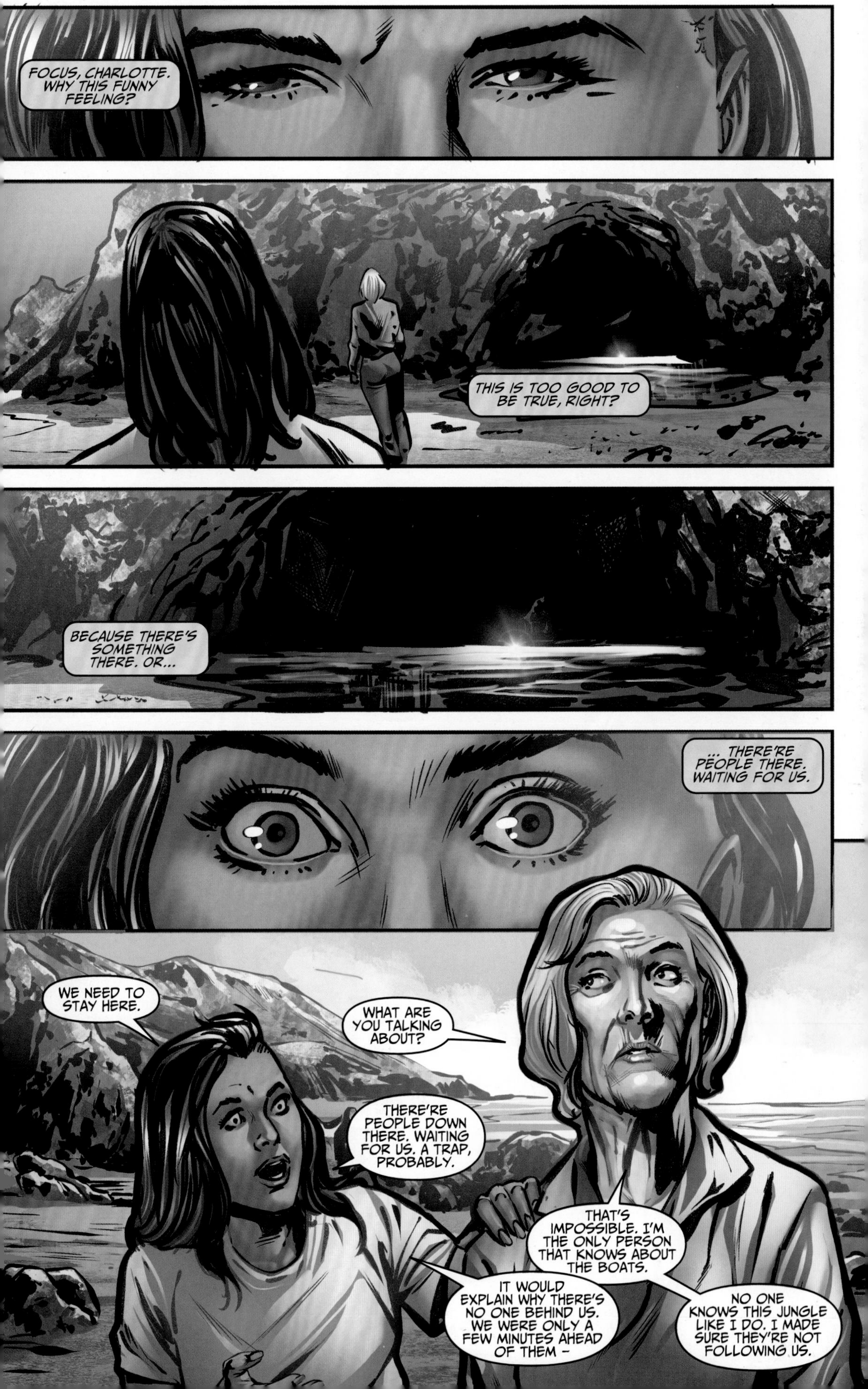
FOCUS, CHARLOTTE. WHY THIS FUNNY FEELING?
THIS IS TOO GOOD TO BE TRUE, RIGHT?
BECAUSE THERE'S SOMETHING THERE. OR...
... THERE'RE PEOPLE THERE. WAITING FOR US.
WE NEED TO STAY HERE.
WHAT ARE YOU TALKING ABOUT?
THERE'RE PEOPLE DOWN THERE. WAITING FOR US. A TRAP, PROBABLY.
THAT'S IMPOSSIBLE. I'M THE ONLY PERSON THAT KNOWS ABOUT THE BOATS.
IT WOULD EXPLAIN WHY THERE'S NO ONE BEHIND US. WE WERE ONLY A FEW MINUTES AHEAD OF THEM –
NO ONE KNOWS THIS JUNGLE LIKE I DO. I MADE SURE THEY'RE NOT FOLLOWING US.

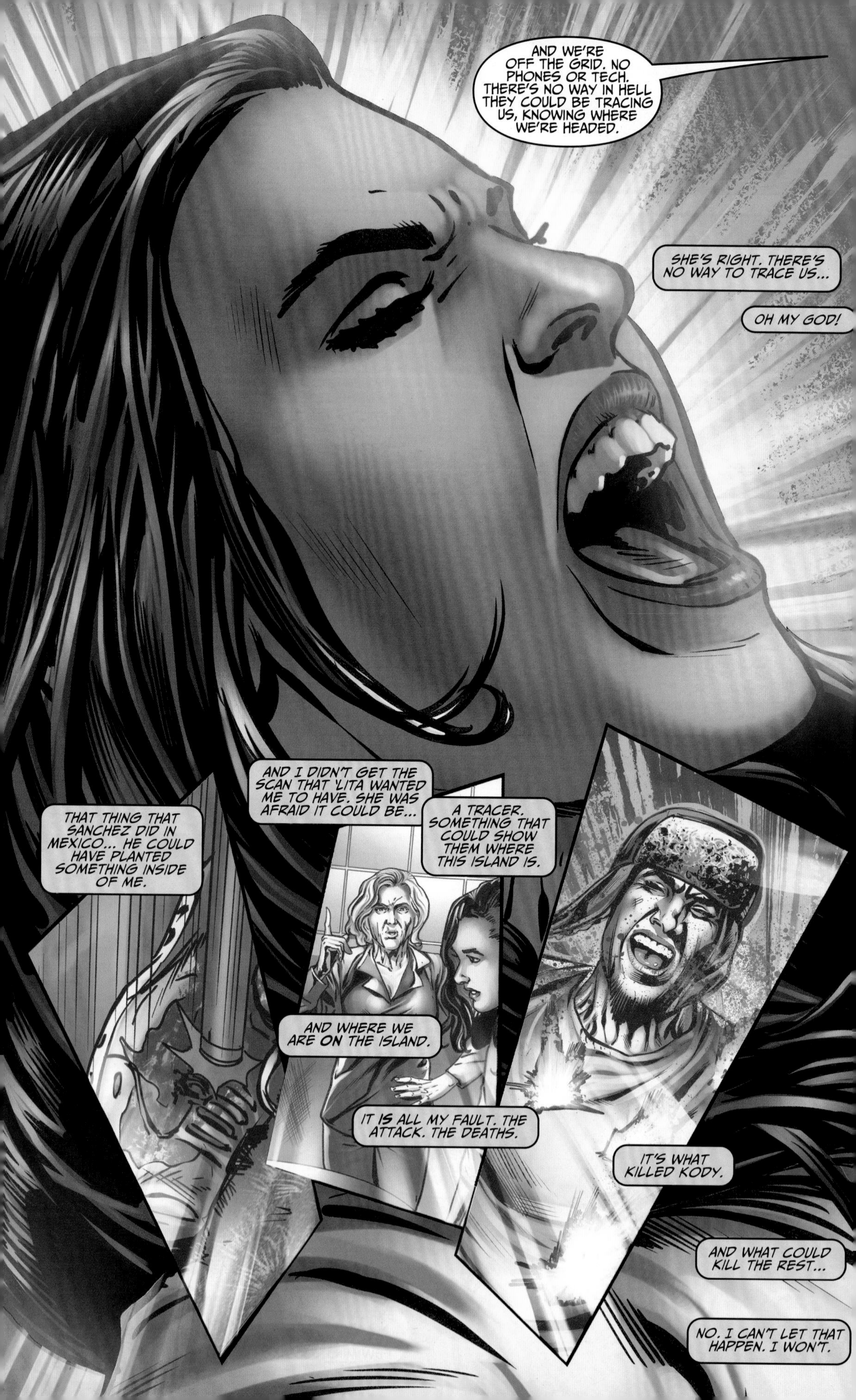
AND WE'RE OFF THE GRID. NO PHONES OR TECH. THERE'S NO WAY IN HELL THEY COULD BE TRACING US, KNOWING WHERE WE'RE HEADED.
SHE'S RIGHT. THERE'S NO WAY TO TRACE US...
OH MY GOD!
THAT THING THAT SANCHEZ DID IN MEXICO... HE COULD HAVE PLANTED SOMETHING INSIDE OF ME.
AND I DIDN'T GET THE SCAN THAT 'LITA WANTED ME TO HAVE. SHE WAS AFRAID IT COULD BE...
A TRACER. SOMETHING THAT COULD SHOW THEM WHERE THIS ISLAND IS.
AND WHERE WE ARE ON THE ISLAND.
IT IS ALL MY FAULT. THE ATTACK. THE DEATHS.
IT'S WHAT KILLED KODY.
AND WHAT COULD KILL THE REST...
NO. I CAN'T LET THAT HAPPEN. I WON'T.

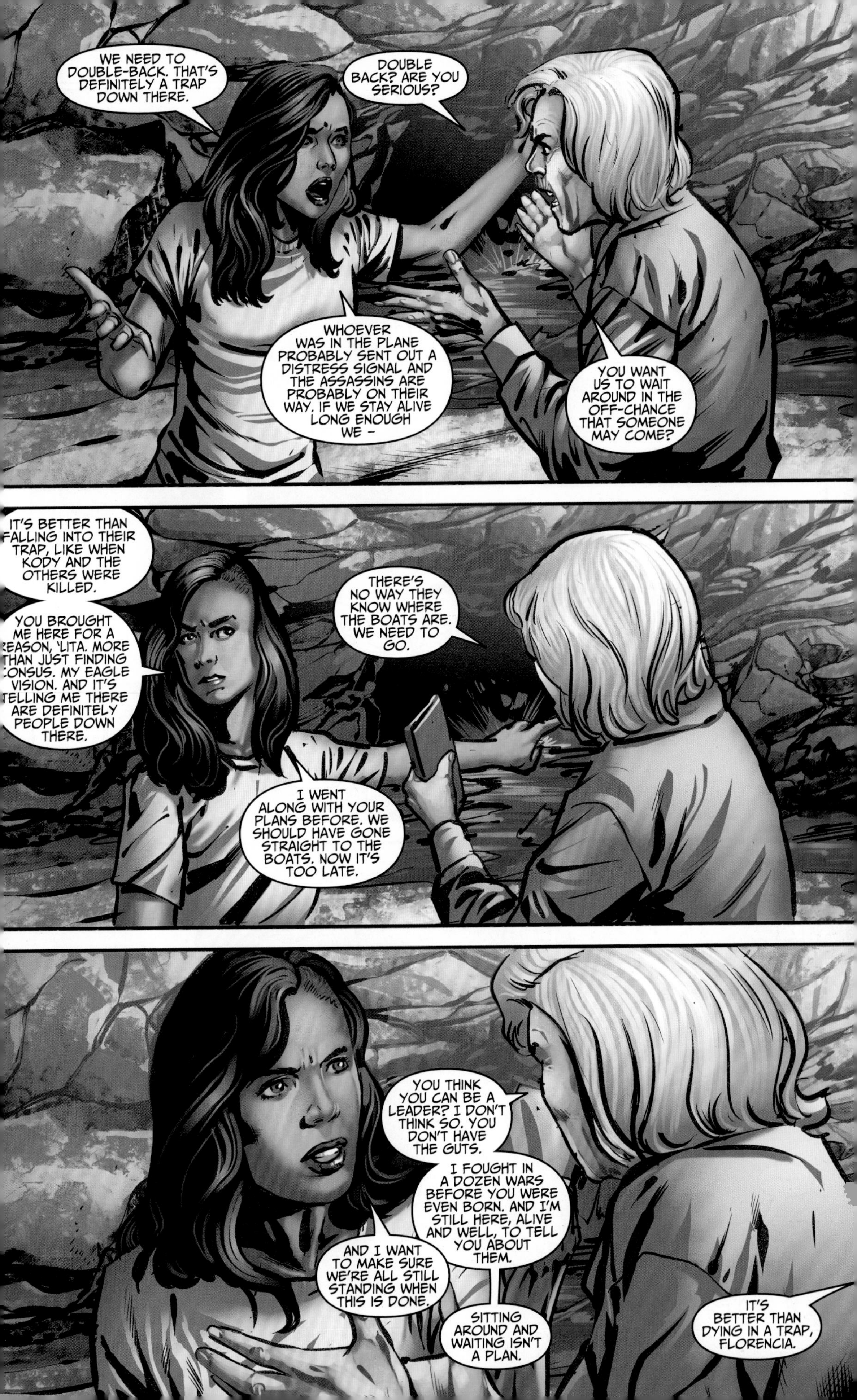
WE NEED TO DOUBLE-BACK. THAT'S DEFINITELY A TRAP DOWN THERE.
DOUBLE BACK? ARE YOU SERIOUS?
WHOEVER WAS IN THE PLANE PROBABLY SENT OUT A DISTRESS SIGNAL AND THE ASSASSINS ARE PROBABLY ON THEIR WAY. IF WE STAY ALIVE LONG ENOUGH WE –
YOU WANT US TO WAIT AROUND IN THE OFF-CHANCE THAT SOMEONE MAY COME?
IT'S BETTER THAN FALLING INTO THEIR TRAP, LIKE WHEN KODY AND THE OTHERS WERE KILLED.
YOU BROUGHT ME HERE FOR A REASON, 'LITA. MORE THAN JUST FINDING CONSUS. MY EAGLE VISION. AND IT'S TELLING ME THERE ARE DEFINITELY PEOPLE DOWN THERE.
THERE'S NO WAY THEY KNOW WHERE THE BOATS ARE. WE NEED TO GO.
I WENT ALONG WITH YOUR PLANS BEFORE. WE SHOULD HAVE GONE STRAIGHT TO THE BOATS. NOW IT'S TOO LATE.
YOU THINK YOU CAN BE A LEADER? I DON'T THINK SO. YOU DON'T HAVE THE GUTS.
I FOUGHT IN A DOZEN WARS BEFORE YOU WERE EVEN BORN. AND I'M STILL HERE, ALIVE AND WELL, TO TELL YOU ABOUT THEM.
AND I WANT TO MAKE SURE WE'RE ALL STILL STANDING WHEN THIS IS DONE.
SITTING AROUND AND WAITING ISN'T A PLAN.
IT'S BETTER THAN DYING IN A TRAP, FLORENCIA.

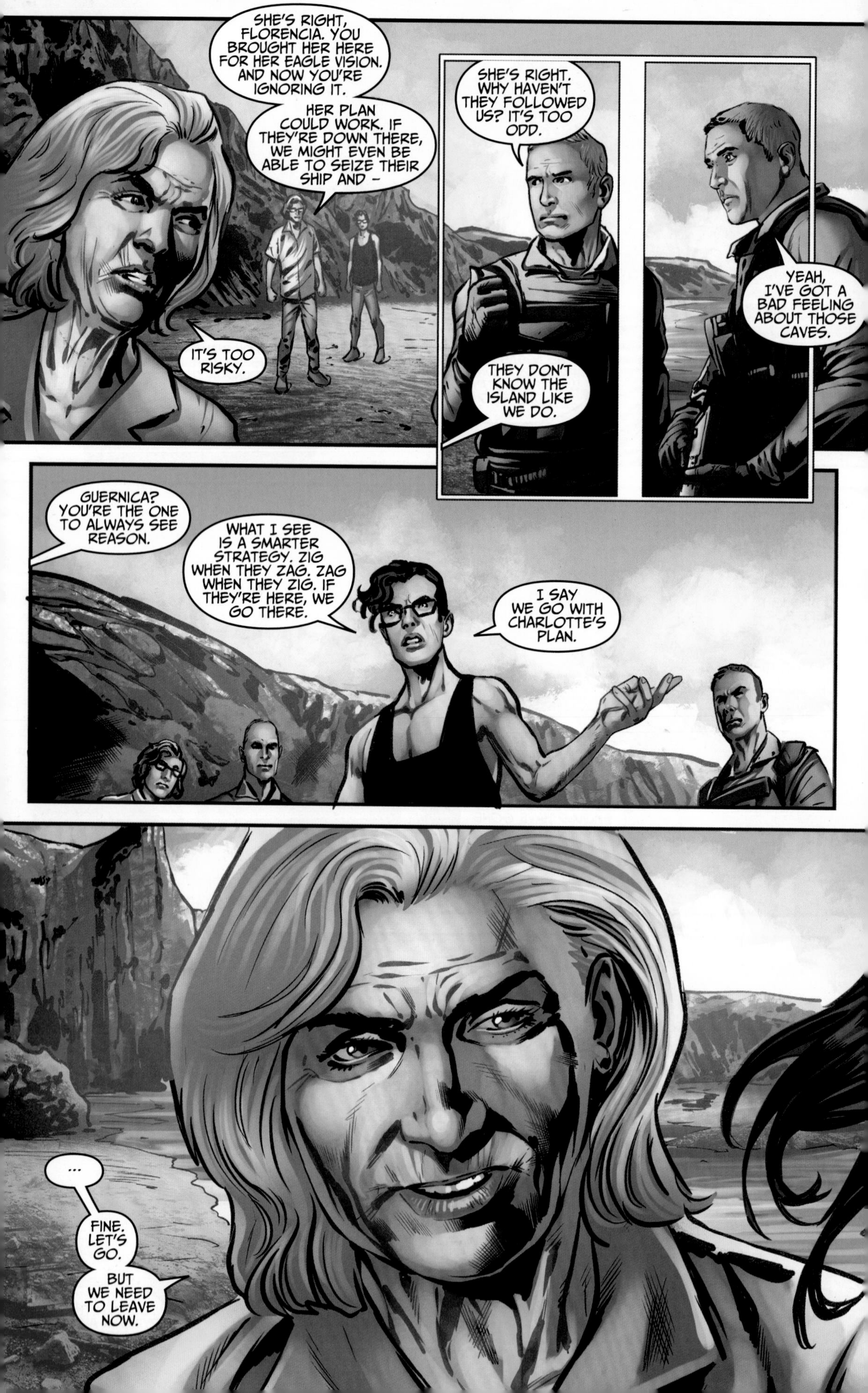

SHE'S RIGHT, FLORENCIA. YOU BROUGHT HER HERE FOR HER EAGLE VISION. AND NOW YOU'RE IGNORING IT.
HER PLAN COULD WORK. IF THEY'RE DOWN THERE, WE MIGHT EVEN BE ABLE TO SEIZE THEIR SHIP AND –
IT'S TOO RISKY.
SHE'S RIGHT. WHY HAVEN'T THEY FOLLOWED US? IT'S TOO ODD.
THEY DON'T KNOW THE ISLAND LIKE WE DO.
YEAH, I'VE GOT A BAD FEELING ABOUT THOSE CAVES.
GUERNICA? YOU'RE THE ONE TO ALWAYS SEE REASON.
WHAT I SEE IS A SMARTER STRATEGY. ZIG WHEN THEY ZAG. ZAG WHEN THEY ZIG. IF THEY'RE HERE, WE GO THERE.
I SAY WE GO WITH CHARLOTTE'S PLAN.
...
FINE. LET'S GO.
BUT WE NEED TO LEAVE NOW.

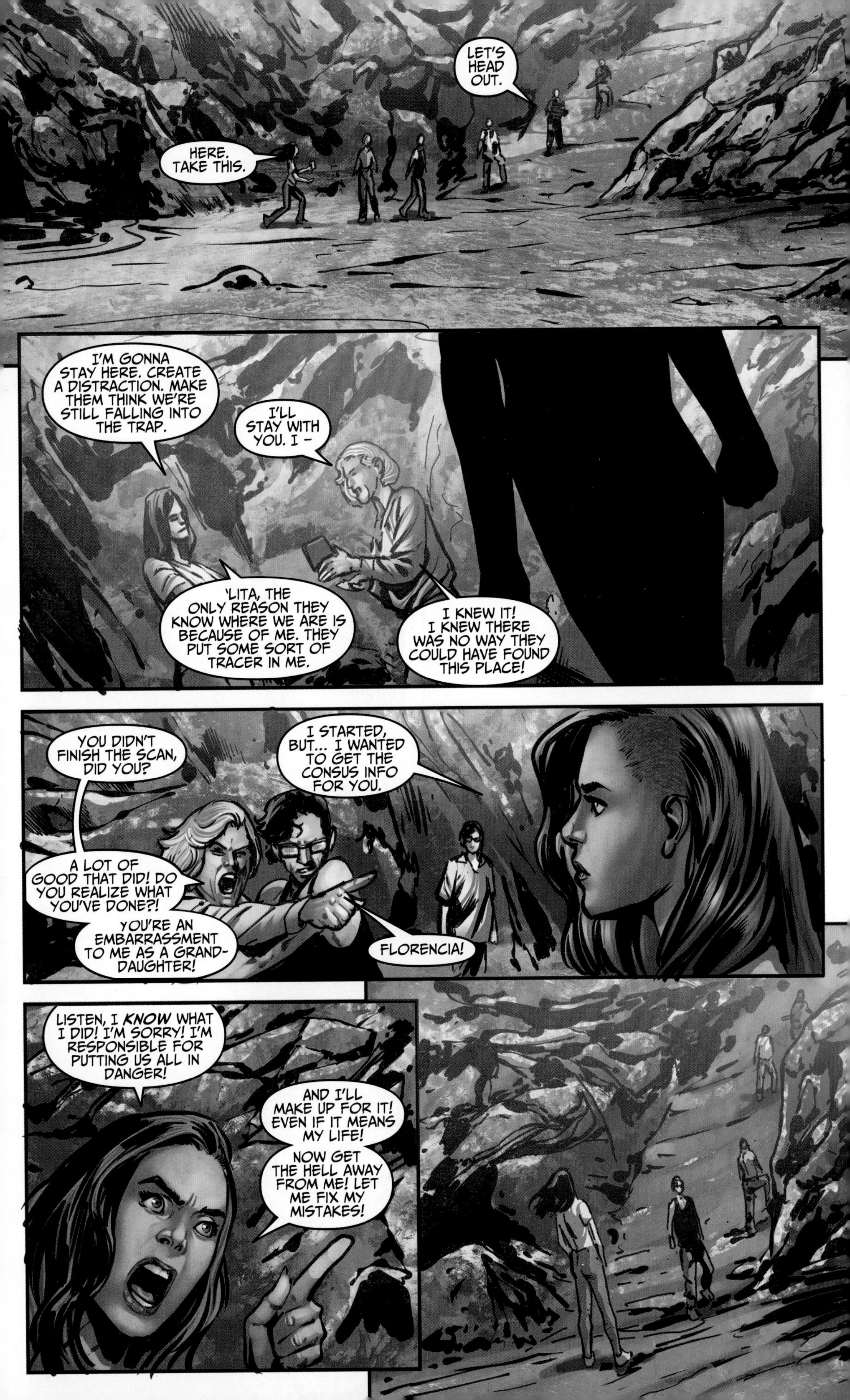
LET'S HEAD OUT.
HERE. TAKE THIS.
I'M GONNA STAY HERE. CREATE A DISTRACTION. MAKE THEM THINK WE'RE STILL FALLING INTO THE TRAP.
I'LL STAY WITH YOU. I –
'LITA, THE ONLY REASON THEY KNOW WHERE WE ARE IS BECAUSE OF ME. THEY PUT SOME SORT OF TRACER IN ME.
I KNEW IT! I KNEW THERE WAS NO WAY THEY COULD HAVE FOUND THIS PLACE!
YOU DIDN'T FINISH THE SCAN, DID YOU?
I STARTED, BUT... I WANTED TO GET THE CONSUS INFO FOR YOU.
A LOT OF GOOD THAT DID! DO YOU REALIZE WHAT YOU'VE DONE?!
YOU'RE AN EMBARRASSMENT TO ME AS A GRAND-DAUGHTER!
FLORENCIA!
LISTEN, I *KNOW* WHAT I DID! I'M SORRY! I'M RESPONSIBLE FOR PUTTING US ALL IN DANGER!
AND I'LL MAKE UP FOR IT! EVEN IF IT MEANS MY LIFE!
NOW GET THE HELL AWAY FROM ME! LET ME FIX MY MISTAKES!

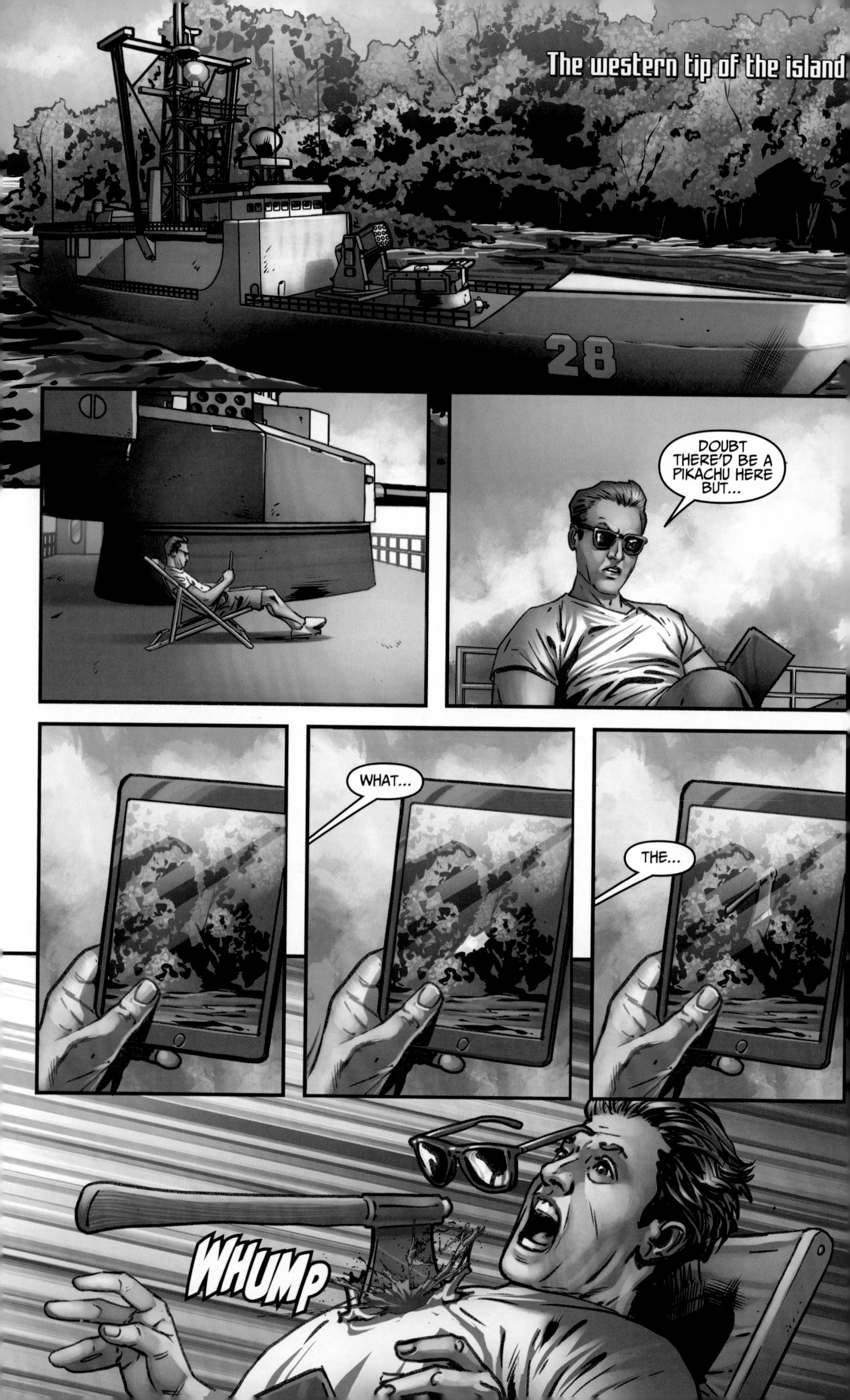
The western tip of the island
28
DOUBT THERE'D BE A PIKACHU HERE BUT...
WHAT...
THE...
WHUMP

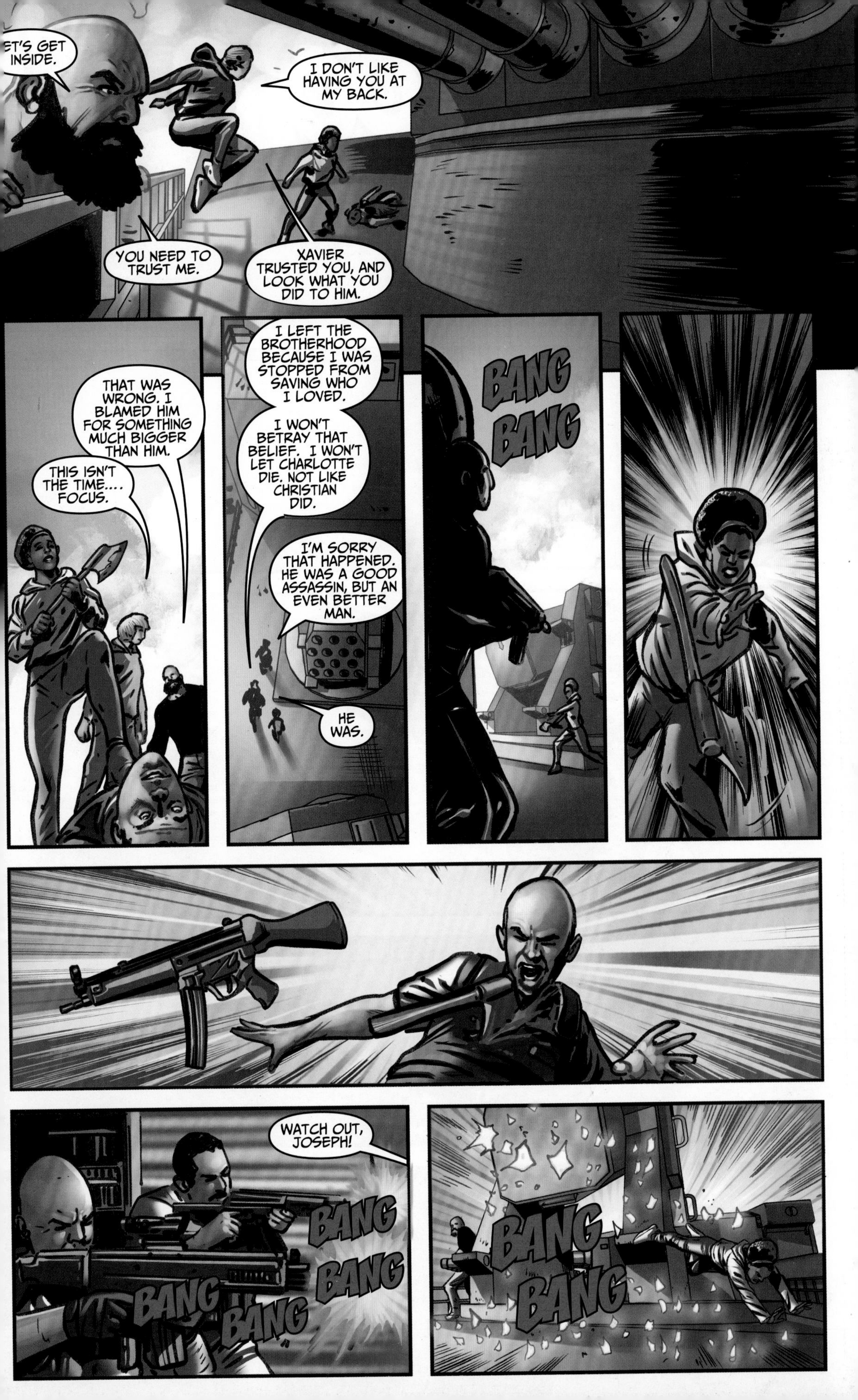
ET'S GET INSIDE.
I DON'T LIKE HAVING YOU AT MY BACK.
YOU NEED TO TRUST ME.
XAVIER TRUSTED YOU, AND LOOK WHAT YOU DID TO HIM.
THAT WAS WRONG. I BLAMED HIM FOR SOMETHING MUCH BIGGER THAN HIM.
THIS ISN'T THE TIME.... FOCUS.
I LEFT THE BROTHERHOOD BECAUSE I WAS STOPPED FROM SAVING WHO I LOVED.
I WON'T BETRAY THAT BELIEF. I WON'T LET CHARLOTTE DIE. NOT LIKE CHRISTIAN DID.
I'M SORRY THAT HAPPENED. HE WAS A GOOD ASSASSIN, BUT AN EVEN BETTER MAN.
HE WAS.
BANG
BANG
WATCH OUT, JOSEPH!
BANG
BANG
BANG
BANG
BANG
BANG

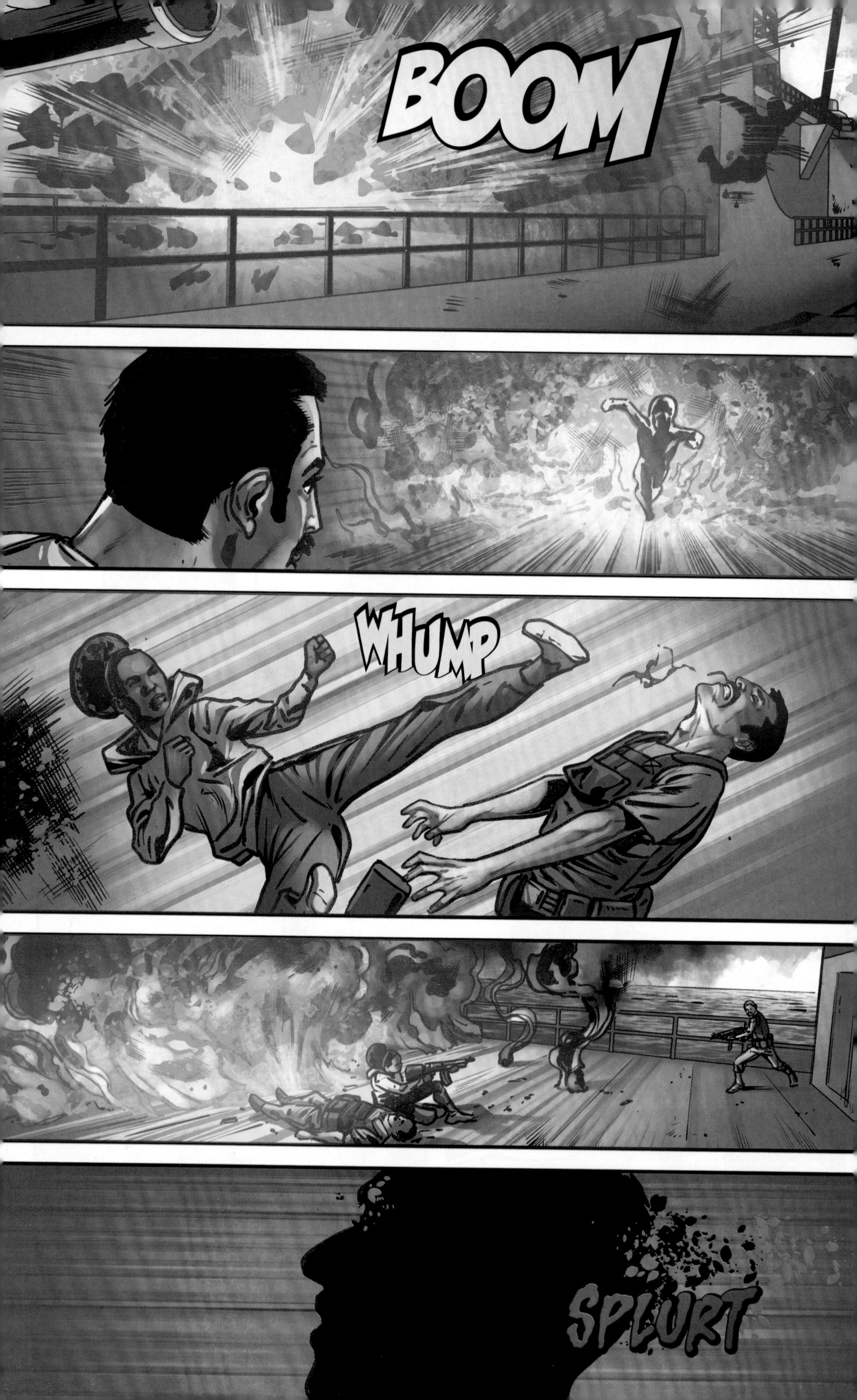
BOOM
WHUMP
SPLURT

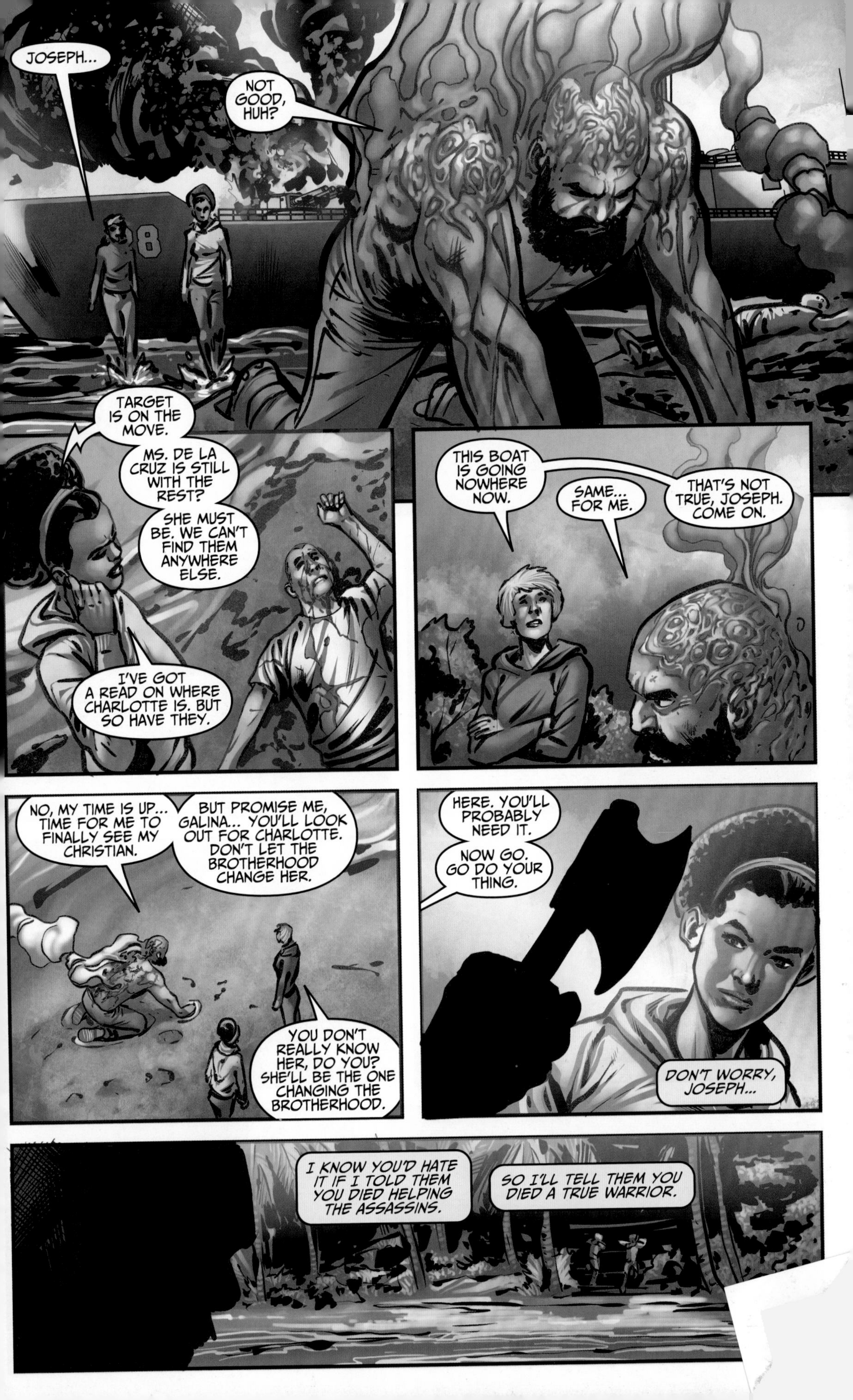
JOSEPH...
NOT GOOD, HUH?
TARGET IS ON THE MOVE.
MS. DE LA CRUZ IS STILL WITH THE REST?
SHE MUST BE. WE CAN'T FIND THEM ANYWHERE ELSE.
I'VE GOT A READ ON WHERE CHARLOTTE IS. BUT SO HAVE THEY.
THIS BOAT IS GOING NOWHERE NOW.
SAME... FOR ME.
THAT'S NOT TRUE, JOSEPH. COME ON.
NO, MY TIME IS UP... TIME FOR ME TO FINALLY SEE MY CHRISTIAN.
BUT PROMISE ME, GALINA... YOU'LL LOOK OUT FOR CHARLOTTE. DON'T LET THE BROTHERHOOD CHANGE HER.
YOU DON'T REALLY KNOW HER, DO YOU? SHE'LL BE THE ONE CHANGING THE BROTHERHOOD.
HERE. YOU'LL PROBABLY NEED IT.
NOW GO. GO DO YOUR THING.
DON'T WORRY, JOSEPH...
I KNOW YOU'D HATE IT IF I TOLD THEM YOU DIED HELPING THE ASSASSINS.
SO I'LL TELL THEM YOU DIED A TRUE WARRIOR.

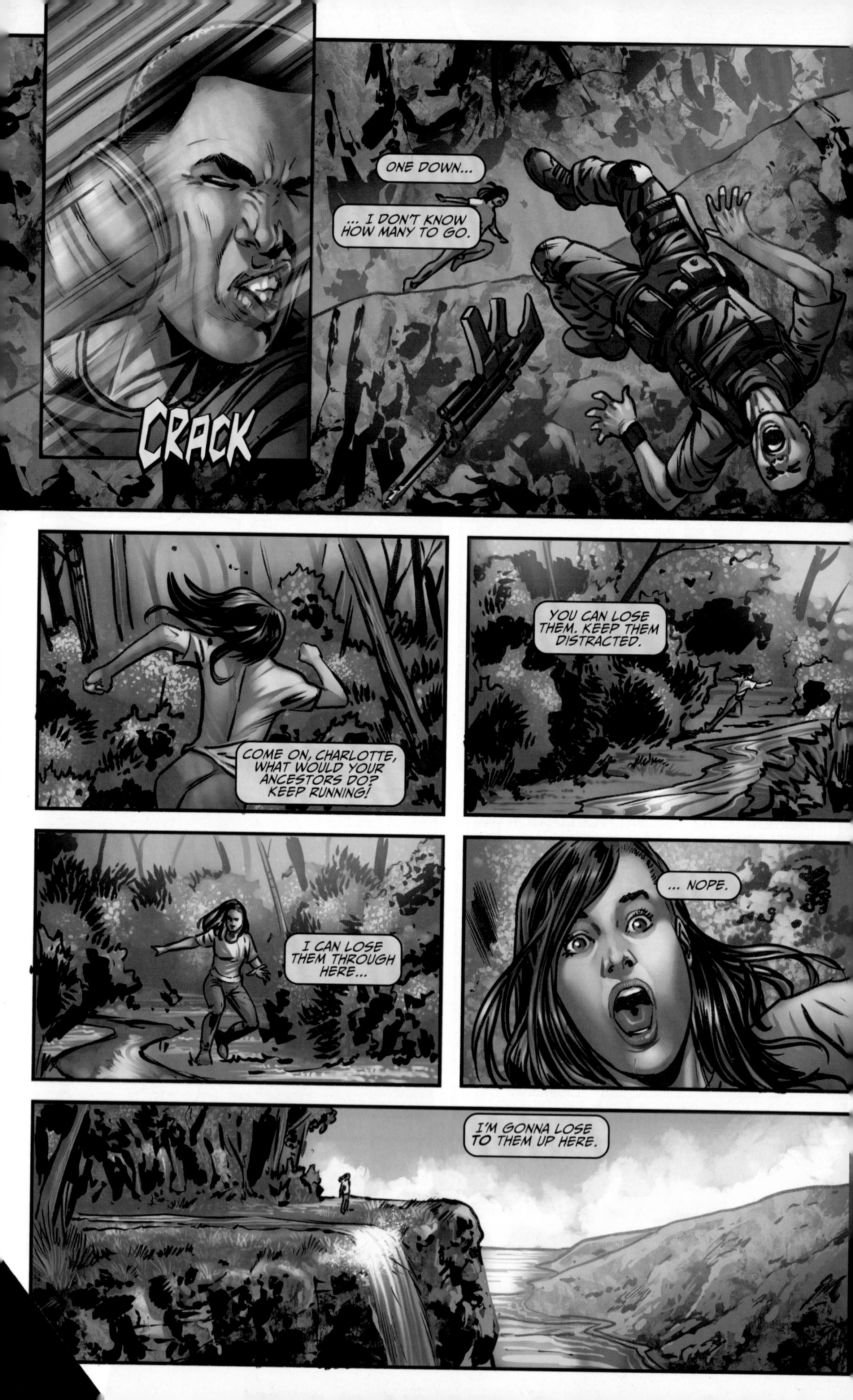
CRACK
ONE DOWN...
... I DON'T KNOW HOW MANY TO GO.
COME ON, CHARLOTTE, WHAT WOULD YOUR ANCESTORS DO? KEEP RUNNING!
YOU CAN LOSE THEM. KEEP THEM DISTRACTED.
I CAN LOSE THEM THROUGH HERE...
... NOPE.
I'M GONNA LOSE TO THEM UP HERE.

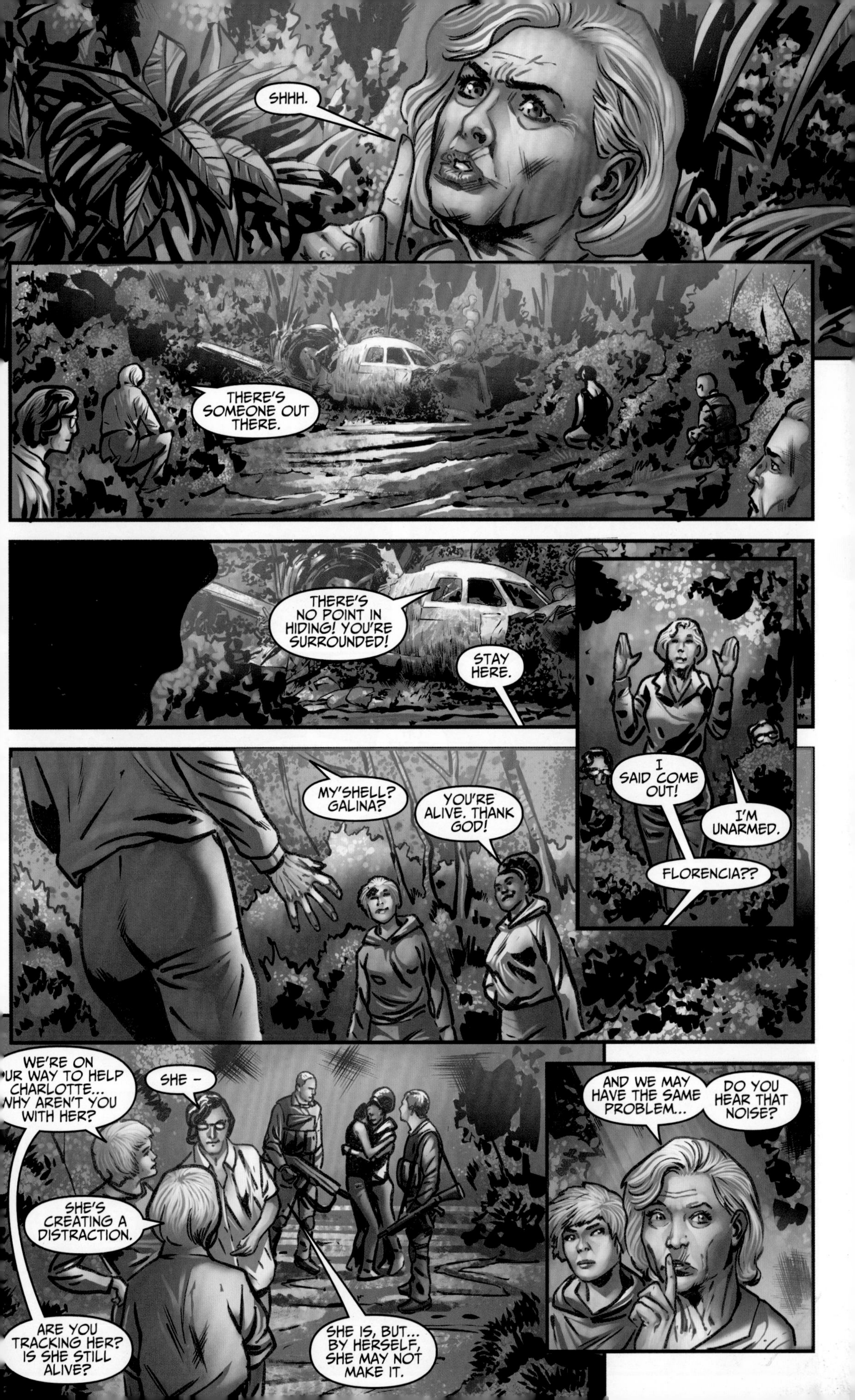
SHHH.
THERE'S SOMEONE OUT THERE.
THERE'S NO POINT IN HIDING! YOU'RE SURROUNDED!
STAY HERE.
I SAID COME OUT!
I'M UNARMED.
FLORENCIA??
MY'SHELL? GALINA?
YOU'RE ALIVE. THANK GOD!
WE'RE ON UR WAY TO HELP CHARLOTTE... HY AREN'T YOU WITH HER?
SHE –
SHE'S CREATING A DISTRACTION.
ARE YOU TRACKING HER? IS SHE STILL ALIVE?
SHE IS, BUT... BY HERSELF, SHE MAY NOT MAKE IT.
AND WE MAY HAVE THE SAME PROBLEM...
DO YOU HEAR THAT NOISE?

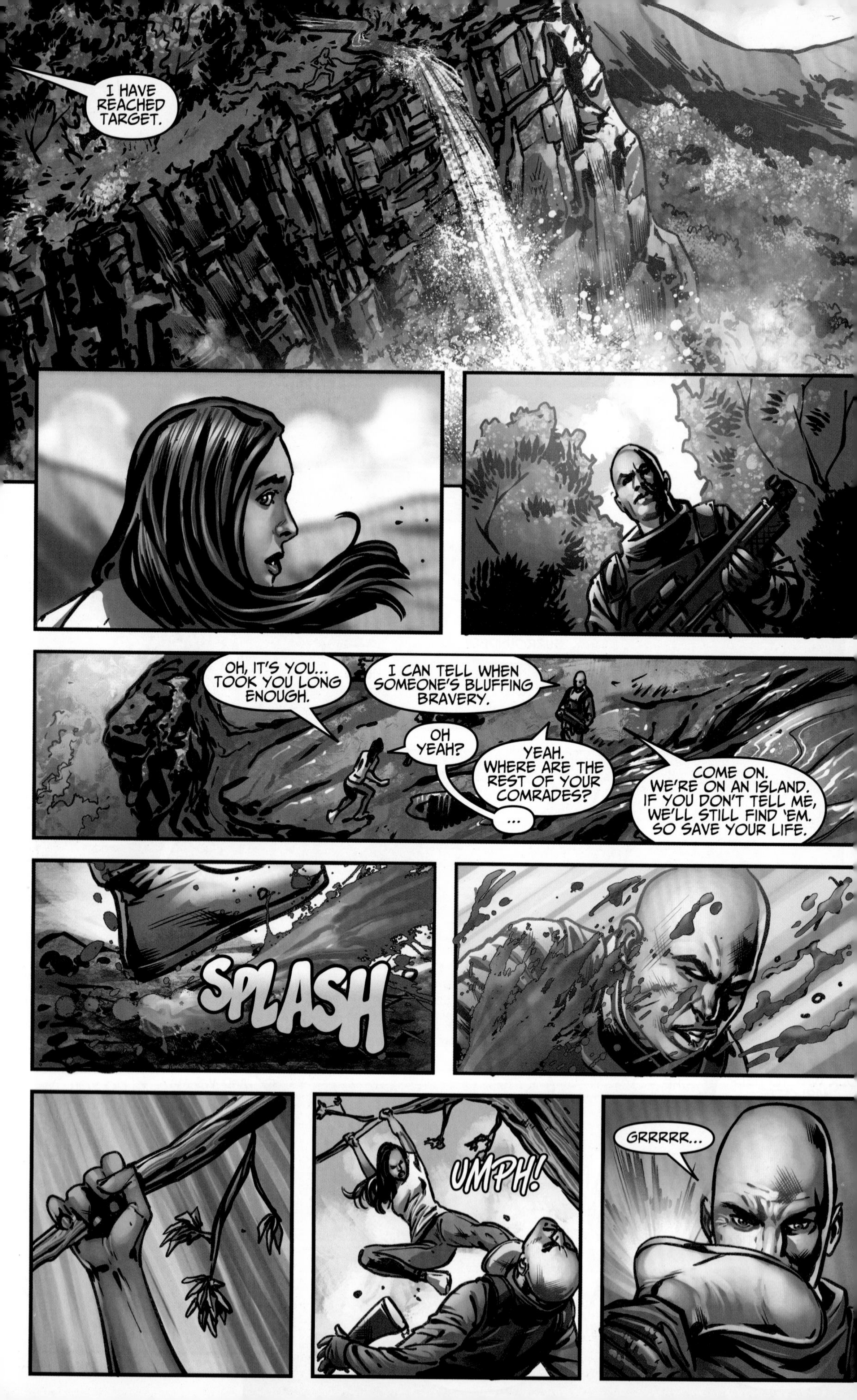
I HAVE REACHED TARGET.
OH, IT'S YOU... TOOK YOU LONG ENOUGH.
I CAN TELL WHEN SOMEONE'S BLUFFING BRAVERY.
OH YEAH?
YEAH. WHERE ARE THE REST OF YOUR COMRADES?
...
COME ON. WE'RE ON AN ISLAND. IF YOU DON'T TELL ME, WE'LL STILL FIND 'EM. SO SAVE YOUR LIFE.
SPLASH
UMPH!
GRRRRR...

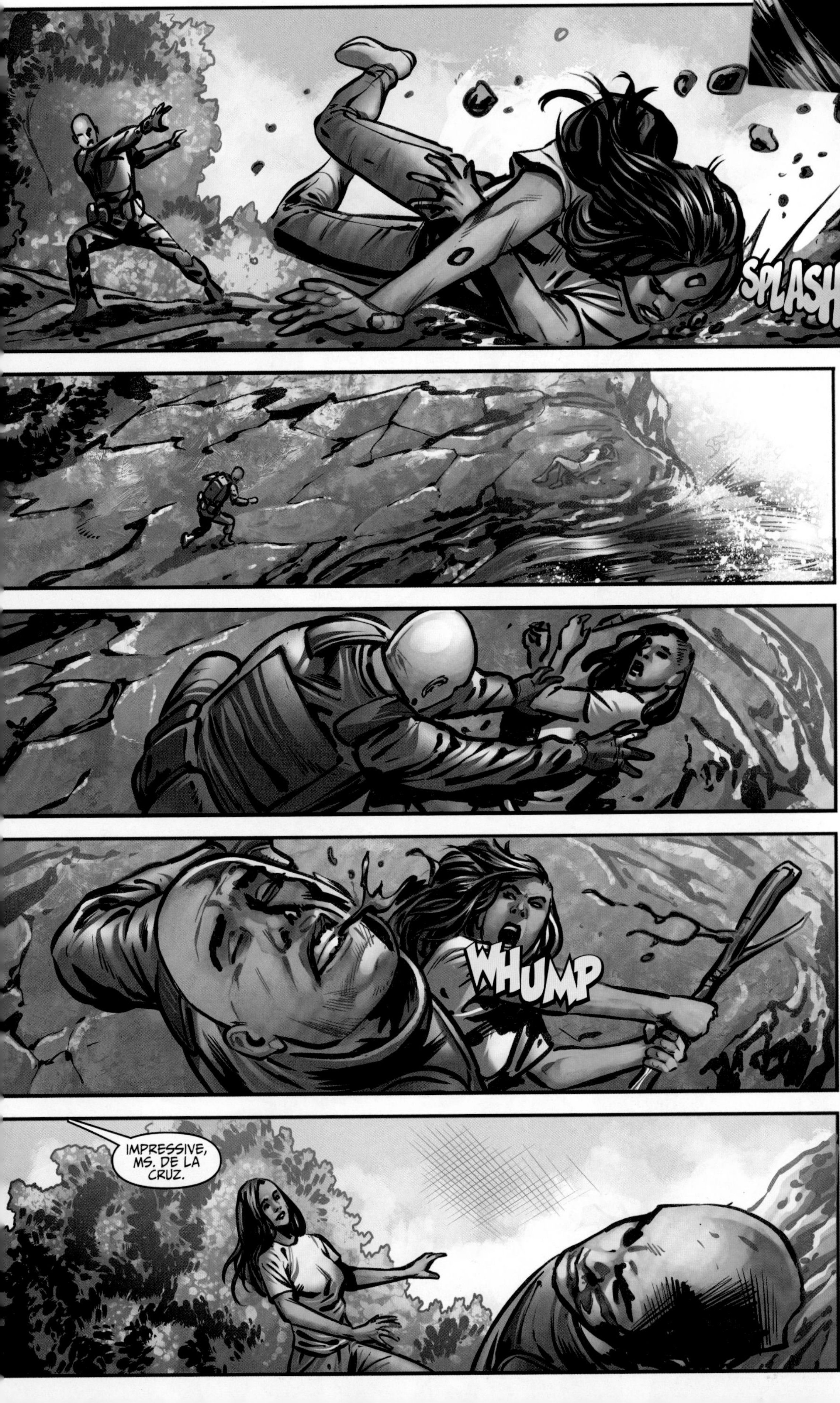
SPLASH
WHUMP
IMPRESSIVE, MS. DE LA CRUZ.

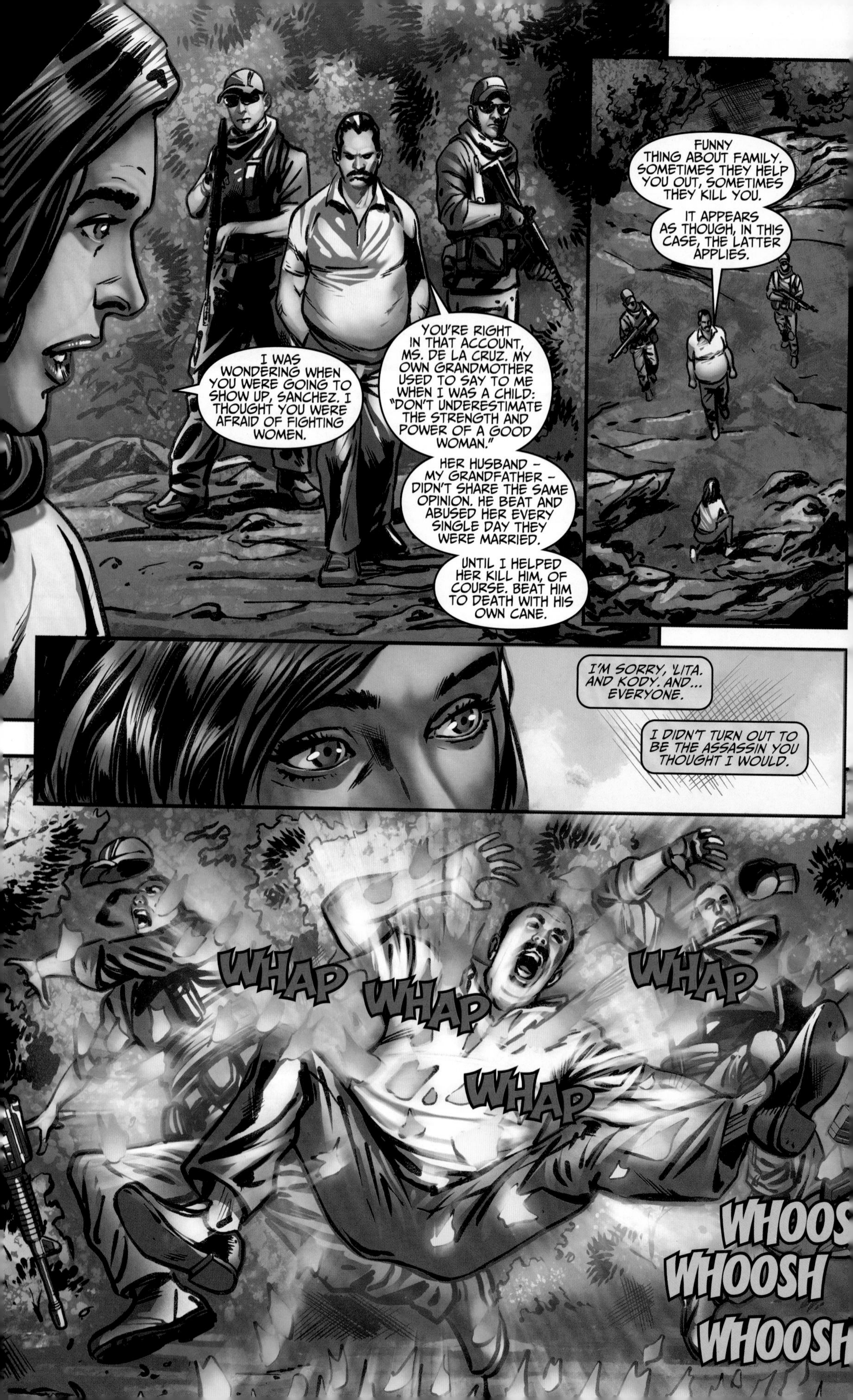
I WAS WONDERING WHEN YOU WERE GOING TO SHOW UP, SANCHEZ. I THOUGHT YOU WERE AFRAID OF FIGHTING WOMEN.
YOU'RE RIGHT IN THAT ACCOUNT, MS. DE LA CRUZ. MY OWN GRANDMOTHER USED TO SAY TO ME WHEN I WAS A CHILD: "DON'T UNDERESTIMATE THE STRENGTH AND POWER OF A GOOD WOMAN."
HER HUSBAND – MY GRANDFATHER – DIDN'T SHARE THE SAME OPINION. HE BEAT AND ABUSED HER EVERY SINGLE DAY THEY WERE MARRIED.
UNTIL I HELPED HER KILL HIM, OF COURSE. BEAT HIM TO DEATH WITH HIS OWN CANE.
FUNNY THING ABOUT FAMILY. SOMETIMES THEY HELP YOU OUT, SOMETIMES THEY KILL YOU.
IT APPEARS AS THOUGH, IN THIS CASE, THE LATTER APPLIES.
I'M SORRY, 'LITA. AND KODY. AND... EVERYONE.
I DIDN'T TURN OUT TO BE THE ASSASSIN YOU THOUGHT I WOULD.
WHAP
WHAP
WHAP
WHAP
WHOOSH
WHOOSH

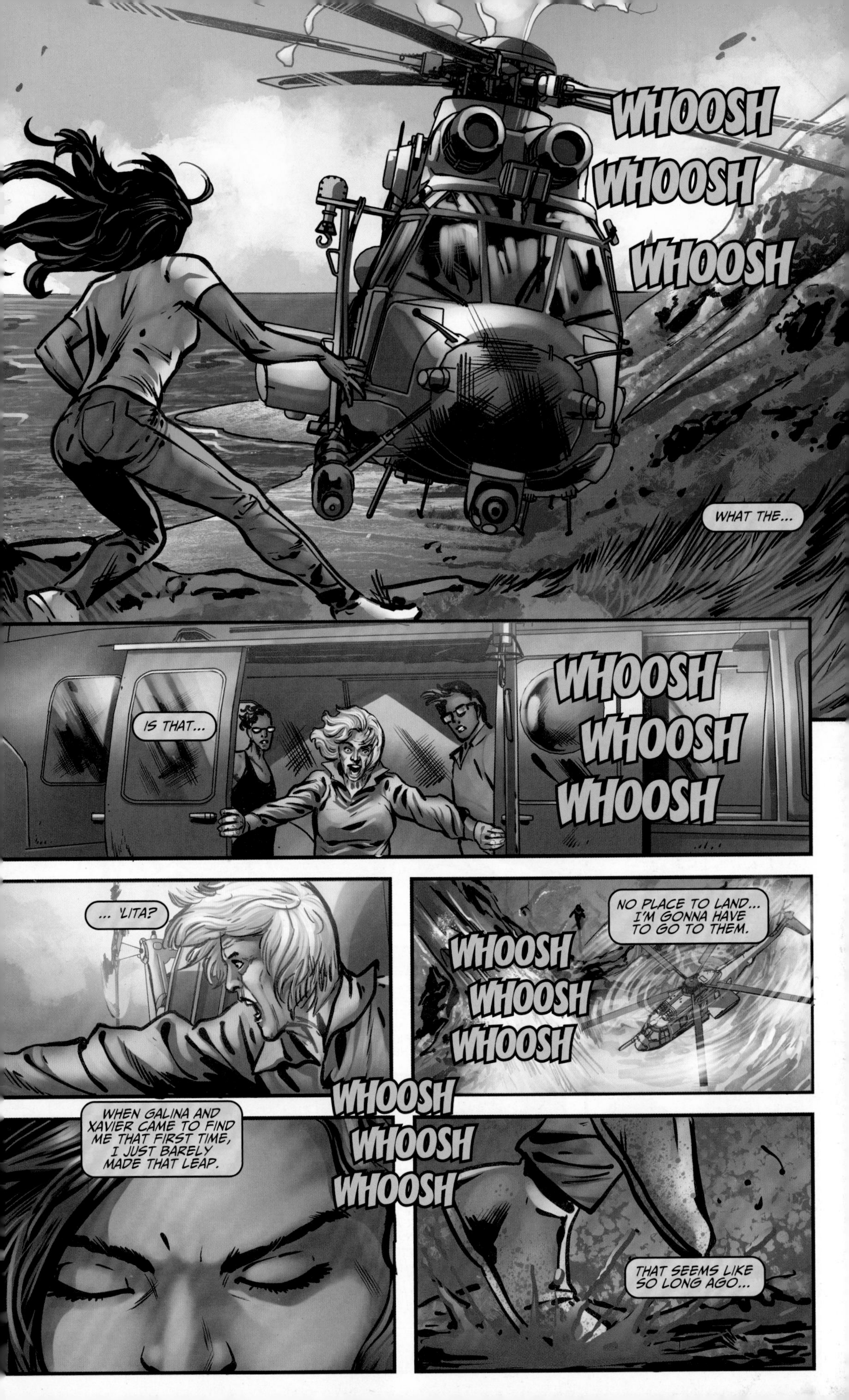
WHOOSH
WHOOSH
WHOOSH
WHAT THE...
IS THAT...
WHOOSH
WHOOSH
WHOOSH
... 'LITA?
NO PLACE TO LAND... I'M GONNA HAVE TO GO TO THEM.
WHOOSH
WHOOSH
WHOOSH
WHOOSH
WHOOSH
WHOOSH
WHEN GALINA AND XAVIER CAME TO FIND ME THAT FIRST TIME, I JUST BARELY MADE THAT LEAP.
THAT SEEMS LIKE SO LONG AGO...

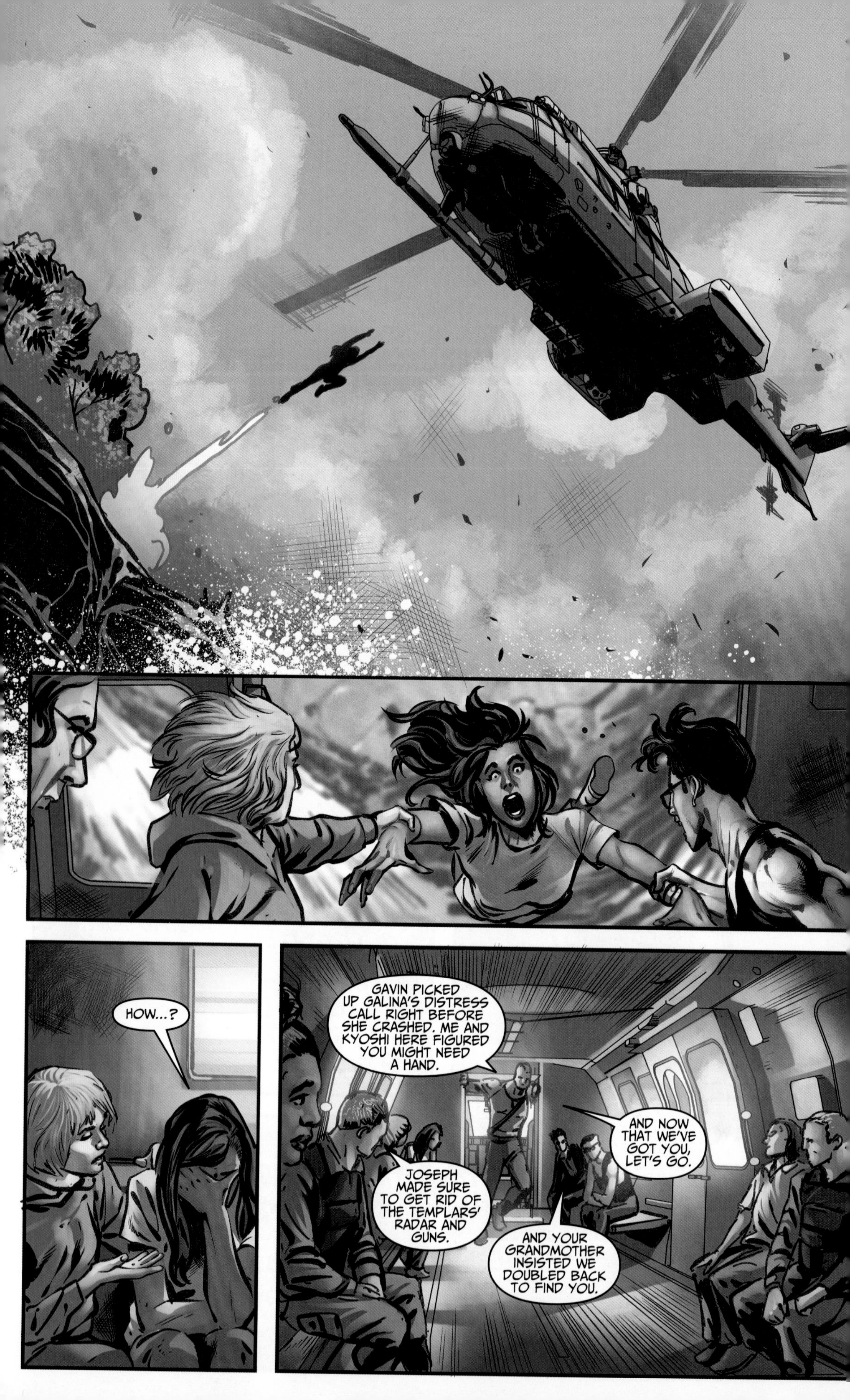
HOW...?
GAVIN PICKED UP GALINA'S DISTRESS CALL RIGHT BEFORE SHE CRASHED. ME AND KYOSHI HERE FIGURED YOU MIGHT NEED A HAND.
AND NOW THAT WE'VE GOT YOU, LET'S GO.
JOSEPH MADE SURE TO GET RID OF THE TEMPLARS' RADAR AND GUNS.
AND YOUR GRANDMOTHER INSISTED WE DOUBLED BACK TO FIND YOU.

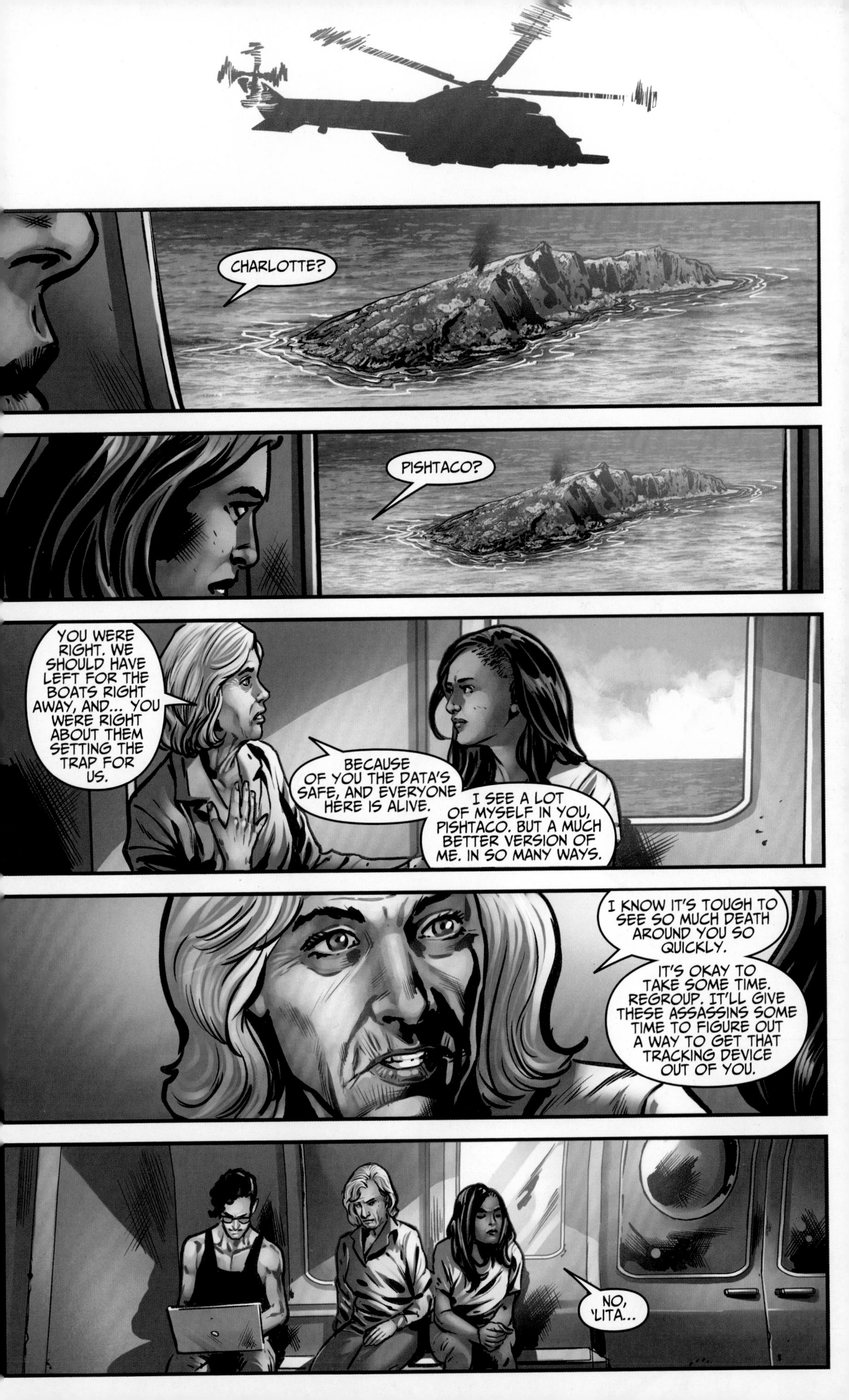
CHARLOTTE?
PISHTACO?
YOU WERE RIGHT. WE SHOULD HAVE LEFT FOR THE BOATS RIGHT AWAY, AND... YOU WERE RIGHT ABOUT THEM SETTING THE TRAP FOR US.
BECAUSE OF YOU THE DATA'S SAFE, AND EVERYONE HERE IS ALIVE.
I SEE A LOT OF MYSELF IN YOU, PISHTACO. BUT A MUCH BETTER VERSION OF ME. IN SO MANY WAYS.
I KNOW IT'S TOUGH TO SEE SO MUCH DEATH AROUND YOU SO QUICKLY.
IT'S OKAY TO TAKE SOME TIME. REGROUP. IT'LL GIVE THESE ASSASSINS SOME TIME TO FIGURE OUT A WAY TO GET THAT TRACKING DEVICE OUT OF YOU.
NO, 'LITA...

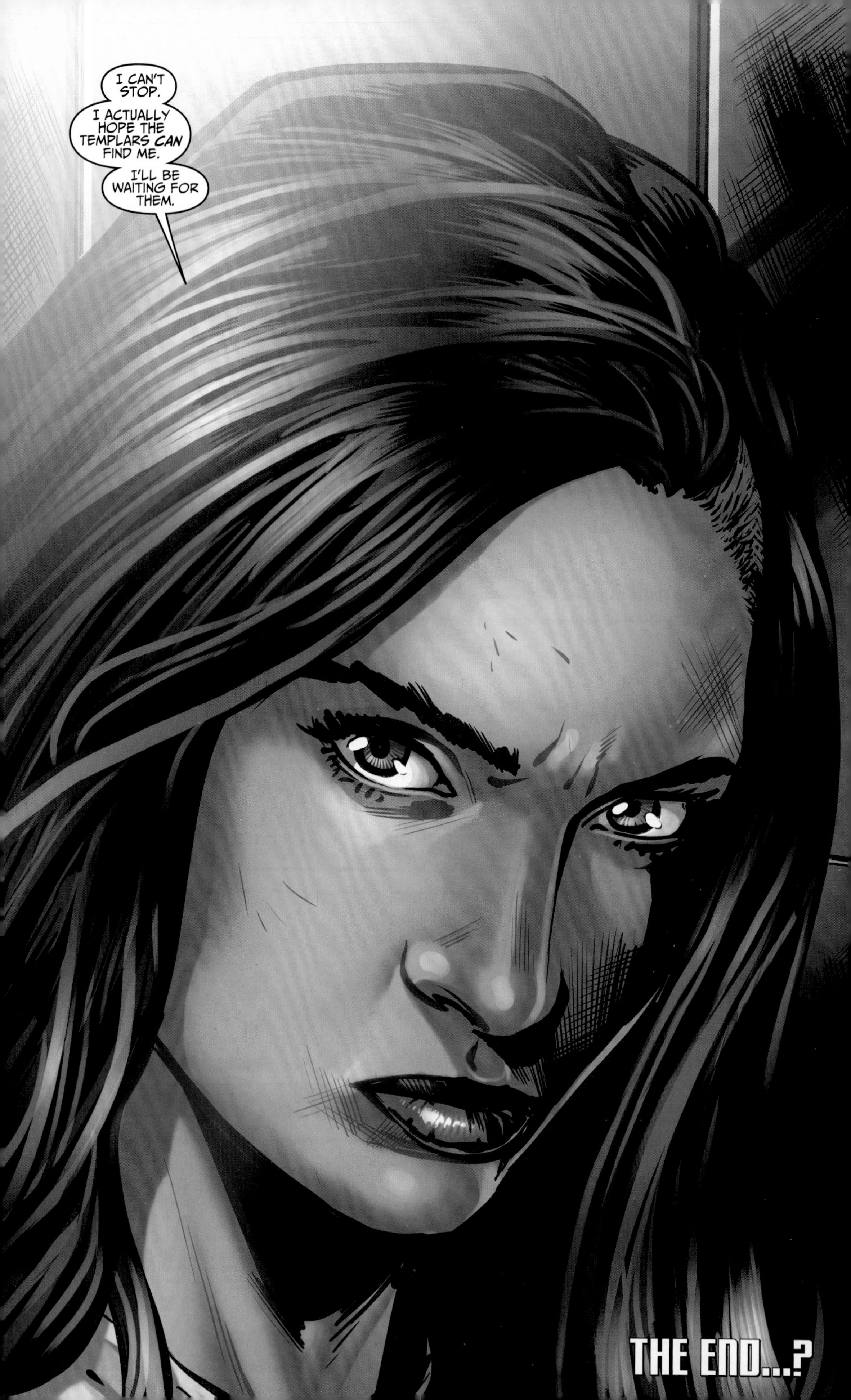
I CAN'T STOP.
I ACTUALLY HOPE THE TEMPLARS *CAN* FIND ME.
I'LL BE WAITING FOR THEM.
THE END...?

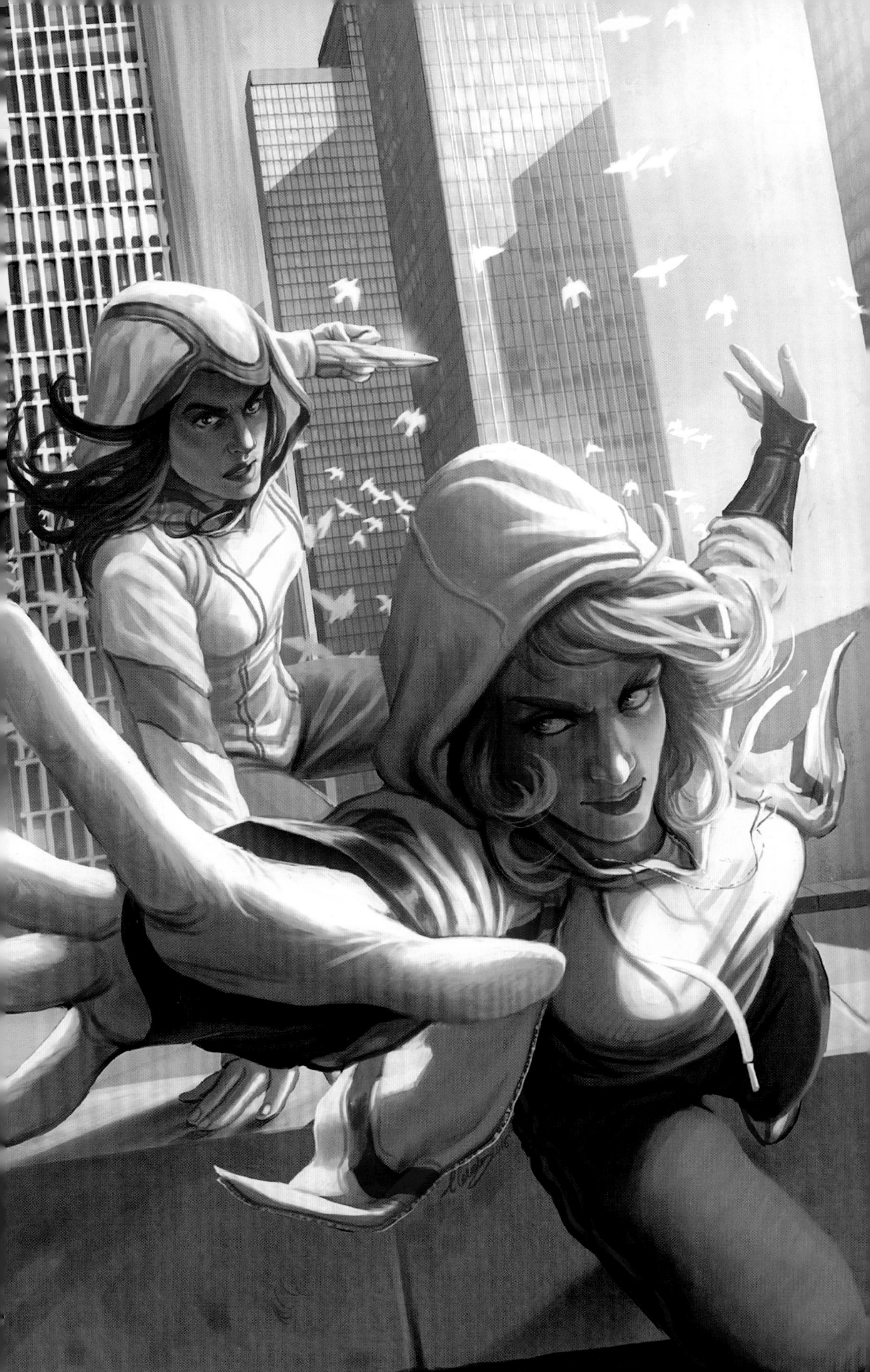

ART BY:
CLAUDIA IANCELLO

FLORENCE

THE CITY THAT SHAPED THE MODERN WESTERN WORLD.

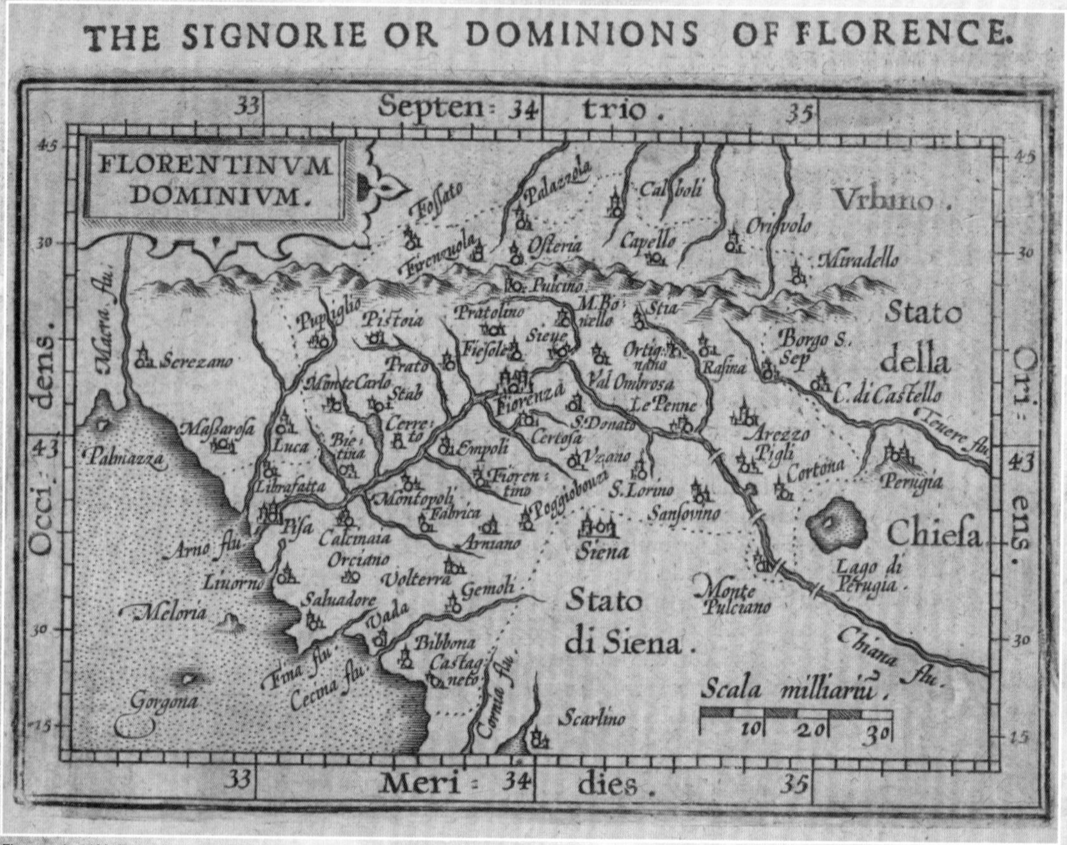
THE SIGNORIE OR DOMINIONS OF FLORENCE.
FLORENTINVM DOMINIVM.
Septen: 34 trio.
Meri: 34 dies.
Occi: dens.
Ori: ens.
Vrbino.
Stato della Chiesa
Stato di Siena.
Fiorenza
Pistoia
Prato
Fiesole
Luca
Pisa
Liuorno
Empoli
Volterra
Siena
Arezzo
Cortona
Perugia
Lago di Perugia
Monte Pulciano
Arno flu.
Chiana flu.
Meloria
Gorgona
Scala milliariu.

Florence in 1608. From the New York Public Library.

Nestled in the hills of Tuscany is Florence. *Firenze*. Founded in 59BCE by Julius Caesar, it survived fear and famine, and became the birthplace of the modern Italian language. By the beginning of the 15th century, it had become one of the largest cities in Europe. It was there that the Renaissance flourished. This was thanks in large part to the Medici family. Originally textile traders, they capitalized on their wealth and rose to prominence in the 15th century, going on to found the Medici Bank, the largest in Europe at the time. This gave them unparalleled power in the region, especially in Florence. They encouraged the arts and humanism to thrive in the city where they made their home, and were visible at every level of government, even producing three Popes. While there were internal difficulties associated with such a large and powerful dynasty, their influence is eternal. Generations of Medici commissioned work from those who would become the great masters of Modern Art: Michaelangelo, Donatello, and Leonardo Da Vinci, to name but a few. In doing so, the Medici family shaped the modern world. ●

GIOTTO'S CAMPANILE

THE LILY OF FIRENZE

Cathedral Santa Maria del Fiore and Giotto's campanile in Florence, Italy.

Marking one of the finest examples of Florentine Gothic architecture, Giotto's Campanile is the free-standing bell tower of the Cathedral di Santa Maria del Fiore, located on the Piazza del Duomo in central Florence.

Clad in white, red and green marble, the resplendent square construction is considered one of the most beautiful campanile in all of Italy. Featuring numerous works of art (including sculptures by Donatello and Andrea Pisano), the building also houses seven bells of varying size.

Conceived by the eminent painter and architect Giotto di Bondone, the first stone was laid on July 19th, 1334, with the tower reaching completion in 1359. Standing at 277.9ft, the tower's summit can be reached by climbing its 414 steps and offers breathtaking views of Florence and its surrounding area.

Creation of Eve by Andrea Pisano - Relief on Giotto's campanile

SKETCHES

DESIGNS FOR GIOVANNI BORGIA AND HIRAM STODDARD

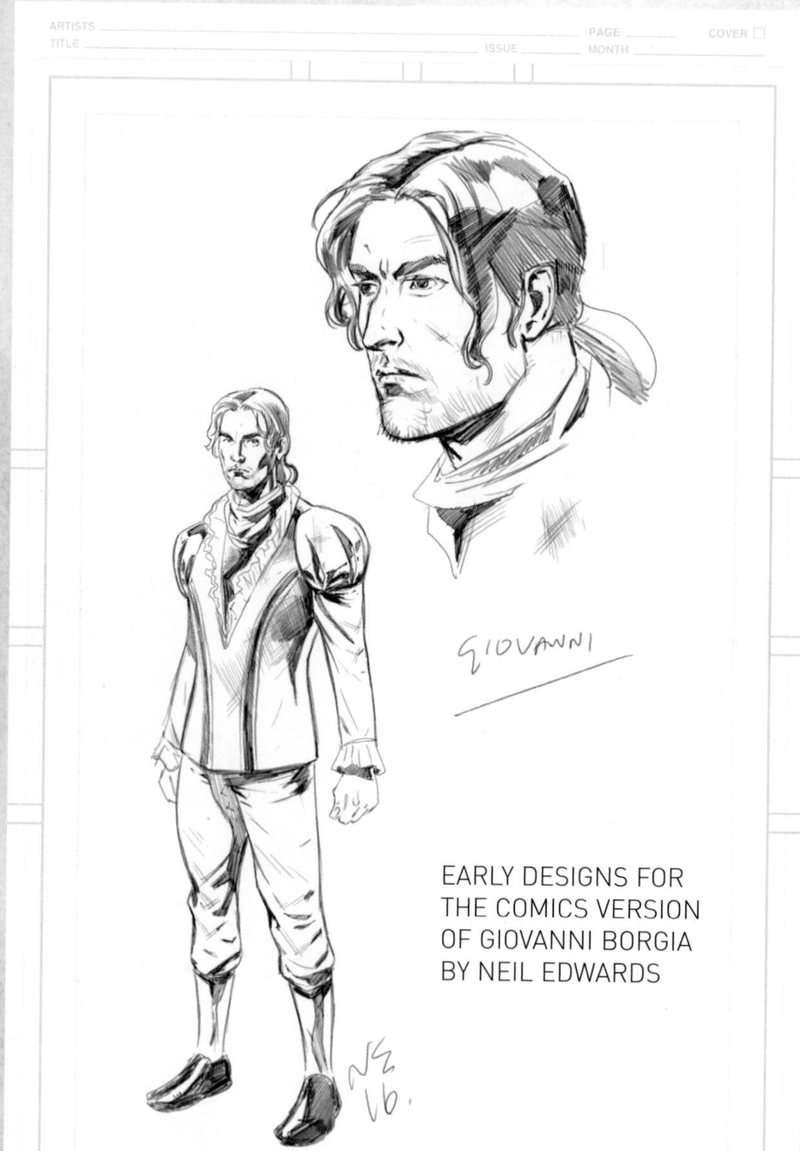
ARTISTS
TITLE
ISSUE
PAGE
MONTH
COVER
GIOVANNI
NE 16.
MAKE SURE NO IMPORTANT ARTWORK IS IN THE BLEED AREA. IT WILL BE CUT OFF!

EARLY DESIGNS FOR THE COMICS VERSION OF GIOVANNI BORGIA BY NEIL EDWARDS

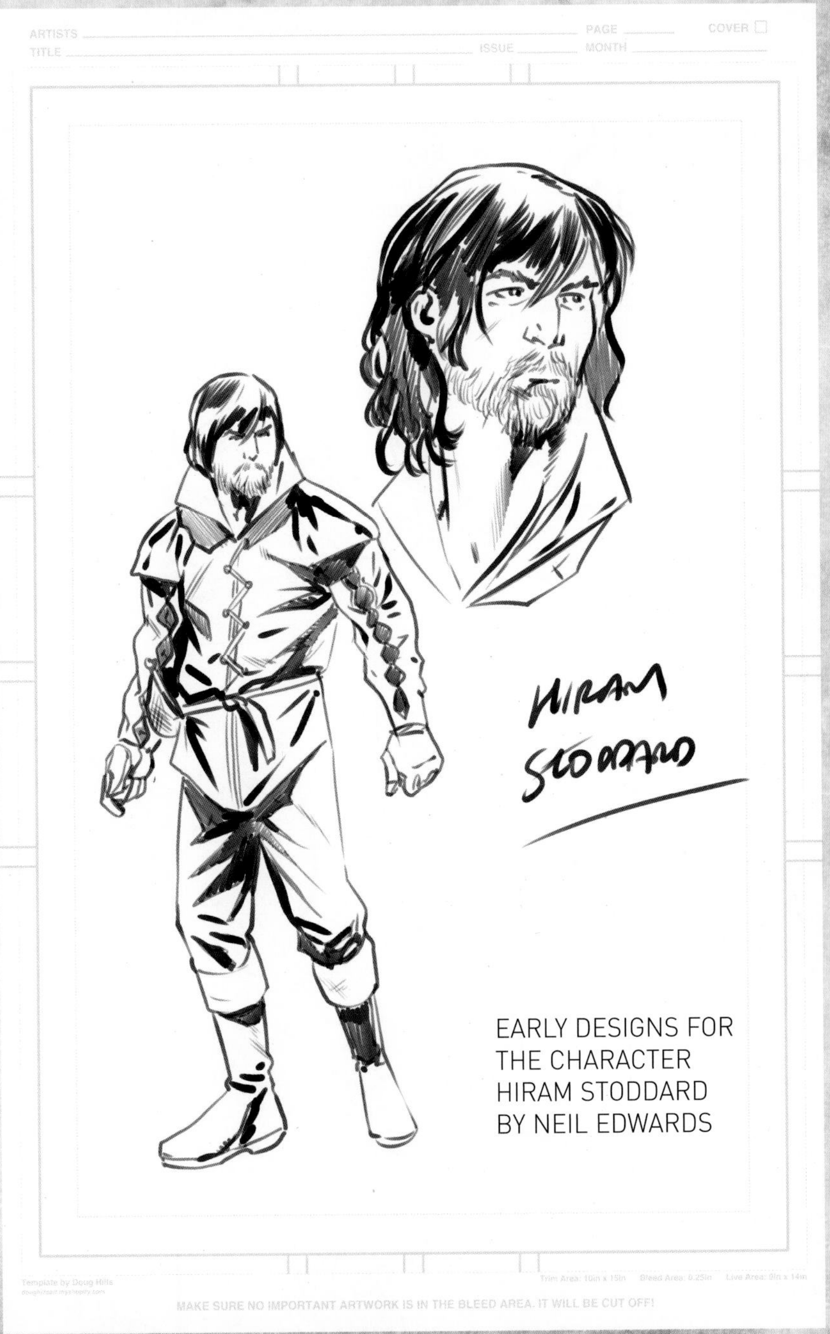
ARTISTS
PAGE
COVER
TITLE
ISSUE
MONTH
HIRAM STODDARD
MAKE SURE NO IMPORTANT ARTWORK IS IN THE BLEED AREA. IT WILL BE CUT OFF!

EARLY DESIGNS FOR THE CHARACTER HIRAM STODDARD BY NEIL EDWARDS

ARTISTIC PROCESS

HERE'S A QUICK LOOK INTO THE COLLABORATIVE EFFORT AND TECHNIQUES USED TO BRING ASSASSIN'S CREED TO THE PAGE.

ASSASSIN'S CREED

PAGE 3

Panel 1: Hiram lunges at Giovanni with his sword. Giovanni is able to narrowly dodge the attack.

Hiram: Shut up!

SFX: SWOOSH!

Panel 2: Hiram takes another swipe at Giovanni with his sword (like an uppercut). But this time he's able to get (some) contact. He slashes Giovanni's shoulder – a small amount of blood flies.

Giovanni: Ugh!

Panel 3: But this has been Giovanni's plan. Using Hiram's momentum against him (exposing his side and chest), Giovanni blocks Hiram's sword-wielding arm while punching him in the face with the other – or hit him with his elbow.

Panel 4: Giovanni kicks Hiram's arm, forcing the sword to go flying through the air.

Panel 5: Giovanni does a round kick directly to Hiram's face, forcing him to fall to the ground, bashing his head hard on the floor.

Panel 6: Hiram holds his head – he's only halfway conscious. Giovanni crouches and looks down at Hiram to check on him.

Hiram: Ugh…

Giovanni: I'm sorry, Hiram.

Giovanni: But we have a Code, to help protect this world…

1. SCRIPT EXCERPT
Beginning with the script, our writers Anthony and Conor set the scene...

PAGE
ISSUE
MONTH
COVER
Template by Doug Hills
Trim Area: 10in x 15in
Bleed Area: 0.25in
Live Area: 9in x 14in
MAKE SURE NO IMPORTANT ARTWORK IS IN THE BLEED AREA. IT WILL BE CUT OFF!

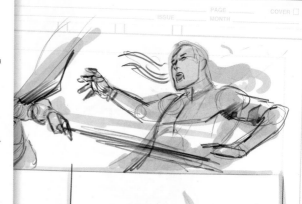

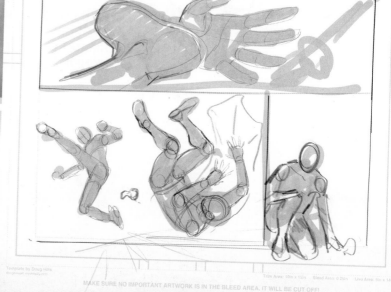

2. ROUGHS
Preliminary layouts from interior artist Neil Edwards allow a first look at the storytelling elements, allowing the editor to adjust as needed.

3. PENCILS
Next comes the pencil stage where the layouts are sharpened and the page begins to take shape (not shown).

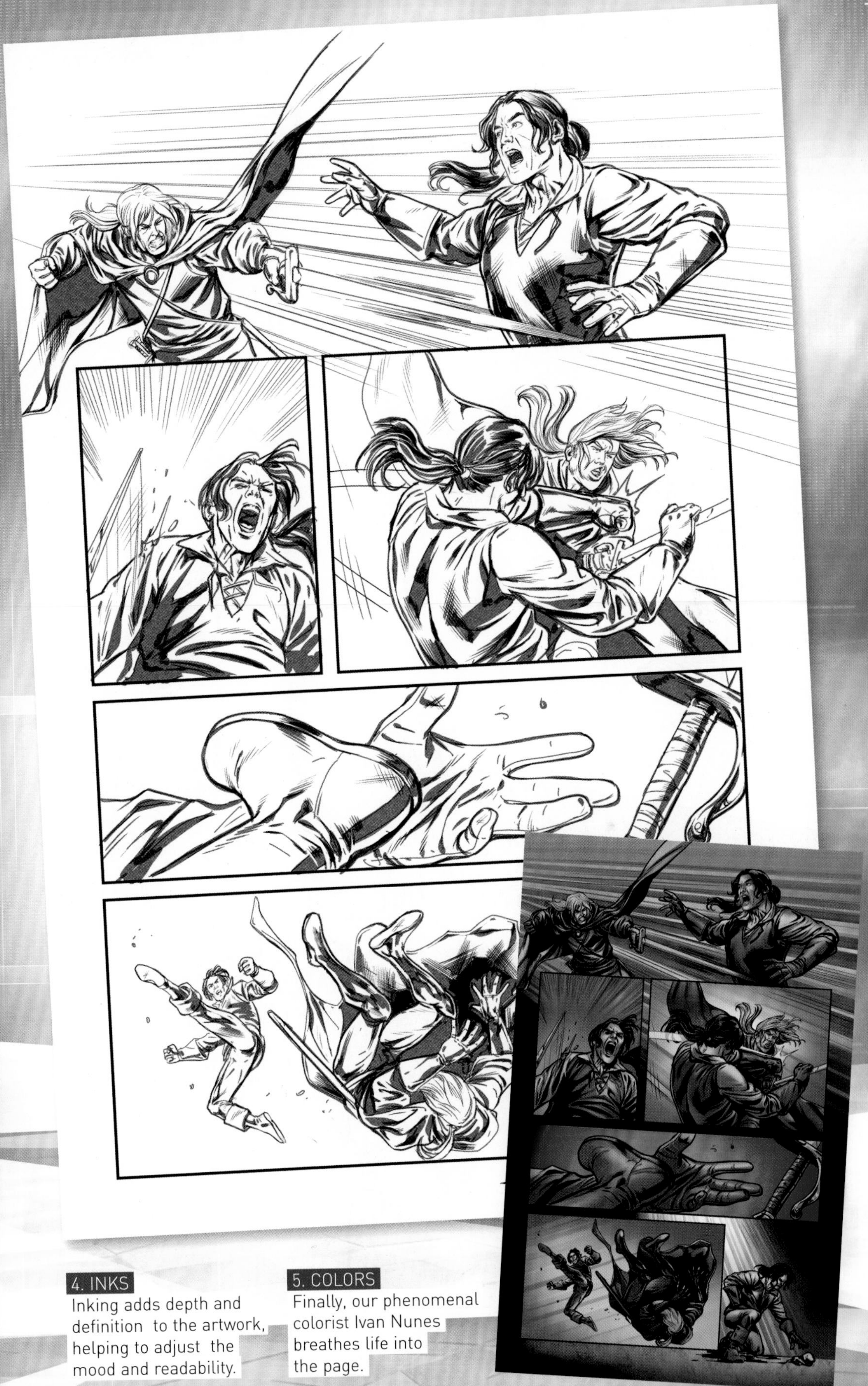

4. INKS

Inking adds depth and definition to the artwork, helping to adjust the mood and readability.

5. COLORS

Finally, our phenomenal colorist Ivan Nunes breathes life into the page.

ANATOMY OF A COVER

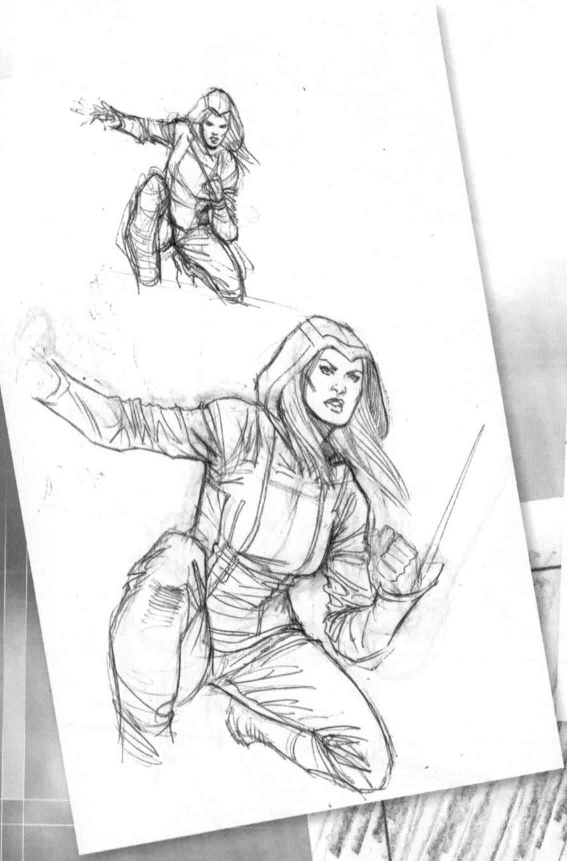

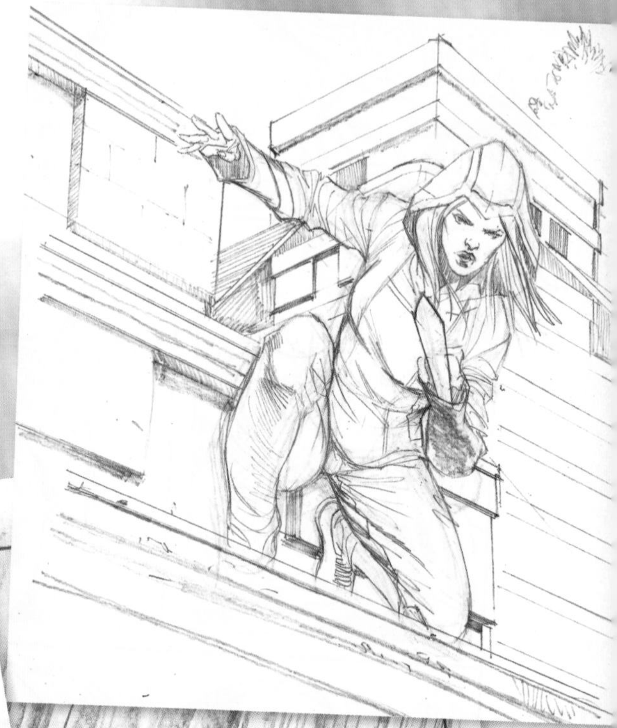

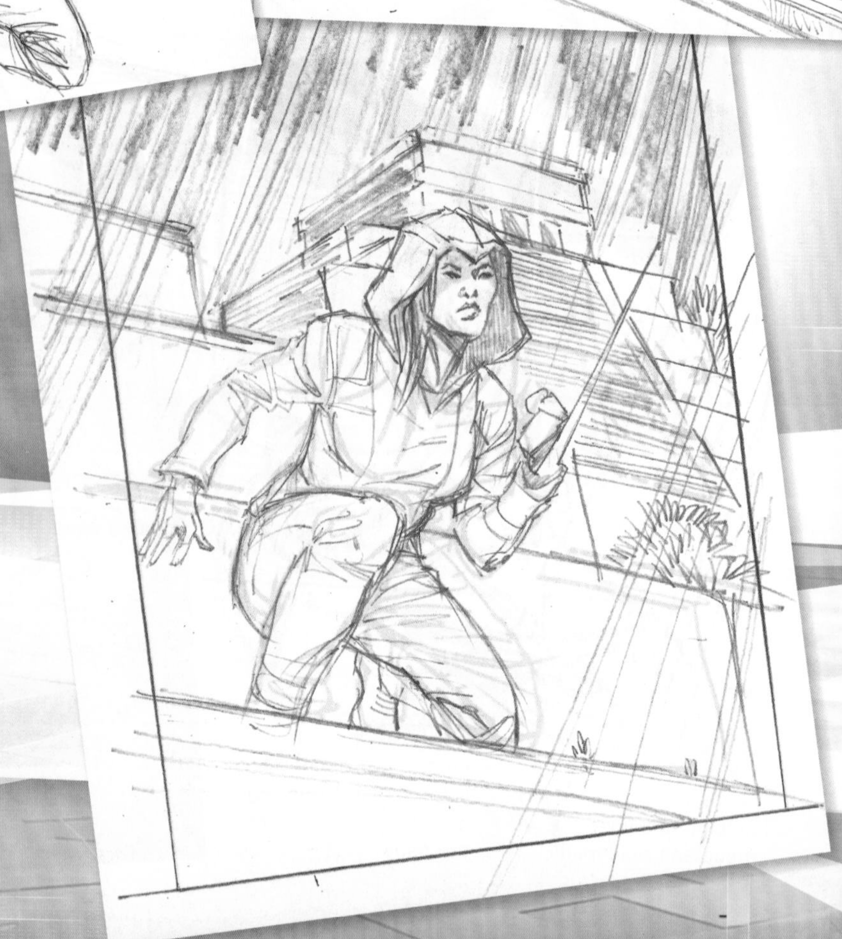

1. THUMBNAILS

Every cover starts with a series of exploratory thumbnails. For our issue #11 cover, artist Staz Johnson provided an initial thumbnail before reworking the pose to something more dynamic. From there, it's a case of refining the rough through several stages.

2. PENCILS

At the pencil stage, the cover begins to take its final shape.

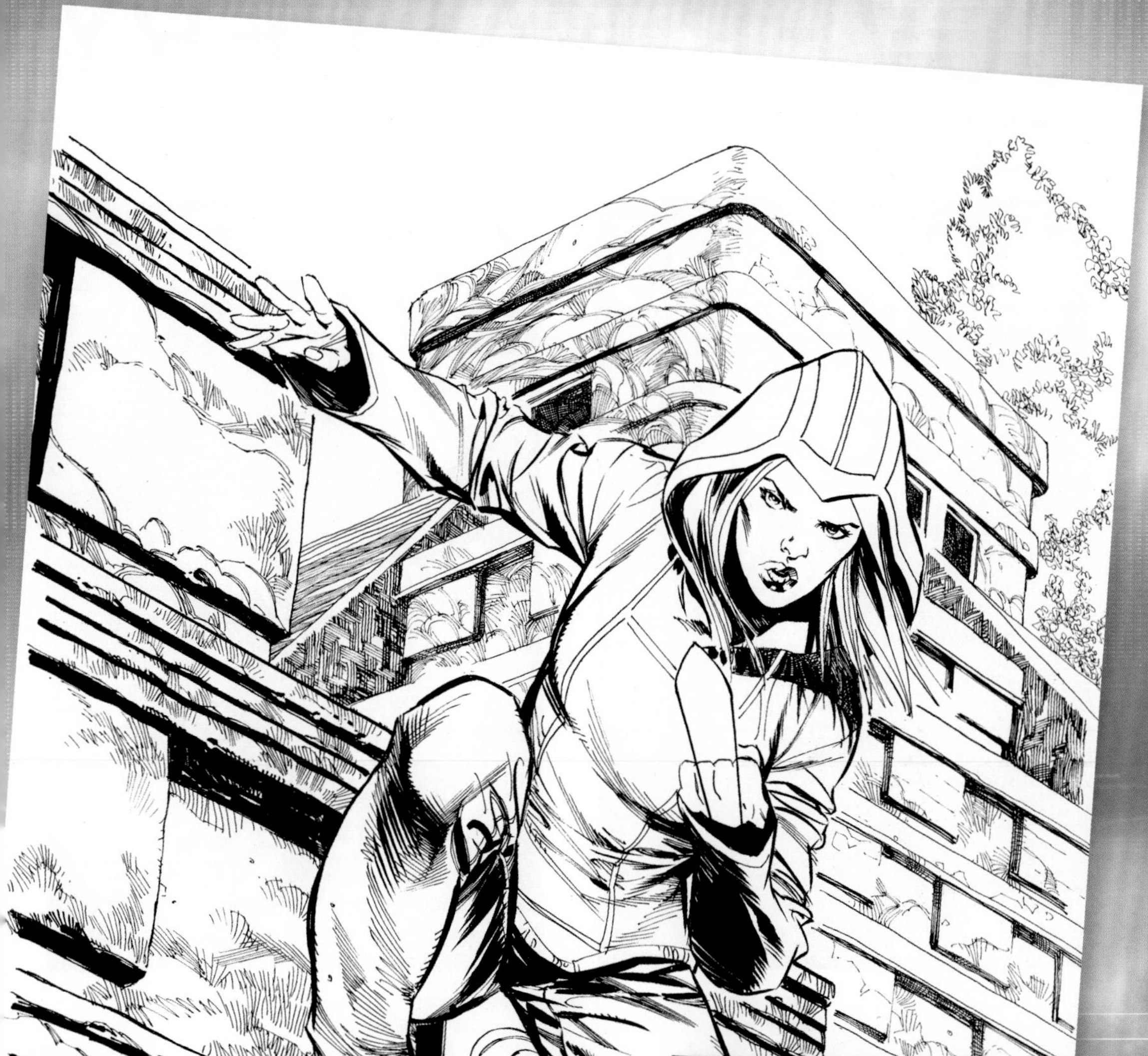

3. INKS

During the inking stage, shading, depth and finer details are added to give the image more definition.

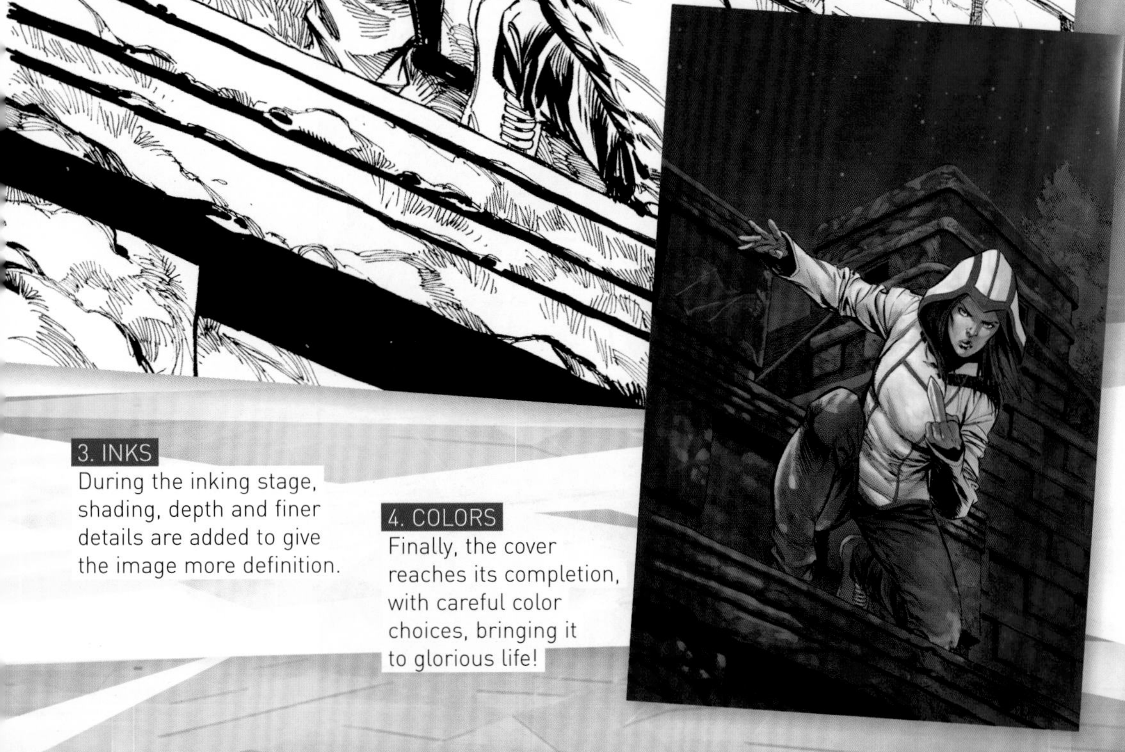

4. COLORS

Finally, the cover reaches its completion, with careful color choices, bringing it to glorious life!

COVER GALLERY

ISSUE 11

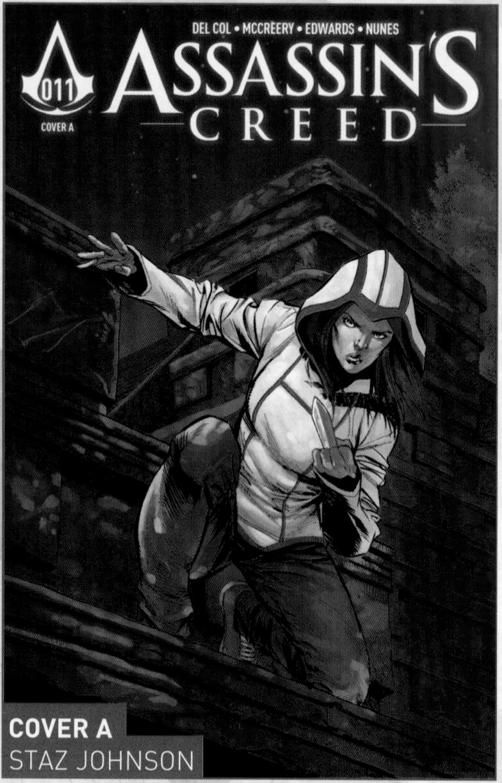
DEL COL • MCCREERY • EDWARDS • NUNES
011
ASSASSIN'S
CREED
COVER A

COVER A
STAZ JOHNSON

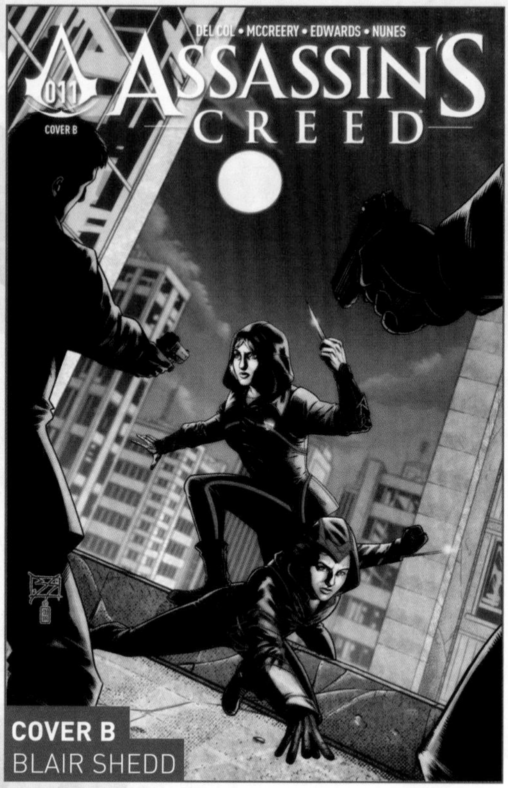
DEL COL • MCCREERY • EDWARDS • NUNES
011
ASSASSIN'S
CREED
COVER B

COVER B
BLAIR SHEDD

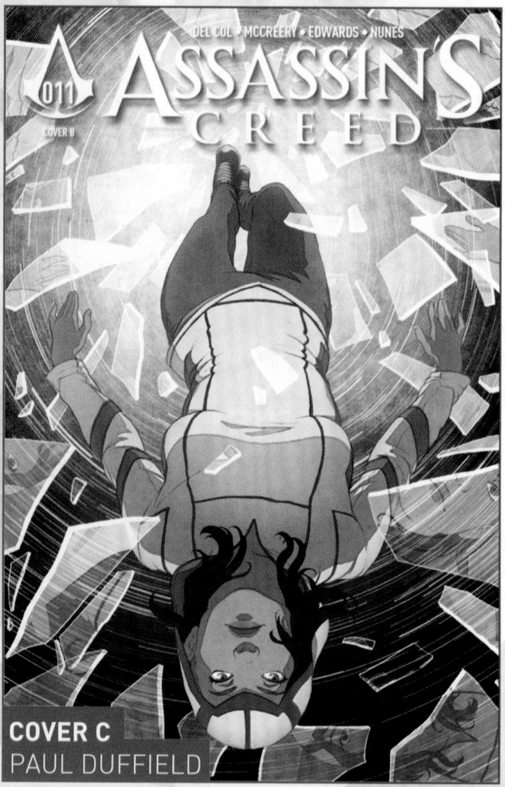
DEL COL • MCCREERY • EDWARDS • NUNES
011
ASSASSIN'S
CREED
COVER B

COVER C
PAUL DUFFIELD

ISSUE 12

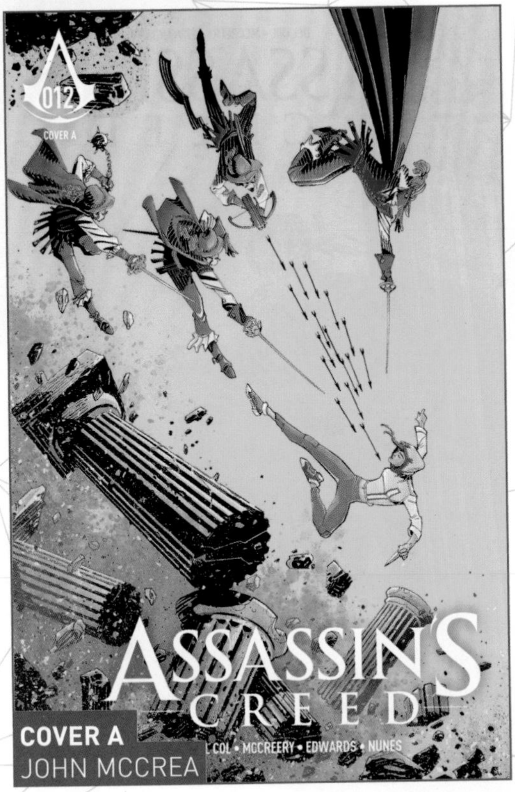
012
COVER A
ASSASSIN'S
CREED
MCCREERY • EDWARDS • NUNES

COVER A
JOHN MCCREA

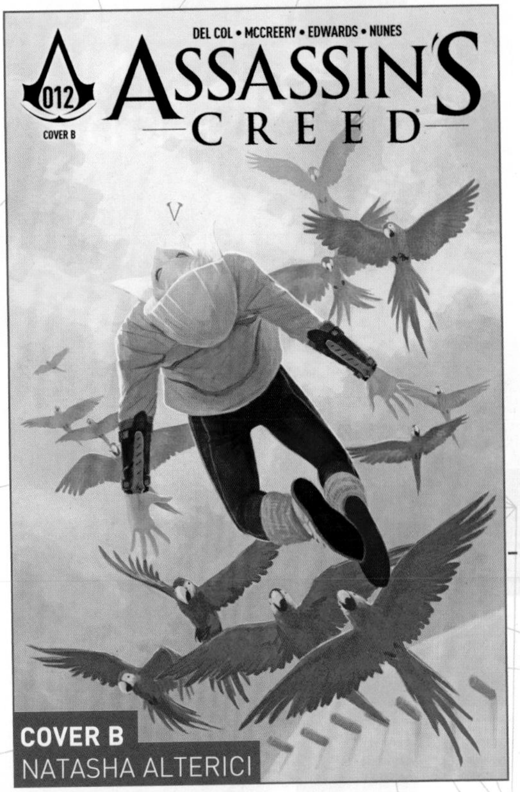
DEL COL • MCCREERY • EDWARDS • NUNES
ASSASSIN'S
CREED
012
COVER B

COVER B
NATASHA ALTERICI

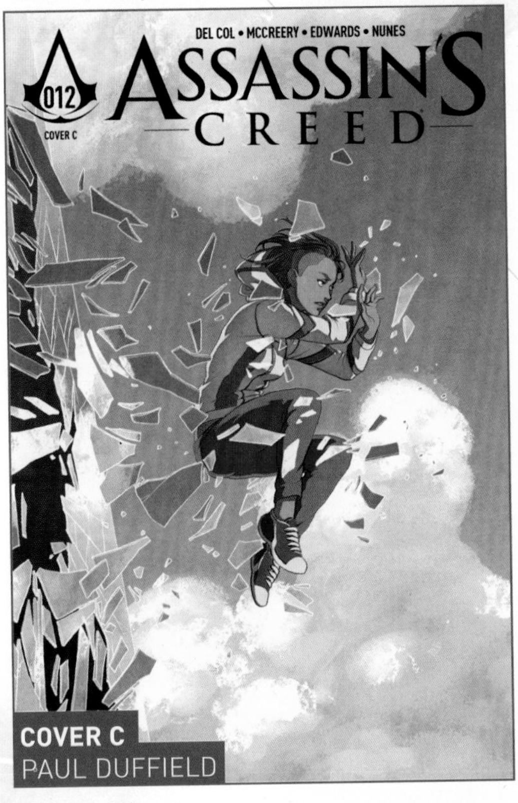
DEL COL • MCCREERY • EDWARDS • NUNES
ASSASSIN'S
CREED
012
COVER C

COVER C
PAUL DUFFIELD

COVER GALLERY

ISSUE 13

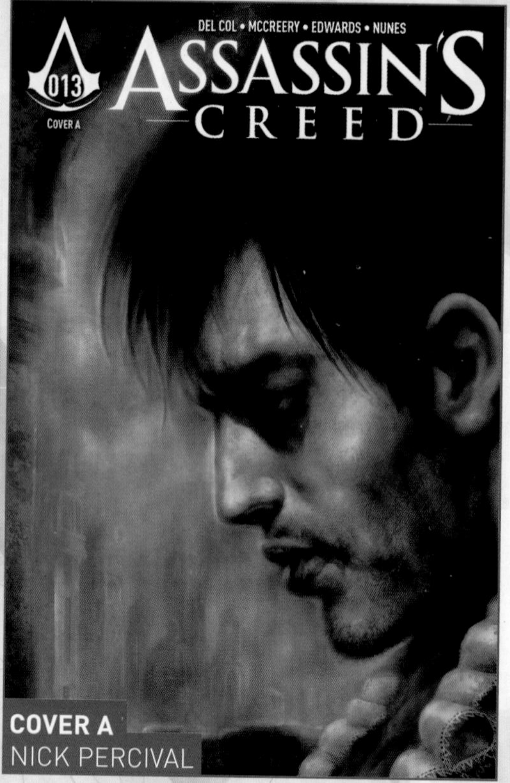

DEL COL • MCCREERY • EDWARDS • NUNES
ASSASSIN'S
CREED
013
COVER A

COVER A
NICK PERCIVAL

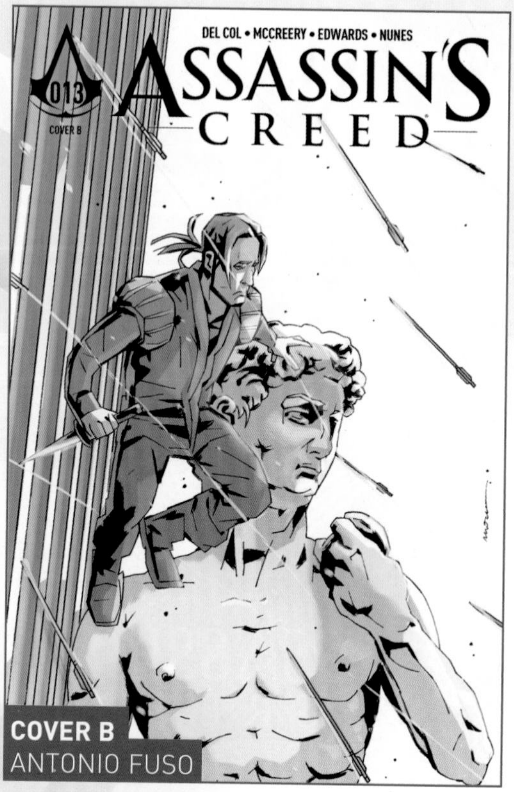

DEL COL • MCCREERY • EDWARDS • NUNES
ASSASSIN'S
CREED
013
COVER B

COVER B
ANTONIO FUSO

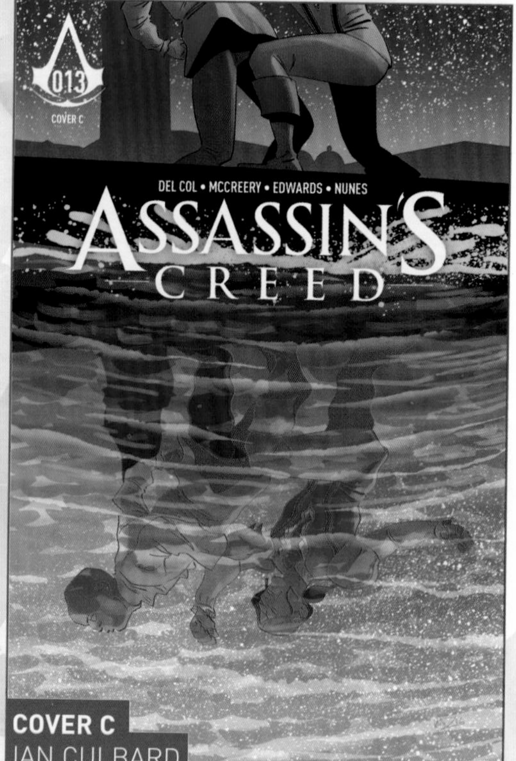

013
COVER C
DEL COL • MCCREERY • EDWARDS • NUNES
ASSASSIN'S
CREED

COVER C
IAN CULBARD

ISSUE 14

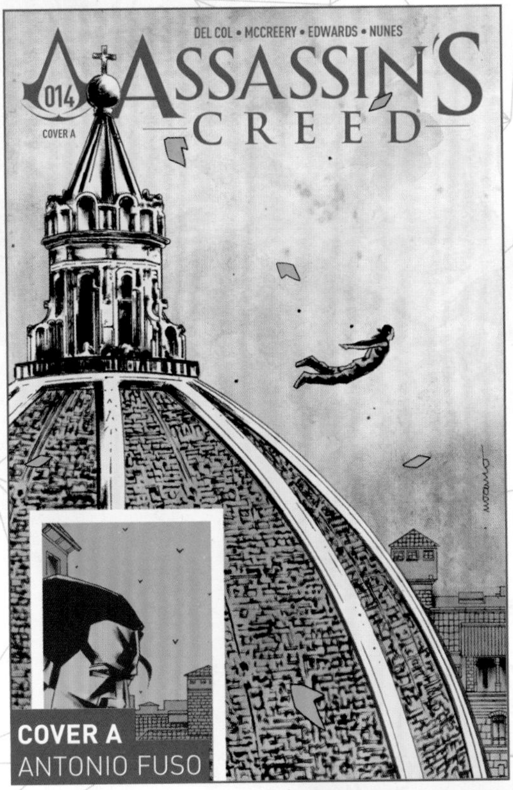
DEL COL • MCCREERY • EDWARDS • NUNES
014
ASSASSIN'S
CREED
COVER A

COVER A
ANTONIO FUSO

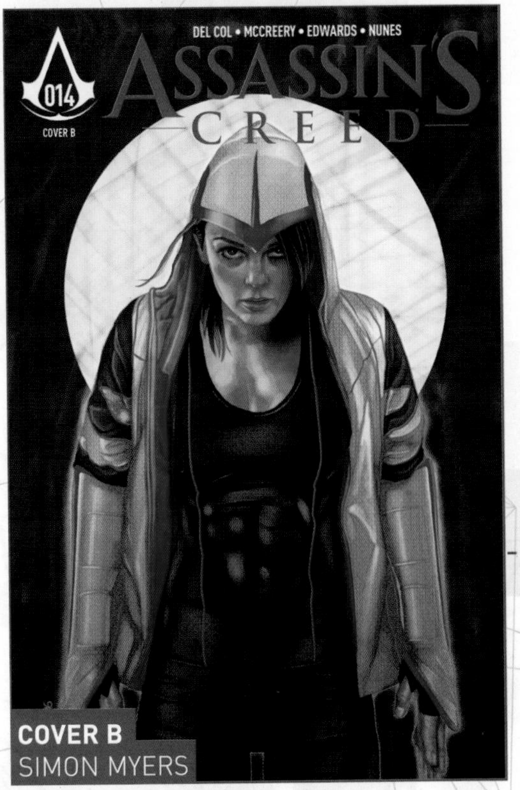
DEL COL • MCCREERY • EDWARDS • NUNES
014
ASSASSIN'S
CREED
COVER B

COVER B
SIMON MYERS

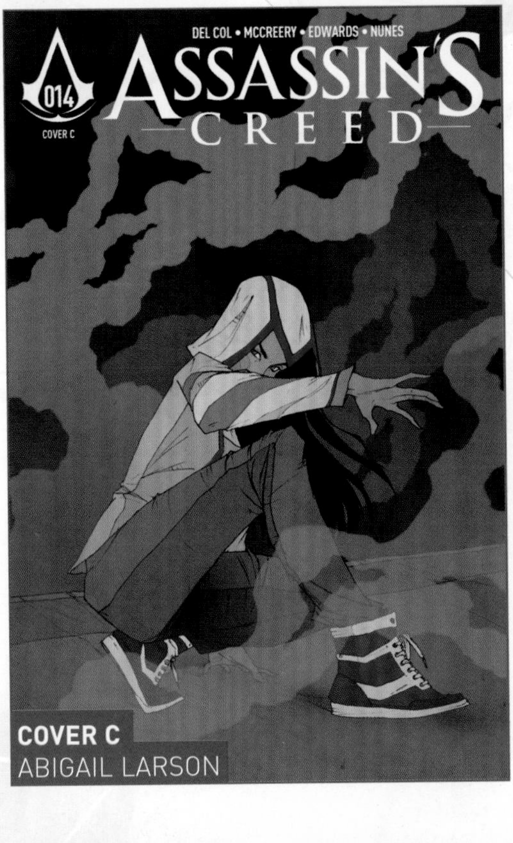
DEL COL • MCCREERY • EDWARDS • NUNES
014
ASSASSIN'S
CREED
COVER C

COVER C
ABIGAIL LARSON

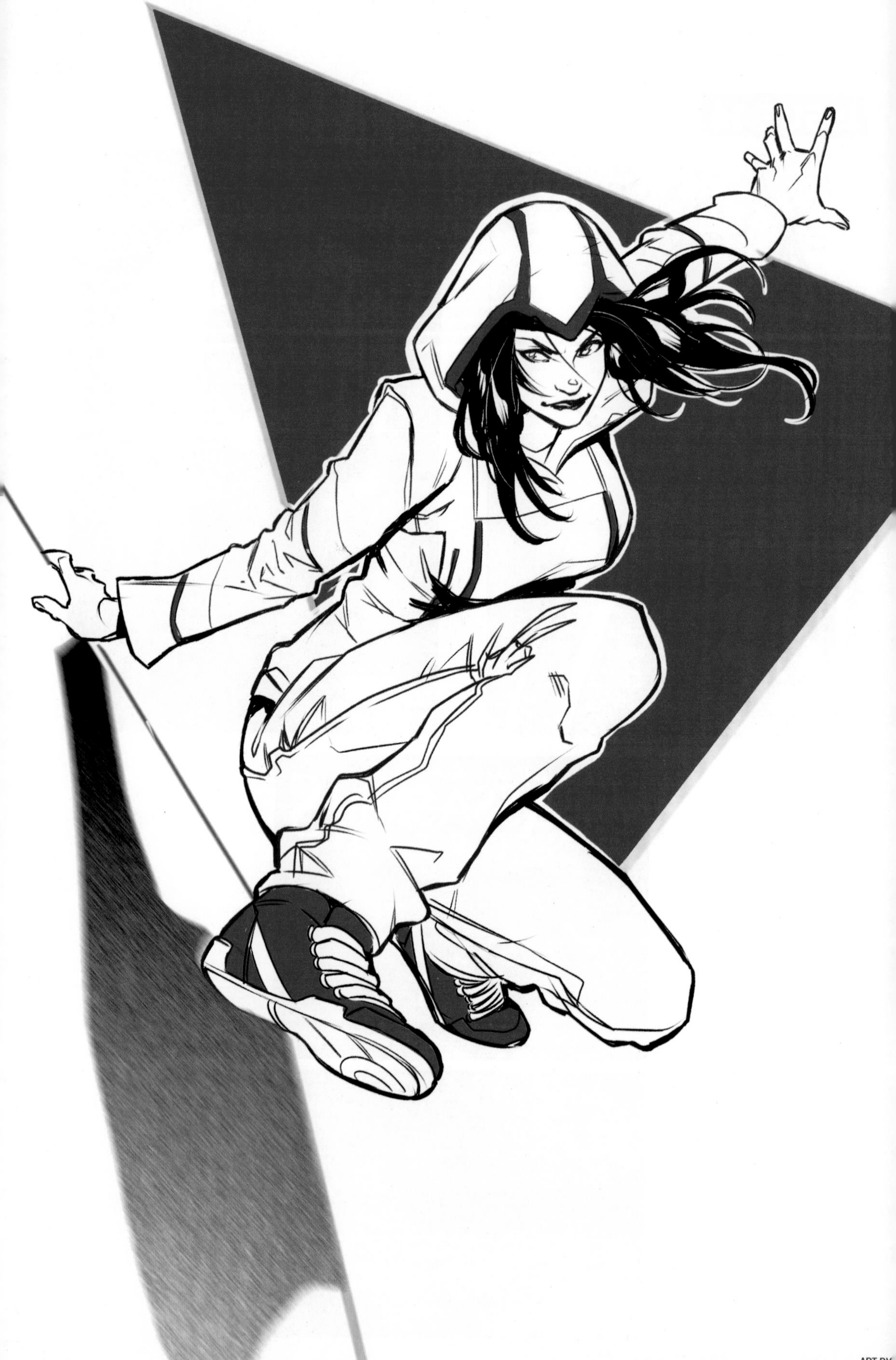

ART BY
VALERIA FAVOCCIA

ASSASSIN'S CREED

BIOS

>Anthony Del Col

Anthony Del Col is a Canadian writer, producer and entrepreneur. A graduate of the Canadian Film Centre, Anthony has worked in the music, film and television industries, producing several independent films and recently assisting with the management of international pop star Nelly Furtado on her world tour. He is the co-creator of the Joe Shuster Award-nominated *Kill Shakespeare* from IDW and Dynamite Entertainment's *Sherlock Homes vs. Harry Houdini*.

>Conor McCreery

Conor McCreery is a Canadian comics writer and journalist. Spending most of his career in film, television and journalism, Conor has covered everything from the NBA, to stock-market apocalypses, with a little dash of celebrity gossip for (questionable) taste. Along with Anthony Del Col, he is the co-creator of the Joe Shuster Award-nominated *Kill Shakespeare* from IDW and Dynamite Entertainment's *Sherlock Homes vs. Harry Houdini*. He lives in Toronto with his fiancée Crystal and two children.

>Neil Edwards

Neil Edwards is a Welsh comic artist who has worked for a variety of publishers including Marvel, DC, 2000AD and Titan Comics. Best known for his work on *Dark Avengers*, *Fantastic Four*, *Justice League* and *Spider-Man*, Neil has also worked on numerous television and film comic adaptions including *Heroes*, *Doctor Who*, *Vampire Diaries*, *Starship Troopers* and *Vikings*.

>Ivan Nunes

Ivan Nunes is a Brazilian comic artist and colorist whose past works have included Marvel's *New Avengers* and *Thor*, Dynamite's *Green Hornet*, *Game of Thrones* and *The Bionic Man*.

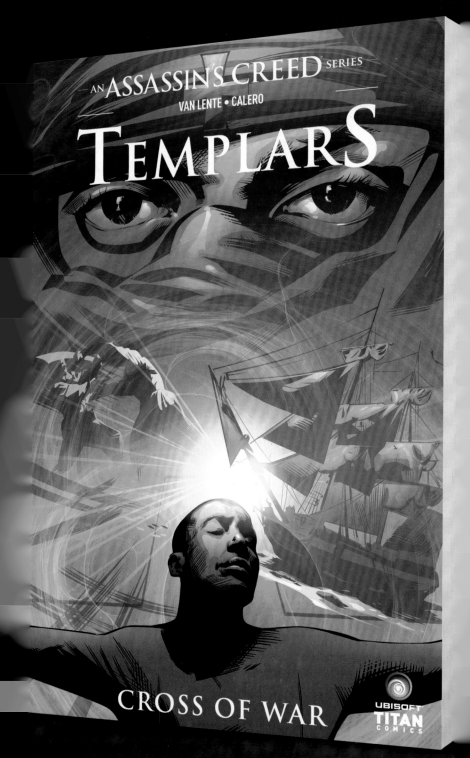

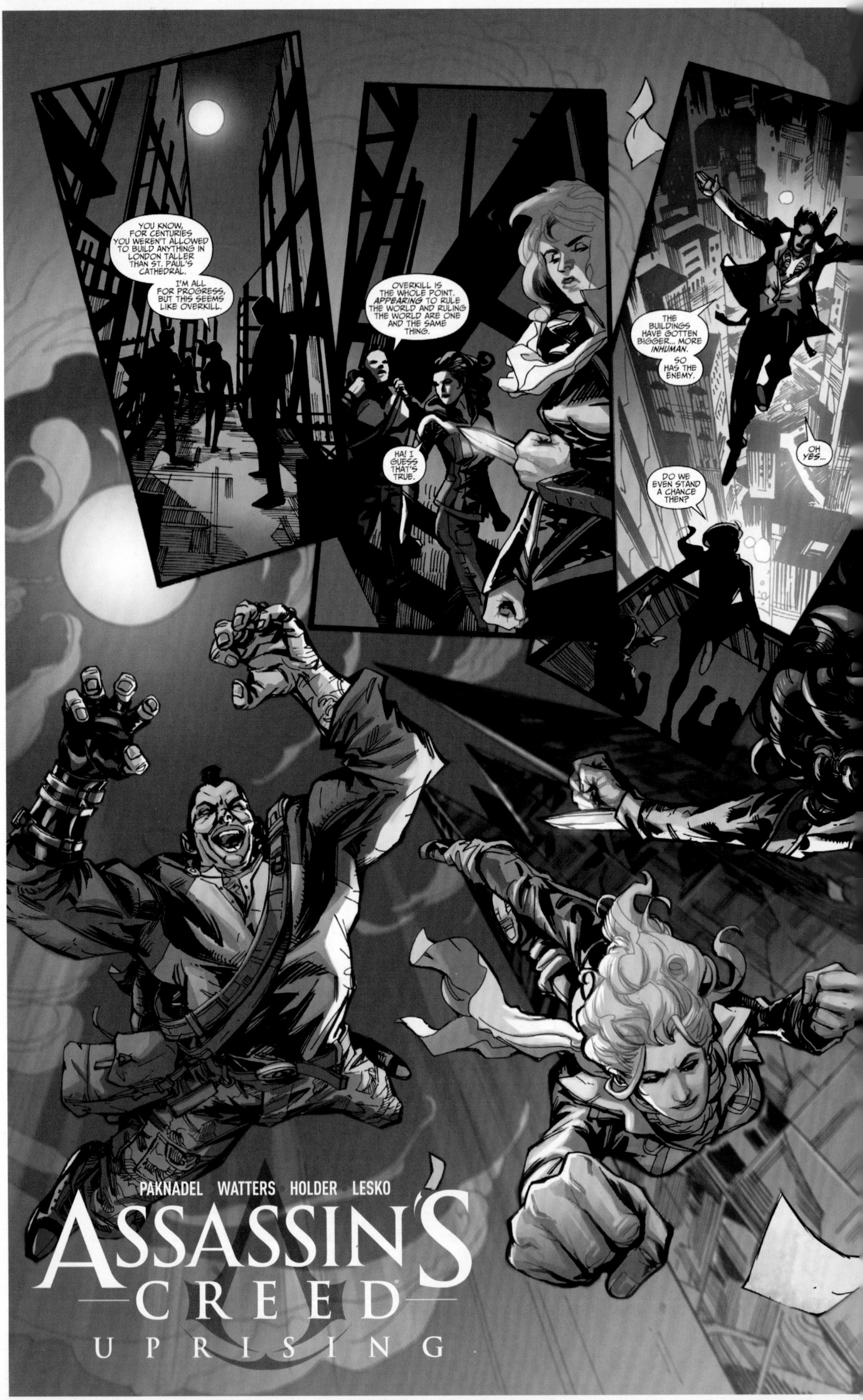
YOU KNOW, FOR CENTURIES YOU WEREN'T ALLOWED TO BUILD ANYTHING IN LONDON TALLER THAN ST. PAUL'S CATHEDRAL.
I'M ALL FOR PROGRESS, BUT THIS SEEMS LIKE OVERKILL.
OVERKILL IS THE WHOLE POINT. *APPEARING* TO RULE THE WORLD AND RULING THE WORLD ARE ONE AND THE SAME THING.
HA! I GUESS THAT'S TRUE.
THE BUILDINGS HAVE GOTTEN BIGGER... MORE *INHUMAN*.
SO HAS THE ENEMY.
OH *YES*...
DO WE EVEN STAND A CHANCE THEN?
PAKNADEL WATTERS HOLDER LESKO
ASSASSIN'S CREED
UPRISING

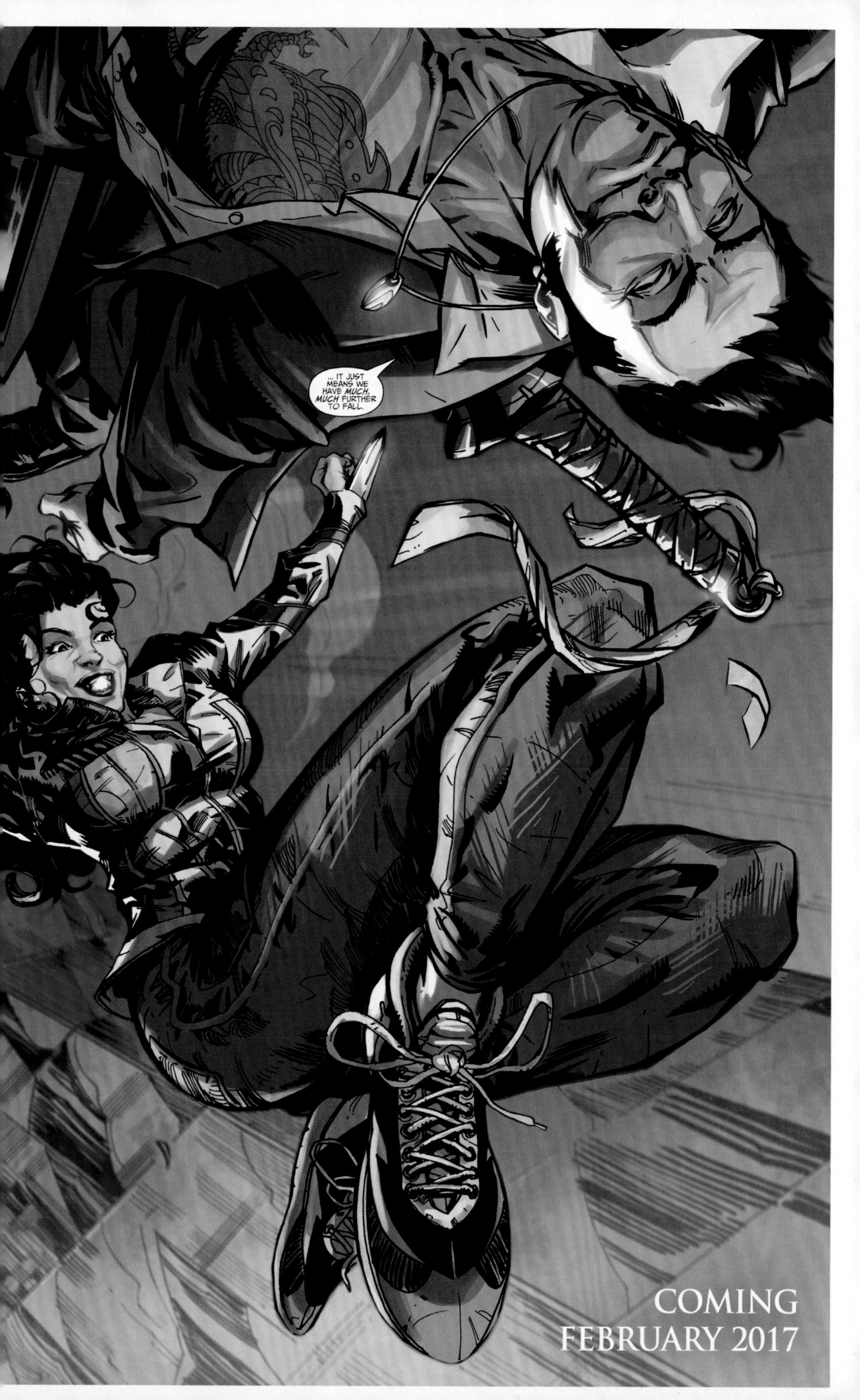
... IT JUST MEANS WE HAVE *MUCH, MUCH* FURTHER TO FALL.
COMING FEBRUARY 2017

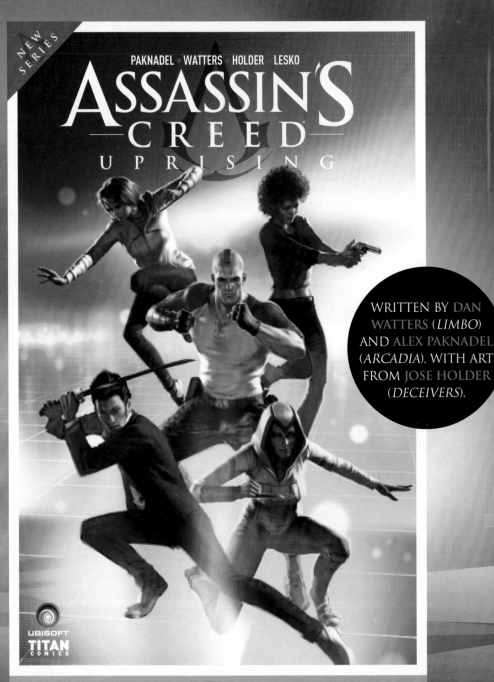